Jazakallah

for op

to the Deen for us all!

Knowledgeseekers '07

Social Justice in Islam

First Edition (1421/2000)

Social Justice in Islam

Dina Abdelkader

International Institute of Islamic Thought
Herndon, Virginia, U.S.A.
1421/2000

Academic Dissertations (8)

The International Institute of Islamic Thought
P.O. Box 669
Herndon, VA 20172-0669, U.S.A.
Tel: (703) 471-1133 Fax (703) 471-3922
E-mail: iiit@iiit.org Website: www.iiit.com

Library of Congress Cataloging-in-Publication Data

Abdelkader, Dina.
Social justice in Islam / Dina Abdelkader.-- 1st ed.
p. cm. -- (Academic dissertations ; 8)
Includes bibliographical references.
ISBN 1-56564-268-6
1. Human rights--Religious aspects--Islam. 2. Civil rights--Religious aspects--Islam. 3. Islam--Social aspects. I. Title. II. Series.

BP173.44. A22 2000
297.2'72--dc21

00-031936

Printed in the United States of America by International Graphics
10710 Tucker Street, Beltsville, Maryland 20705-2223-USA
Tel: (301) 595-5999 Fax: (301) 595-5888
Email: ig@igprinting.com

Contents

Preface

The issue of using *uṣūl al fiqh* (the sources of Islamic law) as a methodological tool for studying social sciences emerged in recent decades as the idea of the Islamization of knowledge reached a more clearly defined and concrete form. Indeed, initial studies were concerned with how to approach the legacy of Islam and attempted to crystallize a methodology for dealing with that legacy. This use of the sources of Islamic law in the study of social sciences stirred up considerable debate among Shari'ah scholars and specialists in the social sciences. Although these differences of opinion have not yet been resolved, several researchers have made serious attempts to test some of these sources—particularly those which are considered "disputed sources" or "rational sources"—by using them in their studies of social issues and phenomena.

Dr. Sayf 'Abd al Fattah was one of the first who embarked on this venture when he used the two sources of *sadd al dharā'i* (preventing the use of lawful means for an unlawful end) and *maṣlaḥah* (the sourcing of an acknowledged interest in the Shari'ah) in his doctoral thesis in political science. He was followed by Dr. Nasr Mohammad Arif, who used *maṣlaḥah* in his study titled *Nadhari'āt al Tanmiyah al Siyāsiyyah al Mu'āṣirah* (Theories of Contemporary Political Development). Dr. Dina Abdelkader also pioneered in this field when she chose to use both *maṣlaḥah* and *maqāṣid* (the intents or end goals of the Shari'ah) as two sources of law to analyze the Islamic awakening and identify the influence of fiqh in the shaping of the contemporary Islamic phenomenon and its discourse.

I had the pleasure of working with Dr. Dina throughout the various stages of conception, preparation, and writing of this book. We met on numerous occasions to discuss a wide range of questions relating to *maqāṣid* and *maṣlaḥah*—two sources that she considered, from the beginning, to be the two most effective methodological tools for her research. Her background in political science and her knowledge of the methodologies of the social sciences helped her to understand these sources and to use them effectively as methodological tools and as sources of law. Indeed, she has successfully incorporated into her study a number of sources of Islamic jurisprudence and concepts from the Shari'ah, and in doing so, provides a good example of how such sources can be used as methodological tools in the study of social phenomena.

In this research, Dr. Dina has carried out an in-depth study of ijtihad and opinion (*ra'i*), and has attempted to analyze the debate between the schools of jurisprudence and the schools of hadith regarding restricted ijtihad and unrestricted opinion. She has also closely examined the sources of Islamic jurisprudence in order to explain the position and role of *maqāṣid* and *maṣlaḥah* as a source of law, as well as in explaining or clarifying other rulings.

Dr. Dina has also succeeded in establishing links between fiqh and its impact in real life, by examining the nature of the interaction that takes place between a legal ruling and practice. She shows that the relationship between fiqh and reality is a quasi-dialectical one: on one hand, fiqh provides the legislation or rule for a given situation—which constitutes an answer to a question posed by reality; on the other hand, when an opinion or fatwa is issued, this has immediate effects on people's lives and their behavior, which, in turn, generates new questions which fiqh is required to answer. Needless to say that not all the specialists in fiqh or of any area of the social sciences understand or appreciate this relationship. However, Dr. Dina, being aware of this dialectical relationship between fiqh and reality, was able to realize that the Shari'ah has instilled social action into its jurisprudential and legislative systems. She also realized that by being based on the dialectical relationship between reality and fiqh, social justice has become part of the reality of Islam. However, this social justice disappears when it separates itself from reality or ignores it in any way; and this, in turn, leads to new attempts to reclaim it and re-establish it in reality.

Furthermore, Dr. Dina was able to link the phenomenon of Islamic awakening and Islamic movements—also known as "political Islam"—with the demand for social justice which the Shari'ah has implanted in the Muslim milieu, and which fiqh has reinforced and made an integral part of Islamic life. This understanding enabled her to avoid what other Muslim and non-Muslim scholars wrongly believed to be an abnormal phenomenon. Indeed, from the outset, she rejected this idea and tried to prove that such a phenomenon is natural, emanating from a society which strives to establish justice by way of its jurisprudential and legislative systems, with the result that justice has become the first and most fundamental objective of the Islamic awakening.

She then set about explaining the contradiction that exists among the Muslim elite, where one group is Westernized and has adopted Western thought, and the other considers Islam as the appropriate means of reform. In doing so, she discovered that both groups have the same objective of realizing social justice. However, whereas the latter aims to realize social justice because it is a requirement of the Shari'ah and fiqh—as it is part of the intents and therefore may on no account be abandoned—the former favors any means advocated by Western thought that aim to bring about social change and social justice (whether it stems from dialectics, the liberal approach, or any other Western trends). Having explained the difference between the Islamists and the secularists in this regard, Dr. Dina then demonstrates that the Islamic approach is more likely to succeed in achieving and restoring social justice than any other imported solution, firstly, because it is linked to the Shari'ah's objectives, and secondly, because it finds support among the members of the Ummah who uphold the Shari'ah and accept its fatwas. As such, the Ummah will also be more enthusiastic about and responsive to the call for social change that will enable social justice to be achieved.

By using the principles of *maqāṣid* and *maṣlaḥah,* Dr. Dina has also shown the weakness and absurdity of the nation-state in the Islamic world and the extent to which it is isolated from and alien to Islamic societies. In doing so, she offers an excuse to those who are unable to feel any sense of belonging in the nation-state and refuse to pledge their allegiance to it because they do not believe it will meet their aims and aspirations. The nation-state is an aberration because it ignores the intents of the Shari'ah, which have become an inseparable part of the people's traditions, customs, cultural heritage and identity. Indeed, the disregard of these realities has caused the Ummah to lose its power and effectiveness and to become preoccupied with internal conflicts, forgetting the issues of development and social justice.

The conflicts that therefore naturally emerged among the different elite groups, as well as between the elite groups as a whole and the state that was seen as something alien to society, make the realization of democracy in these states virtually impossible. Indeed, by abandoning the Shari'ah and neglecting its objectives, these so-called nation-states are causing friction to arise among their peoples and creating a rift between the rulers and the ruled. This leaves no chance for the establishment of any consultative or democratic system capable of organizing the available forces and achieving social justice, which is the alternative to the concept of welfare celebrated by capitalism.

Finally, this research also examines the Western theoretical approaches that have led the West to misunderstand the contemporary Muslim world. Indeed, Dr. Dina shows that writers and researchers in the West—whether they are Westerners or Muslims who have adopted western methodologies and approaches—have opted for methods of modernization, development, social progress and social interaction that have led them to produce studies and analyses that are out of touch with reality, and that do not even come close to understanding the actuality of the phenomenon, let alone providing a means to formulate a suitable opinion about it.

By following these methodologies, Dr. Dina has managed to produce results that not many researchers have been able to achieve by using other methodological approaches in the study of this phenomenon. Thus, her conclusions not only support the assertions of those who say that Islamic jurisprudence has methodologies and tools that can be used successfully for the study of social phenomena throughout the Muslim world; they also form the nucleus of an Islamic methodology that can be further developed to enable it to bring about the progress, that the social sciences are still striving to achieve. In this sense, we can say that this study provides useful guidelines for the revival of the Islamic discourse, as well as for achieving the social progress that the western world is endeavoring to introduce into the Islamic world. Indeed, social progress and dynamism cannot stem from sources that are alien to the beliefs, culture, and identity of the Ummah. Rather, the sources of Islamic jurisprudence which overlap with the Ummah's beliefs, aspirations, customs, and traditions can generate the dynamism that is an essential pre-condition for the emergence of any social development, change, progress or reform.

I believe the present research can constitute a working model for the study of social phenomena in the Islamic world. It can also show those who have opted for a Western approach how a great deal of resources have been wasted in studies that have only succeeded in adding to the confusion and ambiguity regarding the phenomenon of Islamic revival, simply because they failed to use the appropriate methodological tools.

May Allah grant success to Dr. Dina Abdelkader and her colleagues, and enable them to undertake and produce further serious and useful studies of this kind. May He also reward the International Institute of Islamic Thought (IIIT) for sponsoring this research, publishing it and making it available to other researchers and scholars.

All success is from Allah. Glorified and exalted is He.

Taha J. Al Alwani
President
Graduate School of Islamic and
Social Sciences, USA

Introduction

The current domestic and international conditions of many Middle Eastern countries have increasingly led to visible Islamic activism or, as it is often called, an Islamic revival.[1] This study will focus on the relationship between the religion-based expectations of Muslim peoples and the current manifestations of Islamic activism. As a guide to the basic notion of social justice in Islam and to aid the reader in understanding the religion-based expectations of Muslim peoples the study will use Islamic jurisprudence (fiqh).[2]

In most calls for an Islamic state, the Shari'ah (Islamic law) is of primary importance for ensuring the legitimacy and justification for governmental change. Numerous ideological themes in Islamic jurisprudential teachings concern government; however, this study will analyze an augmentation to one of the sources of the law, namely, *maqāṣid al shari'ah* (the goals of the Shari'ah).

There are four sources of law in the Shari'ah: the Qur'an, the Hadith and Sunnah,[3] ijmā' (the consensus of *fuqahā'*/muftis on a decision), and *qiyās* (syllogism).

---

1. *Revival* has become a generic term often used in the literature on Islamic movements; however, it is important to note that it implies that those movements are regressive or that they are an attempt to reactivate Islamic sentiment. Accordingly, the term *activism* is relatively impartial since it does not carry the same connotations about the movement in terms of direction, development, or time.

2. Fiqh, Shari'ah, and other words related to Islamic law will be defined later when they are analyzed in depth in the chapter on Islamic jurisprudence (Chapter 2).

3. Sunnah is an embodiment of the Prophet's sayings and practice, which are taken as a guide for Islamic law. It is important to note that Hadith means the sayings of the Prophet, while the Sunnah embodies his words and deeds. Therefore, the Sunnah represents a larger body of reference for Muslims.

The last source of law, especially, allows for the exercise of human reasoning. (This does not presume that the other three do not allow for human reasoning; however, relatively speaking, *qiyās* is the source of law that requires human deduction or inference.) *Qiyās* as a source of law has brought about notions such as ijtihād[4] and *ra'i*[5] in the formation of the Shari'ah. As a source of law, *qiyās* and its extensions provided a lively debate among *fuqahā'* throughout Islamic history. Among such extensions is the concept of *maqāṣid al shari'ah,* which provides the theoretical base for the study of Islamic activism in this research.

My study examines the supposition that, in Islamic societies, Islamic activism is a function of the extent to which state performance falls short of the principles of Islamic social justice as embodied in the *maqāṣid.* The later chapters contain case studies that are designed to clarify the broad lines of development of such movements and to suggest how Muslim societies may change under their influence. In many Muslims countries, Islamic activism is a social phenomenon that is gaining acceptance among the populace. However, tensions between the secular elite and Islamic activists exist, and the case studies will further explore those tensions. Although there are different opinions on the role of the state, research needs to examine how widespread support is for Islamic activism and whether its popularity is linked to the failure of the state to fulfill people's needs and address their grievances. Islamic activism includes all degrees and shades of political activism, from nonviolent demonstrations to violent attempts on public figures' lives, as well as threats to Western interests in each of the three countries being examined.

Another concept important to my research is Islamic social justice. Social justice in Islam, as mentioned earlier, is embodied in the Shari'ah. The Shari'ah's rules and mores are derived from the Qur'an and Sunnah (the Prophet's behavior in word and deed). The spirit of the Shari'ah was further explained by numerous *fuqahā'* (Muslim legal scholars). Exploration of the Shari'ah's essence has led many scholars to believe that some basic needs and rights are safeguarded by its rules. Those basic needs and rights were later compiled and developed by a number of Muslim scholars. However,

4. According to Netton, ijtihād is defined as: "In jurisprudence this term means the exercise of independent judgment unfettered by case law or past precedent. Its opposite is *taqlīd,* which means, literally, imitation. The word *ijtihād* derives from the same Arabic root as jihad." Netton, *A Popular Dictionary of Islam* (1992, p. 117).

5. Netton's definition of *ra'i* is "Opinion, idea. In Islamic law *al ra'i* has the sense of personal opinion, individual judgment, or speculation not based on a recognized source of law." (Ibid., p. 212).

my study focuses on the role of the *maqāṣid* in explaining Islamic activism. Therefore, the state's performance will be measured by its ability to safeguard the tenets of the *maqāṣid*. The basic proposition is that Islamic activism is a function of the state's performance according to the Shari'ah's goals, which are the *maqāṣid*.

A review of Western social science literature reveals three theoretical approaches pertinent to analyzing current activism: modernization/economic development, cultural studies, and popular discontent/mass mobilization. Though the approaches overlap, for the purpose of analyzing and reviewing the literature, I will characterize each approach by referring to its most distinctive elements.

CHAPTER 1

Islamic Activism in Search of a Theory: A Review of the Literature

Introduction

Several theoretical approaches have been used to explain Islamic activism as a social phenomenon. The modernization/economic development approach to Islamic activism focuses on the effect of modernization and the possibilities of development in Muslim societies. The popular discontent approach focuses on the sources and degree of mobilization of Islamic activism. Cultural studies emphasize the customs and traditions of Islamic activism. Whether studies use the modernization/economic development, the mass mobilization, or the cultural and historical approach to explain Islamic activism, each approach includes elements of the others. They differ in the degree of focus and weight given to certain variables.

The research in this book emphasizes the importance of the cultural and historical backgrounds of Muslim peoples as sources of the current Islamic activist movements. That is, I look at Islamic activism through an understanding of Muslim societies' expectations of political systems and deduce the implications for development. Therefore, it is necessary to review the literature on "revival," as it is popularly termed, before further conjecture.

Current literature on Islam and Islamic revival can be divided by two normative positions. The first normative stance is characterized by the researcher's empathy with the culture of Muslim people and Islamic activism, while the second normative position ridicules Islamic activism, mainly by stressing its violent elements.

The first normative stance is clearly exemplified in Burke and Lapidus's writing. For example, Burke (Burke and Lapidus 1988, p. 18) writes:

> In this mood of sober reexamination, it is appropriate to note a related factor that shapes the development of the field. The epistemological ground on which studies of popular political action in Islamic societies [are] situated is notoriously spongy and subject to periodic cave-ins. Not only is it difficult to spot a trend except by hindsight, because of the extent to which we are all prisoners of present ways of thinking, but it is also perilous to advance an explication of the so-called Islamic revival without reproducing the concerns of the ambient political culture of our own society with its deeply grounded fears and phantasms about Islam. The discourse on the Other, especially the Muslim Other, is politically saturated. This is not to disqualify non-Muslim appreciations of Islamic social movements, however. The views of the cultural outsider will invariably differ to some degree from those of an insider, but this fact by no means invalidates them. While we cannot escape completely from these constraints, a degree of methodological self-consciousness is indispensable.

Burke's "methodological self-consciousness" has affected mainly cultural studies on Islamic activism. The studies of modernization/economic development have been less susceptible to this change.

Modernization/Economic Development and Islamic Activism

A review of the literature on the causes of Islamic activism makes it increasingly evident that most contributions relate Islamic activism to modernization/economic development issues. Thus, my literature review will focus mainly on writings that link modernization to Islamic activism. The modernization/economic development explanation of Islamic activism basically reduces the process of development to the economic difficulties that many Third World countries are facing in the 1990s. This explanation characterizes the "universal crisis of modernity" or the "disruptive effect of modernization" as the main causal variable that explains the social phenomenon of Islamic activism. Therefore, the modernization/economic development approach overlooks the particular effect of religion on Islamic activism.

The modernization/economic development approach represents a general framework that would apply in many Third World countries. However, the approach needed in studying Islamic activism requires some degree of sensitivity to the religious specifics of the movement.

An example of the modernization/economic development approach is the latest work of Piscatori (1986, pp. 26–32), in which he identifies the causes of "revival" as follows:

> First, the defeat of Egypt, Syria, and Jordan in the 1967 [war] with Israel shattered the morale not only of the Arabs, who lost in a head to head fight with the enemy, but also of most Muslims, who lost the holy city of Jerusalem. Second, the process of development has been a contributing factor. It has stimulated the revival in two main ways: (a) it has often strained the social and political fabric, thereby leading people to turn to traditional symbols and rites as a way of comforting and orienting themselves, and (b) it has provided the means of speedy communication and easy dissemination of both domestic and international information. The third general reason for the present revival in addition to the intellectual and spiritual malaise since the 1967 war and the effects of the development process is that Muslim societies have been caught up in the universal crisis of modernity. Finally, the fourth general reason for the revival is that the conditions of political development in these societies have tended to heighten the importance of Islam as a political ideology. Because most of these societies are poor in institutions and dominated by unelected rulers, it is natural for those in power to look for a way of legitimating themselves.

Piscatori's last three reasons for revival connect the current movement with the "development process," "the universal crisis of modernity," and "conditions of political development."

Similarly, Dessouki and Cudsi (1981, p. 113) write, "The main hypothesis of [*Islam and Power*] is that the revival of Islamic groups and associations is invited by a particular social environment. It is a product of a crisis situation characterized by economic difficulties, moral and ideological confusion, and political instability."

In agreement with Dessouki, Vatikiotis (1981, p. 193) suggests:

> The current Islamic resurgence, with its reassertion of an essentially religious political identity in the sense of a declared adher-

> ence to the ethic and values of Islam, is the result of the disorientation caused by rapid economic development and the disaffection with social change brought about by the transplantation of certain aspects and appurtenances of modernity.

The "disruptive effects of modernization" as a causal variable are also discussed by Munson (1988, pp. 111–114), who describes those effects as (1) rapid economic growth, (2) education, (3) rural–urban migration, and (4) the demand for political participation.

The latest work of Tibi (1990, p. 127) identifies the North–South conflict, rapid social change, and a "legitimacy crisis with secular-oriented political systems," as the causes for Islamic activism. The first two reasons for Islamic activism are characteristic of the modernization/economic development theoretical analysis of Islamic activism.

In describing Islamic activists' backgrounds, Burell[6] (1989, p. 7) suggests that as a result of the growth of the population (especially youth),

> As individuals migrate from villages to overcrowded urban slums they face many problems and great hardship. Old friendships are broken and established ways of life are abandoned. It is, perhaps, not surprising that religion—with its promise of salvation—should become a more prominent feature in such uprooted communities.

Burrell thus assumes that the usual urbanization/modernization problems and the resulting feeling of anomie are causal to the rise of Islamic activism. In describing Sadat's assassins, Kepel (1985, p. 235) comments, "Education has taught them the mannerisms of modern life but not its techniques or spirit."

Hiro is yet another author who links modernization/economic development to Islamic activism. He explains that because of migration from rural to urban settings, there is an increase in Islamic activism. Hiro (1989, p. 274) says of Islamic activists that

> [the] reservoir of alienated masses packed into the poor quarters of urban centers provides a ready audience and recruiting ground for radical and revolutionary groups, secular and religious. Muslim fundamentalists try to rally the alienated and underprivileged on the basis of Islam.

6. Burrell's depiction of Islamic activists is similar to that of Munson (1989, pp. 111–114).

Burke and Lapidus (1989, pp. 26–27) include three types of change that cause Islamic activism:

(1) the "indigenous" movement in a region, a rebound reaction to colonialism,
(2) the "incorporation" of the region into the world's market economy, and
(3) the legitimacy crisis of local elites who are viewed as agents of European power and hegemony.

All these authors have a common set of suppositions. First, as Dessouki writes, there is the shared assumption that Islamic activism is a "product" of a "crisis situation." The crisis situation is defined as the "universal crisis of modernity," "the process of development," "political development," "rapid social/economic change," or the "rapid process of urbanization." By defining Islamic activism as a product or reaction, the analyst implicitly judges the Islamic activist movement as an adverse and inimical reaction to modernization and development. That is, by assuming that Islamic activism is caused by the discomfort of modernization, such explanations also assume that Islamic activism, as a social movement, is discordant with modernization and development. This point is emphasized by Sarayi (1984, p. 120), who makes a distinction between Islam as the "principal depository" of tradition in the Middle East or "as being in opposition to scientific rationality, technological progress and even socio-economic development."

Second, the supposition that Islamic activists share "moral and ideological confusion," "disorientation, . . . and disaffection," and are perceived as "uprooted," "alienated and underprivileged" masses reflects the value-laden discourse of analysis, i.e., there is an assumption that Islamic activists are estranged from their creed, a temporary manifestation of social malaise and ideological incompetence.

Third, the perception that Islamic activism is a product of the rapid modernization/economic development process or that the actors involved in Islamic activism are "ideologically confused" assumes that Islamic activism is, for better or for worse, an aberration of sorts in the history of Muslim societies. Historically, however, the call for a return to Islamic mores, whether violent or nonviolent, has manifested itself in Muslim societies long before the advent of the so-called rapid modernization process, rapid social change, and rural–urban migration.

Fourth, the idea that Islamic activism is related to the North–South conflict or to the incorporation of the region into the world's market economy is limited to economic differences and the resultant dynamics. It does not address the norms and cultural differences that must be taken into consideration when analyzing Muslim Third World countries and differentiating them from their counterparts in South American, Asian, or American Third World peoples.

Last, the definitions of modernization and development are not clear theoretically, and comparative studies differ on what development and change pertain to in any Third World country. Assuming that rapid change, development, and modernization are causal factors in Islamic activism is theoretically dubious, since there is no clear conception of a unilateral schema for modernization/economic development. In relation to the first common supposition previously mentioned, Islamic activism is perceived as a regressive force even though there are no clear definitions or empirical studies that specify what constitutes a "rapid modernization process." In other words, even though there are numerous studies on the stagnation of development in the Middle East/Muslim region, Islamic activism is not theoretically analyzed as a vehicle of change. Rather, the authors cited see Islamic activism as a regressive, traditionalist, and stagnant movement against the forces of development and change.

After discussing the general aspects of the modernization/economic development approach, it is necessary to focus on some specific assumptions that underlie this approach. By the phrases "Weberian school of analysis," "the Weberian paradigm," and "Weberian tradition," I mean the sociological school that used Weber's works to analyze developing societies—in other words, the social scientists who have linked Weber's theory to development at large. In Davis's[7] extrapolation of Weber's theory, for example, he explains that Weber studies development as a unilateral obstacle course that starts with traditional societies and ends with modern societies. However, Weber never characterized current Islamic activism as a traditional force. Contemporary social scientists such as Deeb (1992) and Dekmejian (1985) link traditionalism and charismatic authority to current Islamic movements and its leaders respectively. Studies that take such an approach link the traditional type of action[8] to Islamic activism. For exam-

7. Winston Davis's article "Religion and Development: Weber and East Asia Experience" is part of Myron Weiner and Samuel Huntington's edited *Understanding Political Development* (1987).

8. The four main types of action, according to Weber, are (1) Rational action related to a certain goal (*Zweckrational*), (2) Rational action related to a certain value (*Wertrational*), (3) Emotional action as a reflex reaction in certain situations, and (4) Traditional action that is related to customs and habit (see Aron, 1967, p. 220). Analysts who choose traditional action to characterize Islamic activism do not take into account that the *Zweckrational* or *Wertrational* Models could also apply to Islamic activism.

ple, Burke (Burke and Lapidus 1988, p. 20) writes: "Until the last few decades, the great majority of studies of social movements in Islamic societies tended to be situated within the Weberian tradition, though often without much methodological self-awareness."

After reviewing a number of development schools, Binder (1988, p. 78) also indicates this Weberian trend:

> [The] classic political mobilization model is pushed to a further extreme when it is argued that, ultimately, the strategic development decisions of the Egyptian political elite under Nasser were expressions of Nasser's personal preference, and were neither ideologically determined nor the resultant of some political process. The ultimate reduction of politics to particularistic psychological properties, especially as applied to the explanation of political underdevelopment in the Islamic world, has ideological implications which are by this time so well understood that they hardly need further repetition here. Suffice it to say that Middle Eastern political studies, despite some superficial change in terminology, remain remarkably impervious to scientific revolution. Twenty years from now we shall probably still be discussing the Nasserist period under the rubric of charismatic leadership.

Another offshoot of the "Weberian" analysis of Islamic activism is separating the rational from the irrational as illustrated by el-Kenz (1991, p. 104):

> One then proceeds to a classification of social ideologies according to the dyad religious base/rational base which are distributed among the various actor categories. To well-formed classes "sufficiently powerful and homogeneous" will correspond ideologies whose rational elements dominate; to the unstable, precarious, distorted classes will correspond those where the irrational element, particularly religion, will dominate.

Deeb makes further use of the Weberian tradition when she first claims, in reference to Islamic activism, that "there is nothing new in such movements." Deeb (1992, p. 55) then quotes Weber's *The Economic Ethic of the World Religions* to support her point:

> The conception of the idea of redemption as such is very old, if one understands by it a liberation from distress, hunger, drought, sickness, and ultimately from suffering and death. Yet redemption

> attained a specific significance only where it expressed a systematic and rationalized "image of the world" and represented a stand in the face of the world.

Weber's analysis points out that "redemption" gains significance when it presents itself as "a systematic and rationalized" field of action. A real stretching of the Weberian paradigm is evident in Dekmejian's work. In *Egypt Under Nasser* (1971), Dekmejian's introduction indicates that he will use "what Weber calls charismatic authority" to analyze Nasser's rule. Dekmejian (1971, p. 3) also mentions that it is hard to conceptualize charisma because of the "inability of democratic man to conceptualize such a foreign experience."

In his most recent work, *Islam in Revolution*, Dekmejian (1985, pp. 27–32) explains that because of "five catalysts: identity, legitimacy, elite misrule, class conflict and military impotence," Islamic activism is on the rise. Dekmejian (1985, p. 25) also writes that

> The ideologies of these movements are both comprehensive and rigid, reflecting the responses of typically charismatic leaders to situations of crisis. It is no mere accident that fundamentalist movements in various political contexts have acquired spiritual and sociopolitical potency when two interrelated conditions are met: the appearance of a leader of charismatic propensity and a society in deep turmoil. Significantly, the Islamist movements of the past have satisfied both of these conditions. The Islamist movements of the present are no exception.

Dekmejian (1985, p. 81) further describes the Egyptian Muslim Brotherhood's Ḥassan al Bannā within the confines of such a framework:

> In keeping with the universal pattern of fundamentalist leadership, the Brotherhood constituted the organizational extension of Bannā's charismatic personality and the institutional reflection of his vision. Bannā's emergence typifies Weber's charismatic leader who appears in times of crisis with a message of social spiritual salvation.

According to Dekmejian, therefore, there are similarities between Nasser's Egypt and current Islamic activists in several Middle Eastern countries (including Egypt).[9] Dekmejian's work runs the risk of oversim-

9. In addition, Donohue (Esposito 1993, pp. 59–60) points out the similarities between Nasser's charismatic leadership (nationalist) and Khomeini's charismatic appeal (Islamist).

plifying the Weberian paradigm, because his argument (about two separate political phenomena in Egypt) claims that any popular movement is a result of charismatic leadership. That is, Dekmejian overlooks the fact that although most movements have their heroes, the appeal of the leader is only a partial explanation for the success of the movement. Also, Dekmejian, like other social scientists of the modernization/economic development school, links the Weberian paradigm (by using "charismatic authority") to his normative stance, which is the foreignness of this type of authority to democratic man. That is, democracy is linked to economic development as a necessary element. Dekmejian's argument, therefore, implies that the dynamics of a grassroots movement are directly related to the irrational processes of a society that run contradictory to rationality and its practice as embodied in "legal rational" institutions, democracy, and the values of liberalism.

Culture as an Interpretation of Islamic Activism

The problems of the modernization/economic development explanation further manifest themselves in the second genre of analysis, cultural studies of Islamic activism. Cultural explanations of Islamic activism emphasize several themes. First, the rejection of Western mores and culture by Islamic activists is interpreted as a sign that Islamic activism is in conflict with all Western values. Second, the separation between the functions of church and state in modern Europe is taken as a condition for modern societies that wish to safeguard equality and egalitarianism. The latter point overlaps with modernization/economic development's causal explanation of Islamic activism because the separation between the private self and the public self, or between the religious self and the secular self, is posed as a condition for becoming part of the modern world. Thus culture, and its subcomponent religion, are taken as contradictory forces that prevent Muslim peoples from joining the "secular" modern world. Culture and religion become a defensive mechanism, a shield that separates the identity of the individual and the society from foreign cultural experiences.

Tibi (1990, p. 130), for example, stresses that the growing need for religion is related to the instability of the environment and that religion maintains the identity of individuals in the process of social change. Tibi (1990, pp. 180–181) clarifies his analytic stance:

> My perspective, a self-confessedly normative one, is based on an egalitarian definition of cultures, even though the latter today displays different levels of development that are leading to the emergence of structures of global dominance among them. Despite my unequivocal rejection of the Islamic claim to dominance on the grounds both of its anachronism and of my inclination toward intercultural open-mindedness based on cultural pluralism (but not relativism).

Tibi (1990, p. 183) qualifies his claim of appreciating "intercultural open-mindedness" and "cultural pluralism" when he describes the current Islamic revival (relating it to North–South tension) as follows:

> This [North–South tension] involves a sociocultural conflict between industrial and nonindustrial cultures, insofar as the former dominate the latter by virtue of their technological scientific character. I may mention in support of this thesis the example of the specialization of the sacred in Muslim societies, insofar as it documents a sociocultural protest movement and a counter-acculturation.

Here Tibi, like writers who take the modernization/economic development approach, has chosen to define Islamic activism as a "counter-acculturation" movement, thus neglecting the history and the ethos of Islamic movements in the Middle East region before Islamic culture encountered the "technological scientific character" of industrial societies. Tibi identifies Islamic activism as a reaction to the forces of modernization in contemporary Muslim societies. He fails to recognize the cultural special elements of the movement because he begins his argument by stating that "North–South tensions" and the "sociocultural conflict between the industrial and nonindustrial cultures" are causal to many movements including Islamic activism.

In agreement with Tibi's ideas, Hunter (1988, p. 281) emphasizes that a sense of perceived threat to Islam and its role in society, along with the "failure of secular governments in many Muslim countries during the past sixty years to recognize the importance of Islam's place in the socio-economic, political and cultural fabric of their respective societies," leads to the reactionary revivalist movements. Hunter's analysis indicates that Islamic activism is a reaction to a perceived cultural threat.

The perception of threat and reaction to it is a thread that links the cultural studies of Islamic activism.

In addition to these notions of "perceived threat" and "counter-acculturation," the Durkheimian "alienation" theme is also used to describe Islamic activism. A stark example can be found in the work of Youssef (1985, p. 115), where he stresses that

> [C]onfusion and a lack of synthesis create a cultural vacuum in which people resort to the most bizarre mechanisms for coping with stress. It is no surprise therefore that al Jihad took advantage of the opportunity to provide an answer and deliver a "promise" to the bewildered population.

The bizarre mechanism referred to ties in with other claims of "irrationality" offered by most development/modernization and some cultural explanations of Islamic activism.

Gellner (1992, p. 72) defines "Muslim fundamentalism" as

> an enormously simple, powerful, earthy, sometimes cruel, absorbing, socially fortifying movement, which gives a sense of direction and orientation to millions of men and women, many of whom live lives of bitter poverty and are subject to harsh oppression. It enables them to adjust to a new anonymous mass society by identifying with the old, long-established High Culture of their own faith, and explaining their own deprivation and humiliation as a punishment for having strayed from the true path, rather than a consequence of never having found it; a disruption and disorientation is thus turned into a social and moral ascension, an attainment of identity and dignity.

Gellner's point at the beginning of the definition "enormously simple . . . movement," underlies the rest of his writing and analysis. The assumption that "Muslim fundamentalists" are bitterly poor is an undocumented claim (especially since Gellner's book was published in 1992). It has become increasingly evident that the poor masses are not the only sympathizers with Islamic activists. Islamic activism cuts across economic and social strata.[10] Gellner, like others, attributes current Islamic

10. Binder (1988, p. 242) argues: "The Islamic resurgence is a movement of laymen. It is a manifestation of an increasingly popular struggle of a growing number of bureaucrats, technicians, professionals, teachers, skilled workers, and even kulaks, who would assert themselves politically and attempt to reshape the state in terms of their own self-image."

activism to deprivation, humiliation, disruption, and discrimination. As a result, Islamic activism is viewed as a temporary malaise of sorts, or a more reaction to the deprivation and humiliation that are imposed on Muslim societies.

Gellner (1992, p. 92) identifies himself as an "enlightenment rationalist fundamentalist" and claims that

> when dealing with serious matters, when human lives and welfare are at stake, when major resources are being committed, the only kind of knowledge which may legitimately be used and invoked is that which satisfies the criteria of Enlightenment philosophy.

The Enlightenment philosophy, according to Gellner (1992, p. 90)

> strove to understand the economic and social success of the first modern societies, and so proposed a secular version of a salvation religion, a naturalistic doctrine of universally valid salvation, in which reason and nature replaced revelation. It did so because it perceived the role of new, secular knowledge in the new social order.

Gellner (1992, pp. 83–84) further claims that the "cognitive ethic" of the Enlightenment treats "all data, all information, all occasions, . . . alike: there are no privileged sources of illumination. The essence of sin is the making of exceptions. In other words, there is no and can be no revelation." On the other hand, Gellner's main argument throughout the book is that the cultural "relativist" and "postmodernist"[11] positions are "laughable": "Their insights apply to decorative rather than the real structural and functional aspects of our life (Gellner 1992, pp. 95–96).

Gellner (1992, p. 95) respects Islamic fundamentalists "both as fellow recognizers of the uniqueness of truth, who avoid the facile self-deception of universal relativism, and as our intellectual ancestors."

Gellner's contribution is theoretically significant because of its analysis of the three main current ideologies of postmodernism, religion (especially Islamic fundamentalism), and "Enlightenment rationalist fundamentalism."[12] His refutation and dismantling of cultural relativism

---

11. Gellner explains that cultural relativists/postmodernists are researchers who stress the need to evaluate norms and mores in their cultural context. That is, the cultural relativists are concerned with the cultural aspects of different societies rather than with the universality of any social issue. Therefore the cultural relativists are more liberal in their interpretations of different societies than are "religious fundamentalists" or "enlightenment rationalist fundamentalists," as explained in Gellner's writing.

12. Gellner uses the term "Enlightenment rationalist fundamentalism" interchangeably with "reason" as the title of his book suggests: *Postmodernism, Religion, and Reason.*

and postmodernism are representative of the normative position mentioned earlier that ridicules and discredits Islamic activists' "rationality" as a social movement.

Binder's writing is similar to Gellner's, although it is focused on development theory rather than on the broader scheme of analysis that Gellner adopts. Thus both Binder and Gellner criticize the cultural relativists' arguments. While Gellner does not directly critique Said's *Orientalism* as Binder does,[13] he implies such criticism throughout his argument against relativists. Binder does not clarify his ideological stance as Gellner does; the latter clearly identifies himself as a "Enlightenment rationalist fundamentalist" which, according to Gellner, means one who does not believe in any privileged sources of information that should direct human behavior. Gellner is against a divine set of rules and mores that guide human behavior. Rather, he appreciates the equality of all sources of knowledge in the Enlightenment period in Europe, which he also qualifies as "rational." Gellner calls for the return to the age of Enlightenment and the adoption of "rationality" as a guideline in complying with social rules and mores.

Both the differentiation between rational and irrational social choices and the line drawn between secular and religious societies affect the evaluation of Islamic activism as a movement. Gellner's attack on cultural relativists represents the epitome of separating the "religious fundamentalists" from the "enlightenment rationalist fundamentalists." Emphasis on the cultural aspects of the Islamic activist movements also overlooks the modernization factors that could have affected them, i.e., neither modernization/economic development nor cultural causation alone is sufficient to explain the complexity and depth of the social phenomenon of Islamic activism.

---

13. In his chapter titled "Deconstructing Orientalism," Binder (1988, p. 120–21) severely criticizes Said's work:

> There are a number of reasons that might explain why Said says nothing about Islam. He might have intended to write only of the West. He might not know enough about Islam. He might have felt that it was sufficient instead to name those of whose work he approves. He might have felt it best to say nothing rather than to say some one thing. He might believe that it is inappropriate or impossible or even hostile for any outsider to speak of a belief system which he does not share. Whatever his reason, Said says nothing and says nothing about why he says nothing, and it is this double silence which suggests an anomaly, a kind of paradox, an *aporia* or the very condition which makes Said's critical discourse possible. Of course it may be true that if Said were to have written anything about Islam, he might have been able to write nothing about orientalism.

The Popular Discontent Approach to Explaining Islamic Activism

A third approach looks on popular discontent/mass mobilization as the main source of current Islamic activism. Few works take this approach, with the exception of studies on the Iranian Islamic movement.[14]

Though the studies that link Islamic activism to popular discontent are few, they explain Islamic activism using multiple causal factors. They have fewer limitations than do other approaches because the concept of popular discontent allows for the inclusion of modernization/economic development problems, cultural differences, basic needs, and human rights issues. Thus popular discontent reflects the cumulative grievances that could have affected the current Islamic activist movements.

One of the most recent studies on the Iranian revolution (Dabashi 1993, p. 489) for example, links the revolution to the general Islamic activism mood:

> Beyond its material causes, the ideological, mythical, and theological dimensions of a revolution give communal expressions to man's most moving precept: *Discontent. A deeply rooted desire to change, to alter, to modify, to transgress, and ultimately to become another seems to lie beneath every veneer of calm civility that the status quo demands and rewards.* Permanent revolution is simply the political expression of a more abiding truth, which is permanent change in one's self-understanding. Here, on this borderline, the conservative, the liberal, and the revolutionary all concur. Re-enacting "Islam itself," the Islamic Ideology is the historical case of the hermeneutic conversation between the authority of the ideological interpreter and the legitimacy of the remembered text—all to (redefine) man's quintessential discontent with merely being in-the-world. The text in the Islamic case is much more than the Quran and the Hadith, etc. It is that palaverous constellation of symbolics and sensibilities, figures and figurations of authority, that at every historical conjunction its believers obediently call "Islam," or, as in the modernity of its manifestation, the Islamic ideology. That term of disenchantment

14. Iran is excluded from my research because it had already gone through its revolution in 1979. That is, the other countries chosen in this study have not gone through massive change brought about by Islamic activists. My research compares countries where Islamic activism is in opposition to current political systems.

> registers the radicality of contemporary Muslims' bewildering discontent.

Dabashi links the disenchantment of Islamic activists in Iran to their discontent with "merely being in-the-world." That is, he offers discontent as a direct cause of the phenomenon of Islamic activism. Thus, unlike modernization/economic development analysts and cultural analysts, he does not treat Islamic activism as a rebound effect of "rapid modernization" or as a cultural defense mechanism. Although Dabashi qualifies this form of discontent as an inherent psychological state of "merely being in-the-world," he addresses the Islamic movement as a dynamic changing force that has existed throughout the years. To Dabashi it is not a novelty, but rather a manifestation of humanity's continued struggle with existentialism and purpose.

Though the reader may object to any mystical, inherent qualifications of discontent (since such notions fail to offer any causality in explaining Islamic activism), it is important to note that Dabashi addresses the continuity of Islamic activism as a phenomenon. Dabashi's contribution to the literature on Islamic activism lies in his emphasis on the discontent of the people as a determining factor in explaining the reasons for and the degree of strength of the movement.

Batran (1989, p. 10) takes Dabashi's ideas a step further when he acknowledges that:

> Islamic revolutions in Africa have a long tradition extending into the eighth century—a theme that runs uninterrupted across the moving frontiers of the history of Islam in Africa. Whenever African Muslims faced critical situations, they invoked that common thread, Islam, to provide the elixir for all their society's ailments.

Batran (1989, p. 39) later expands his explanation: "Hence mass sufferings, popular indignation and frustrated nationalistic sentiments were often times released, under the direction of self-proclaimed Mahdis or Mujaddids (Renewers), in waves of revolutionary action." Batran does not link Dabashi's discontent to an inherent mystical form of disenchantment. Rather, he links it to specific conditions: "mass sufferings, popular indignation and frustrated nationalist sentiments." This is a unique stance, distinguishable from modernization/economic development and cultural causal explanations. Batran stresses an element seldom recognized by the modernization/economic development and cultural explanations: mass suffering and popular indignation. Modernization/economic development explanations usually describe such movements as irrational, traditional reactions to a perceived threat of modernization, development, and democratic practice.

Goldberg (1992) challenges the theoretical suppositions of modernization/economic development and the cultural explanations of Islamic activism (especially the first). Goldberg (1992, p. 211) compares Calvin's movement to the Muslim Brotherhood's religious ideas in Egypt, beginning with this observation:

> Egypt has experienced inflation, stagnation, low productivity, crowding and increased income inequity in the very recent period. Gilles Kepel and Eric Davis argue that the Islamist program arises from the declining economic situation of group members or (in Davis' words) "pressurization." Such arguments . . . unfortunately do not explain the development of this ideology in the 1950s and 1960s, when the economic situation was improving for all Egyptians. It also cannot explain the militants' manifest and self-conscious understanding that their movement is the result of Nasserism's political victory rather than its economic failure.

Goldberg (1992, p. 213) further clarifies his argument:

> It therefore seems to me to make less sense to argue that these groups respond to social or economic "pressure" than they responded—as did the early Protestant groups—to the process of political centralization that enhanced the arbitrary power of the political elite and especially the head of state.

Goldberg's challenge to current literature on Islamic activism distinguishes his study because he does not ignore the existence of Islamic activism in the 1950s and 1960s, when Egyptian society briefly tasted the fruits of a growing economy. Goldberg thus magnifies the problems that the modernization/economic development approach encounters when explaining Islamic activism. Instead, he relies on the historical existence of such movements when "economic pressurization" was not a factor affecting Islamic activism.

An Analysis of the Literature

In summation of the aforementioned approaches used to explain Islamic activism, I will attempt to clarify some limitations of each analytical perspective. As described above, two normative stands underlie the analysis of Islamic activism. One tends to sympathize with the cultural component of Islamic activism (e.g., Esposito, Lapidus and Burke, and Haddad); the other rejects the movements' premises, not to mention their thought, i.e., it rejects Islamic activists' attachment to religious values and therefore rejects the ideas that are propagated by Islamic activists (e.g., Tibi, Binder, Lawrence, Kepel, and Gellner).

Three major approaches explain Islamic activism: modernization/economic development, cultural, and popular discontent. The first two approaches are the more prominent and frequently used explanations for Islamic activism, as indicated in the literature review.

The popular discontent explanation is a distinctive approach to understanding Islamic activism, because it addresses the phenomenon with the awareness that the movement has a wide popular base. The movement is related to social, psychological, economic, and cultural variables (i.e., it recognizes the holistic nature of mankind and, therefore, their cumulative grievances that invoke in them the need to change). Another important element in the popular discontent approach is that it recognizes the state's failure to perform, which constitutes the basic hypothesis for my study.

The three causal theories of Islamic activism coexist in current literature. A graphic presentation of the literature on Islamic activism is presented in Diagram 1 on page 18.

The two more common approaches share an important factor, which I shall use as a point of departure. Whether one considers the sympathetic/relativist or the conservative view in Islamic activism literature, one finds rigidly drawn lines of duality, of differentiation, of Us versus Them. This duality is captured by Binder (1988, p. 5):

> the outstanding characteristic of Islamic political revival . . . is its rejection of Western liberal pretensions and practices. The outstanding characteristic of the contemporary Islamic political revival is that it points toward the end of a dialogue.

Diagram 1

The Effect of Normative Underpinnings
on Causal Approaches of Islamic Activism

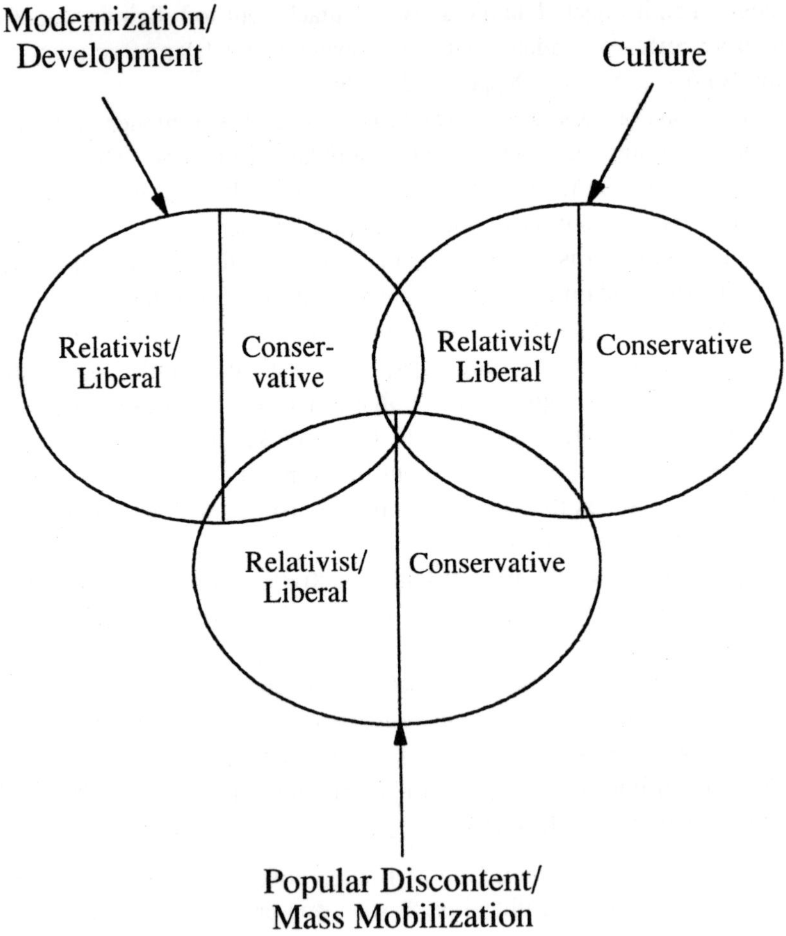

It is precisely the alleged "end of a dialogue" that draws attention to the danger of utilizing the endless dualism of rational versus irrational, developed versus underdeveloped, sacred versus profane, secular versus religious. "The end of a dialogue" adds a pessimistic hue to current and future studies of Islamic activism. A more optimistic stance will allow for an understanding of the common ground between "Western liberal pretensions" and the "Islamic political revival."

Stressing the duality of modes of thought and action, and differentiating between societies by claiming that the relativity of action and thought is particular to each society, becomes a way of escaping from dialog with the Other. Engaging with the Other in dialog requires a balanced position, whereby one is neither too much of a cultural relativist nor a cultural conservative. Therefore, I will attempt to tread a careful balance in order to understand Islamic activism in both its universal and relative aspects. My goal is to comprehend, explain, and—most importantly—engage in a dialog with the Other, the Muslim activists, by analyzing their expressed grievances and expectations.

Whether one considers issues of modernization or cultural phenomena, one would finally end up using some measure of normative judgment. If scholars assume a priori that Islamic activism is a reaction either to modernization problems or to cultural disorientation, they implicitly accept either a fundamentalist or cultural relativist position. Arguments that either modernization or culture is causal to Islamic activism make it harder to analyze the phenomenon. Therefore, by using popular discontent to explain Islamic activism, one avoids the normative constraints that accompany the other two approaches.

The popular discontent/mass mobilization approach also provides an analytical framework that can explain change. While the modernization/economic development and cultural approaches imply that Islamic activism is an aberration of sorts, a reflex reaction to "modernization," "urbanization," and "counter-acculturation," emphasizing popular discontent/mass mobilization directs attention to all the dynamics of change that prevail in Muslim societies today.

My basic hypothesis is that the extent of Islamic activism is a function of the extent to which state performance in Islamic societies falls short of the principles of Islamic social justice as embodied in the *maqāṣid*. Analysis of the case studies will help in envisioning the broad lines of the development of such movements and how Muslim societies will thereby change.

The Link between Popular Discontent/Mass Mobilization Theory and the Analytical Framework of the Proposed Study

Though there are good reasons for emphasizing popular discontent as a cause of Islamic activism, one has to be cautious regarding a pitfall of this approach. The popular discontent approach to explaining Islamic activism has not yet been connected to mass mobilization/mass movement theory.

It is necessary now to link the idea that Islamic activism is caused by popular discontent to the theoretical literature on mass movements. Dabashi (1993) writes about the psychological component of discontent and relates it to the state of "merely being in-the-world" while Batran (1989) comes closer to linking mass mobilization theory to his work. However, the comparative analytical framework offered in Goldstone, Gurr, and Moshiri (1991, p. 37) encourages the need to study Islamic activism from such a perspective.

Goldstone defines three conditions as indicators of state breakdown and the simultaneous and consequent process of revolution: "(1) fiscal distress, (2) elite alienation and conflict, and (3) a high potential for mobilization of the populace."[15] These three conditions are mentioned in a number of works on Islamic activist movements. Haddad (1991, p. 10), for example, indicates that "the discussion of religious topics has entered the public realm" and that the "revivalist movement itself is very much that of the lay population." Binder (1988, p. 242) also writes: "The Islamic resurgence is a movement of laymen. It is a manifestation of an increasingly popular struggle of a growing number of bureaucrats, technicians, profes-

15. Gurr and Goldstone (Goldstone, Gurr, and Moshiri 1991, pp. 346–347) also conclude,

> Concrete signs of impending state crisis are not invisible, although the actual attitudes of people may be concealed. Thus, rather than wait for clear signs of widespread overt opposition, superpowers should realize that regimes that show multiple symptoms of an impending crisis, such as a lack of positive accomplishments, inadequate resources or foreign dependency, corruption, exclusion, and counter-mobilization, are in deep trouble and cannot be shored up indefinitely. If the basic regime attitudes and structures that produced these symptoms cannot be rectified, one should brace for the emergence of a revolutionary struggle in such states.

The authors' remark is also adequate and applicable in reference to current Islamic Activist (IA) movements throughout the Middle East with regard to US foreign policy in particular and a number of European countries' foreign policy (e.g., French policy in North African countries).

sionals, teachers, skilled workers, and even kulaks, who would assert themselves politically and attempt to reshape the state in terms of their own self-image."

Michael Hudson (1980, p. 24) writes that Islam is gaining acceptance as a political ideology for opposition movements, because it is somewhat congenial to other political ideologies. Hudson stresses the potency of Islam as an ideology that is capable of mobilizing the masses. In agreement with Hudson, Williams (1980, pp. 84–85) concludes his research on Islamic activism in Egypt by pointing out the reasons that impel people to examine the possibilities for change. He emphasizes that frustration, despair, loss, and the inability of the government to provide for the people's needs will lead to "a new Egyptian revolution."[16]

Esposito's later work (1992, pp. 22–23) also points out the strength of Islamic activism as a mass movement:

> In the nineties Islamic revivalism has ceased to be restricted to small, marginal organizations on the periphery of society and instead has become part of mainstream Muslim society, producing a new class of modern-educated but Islamically oriented elites who work alongside, and at times in coalitions with, their secular counterparts. Revivalism continues to grow as a broad-based socio-religious movement, functioning today in virtually every Muslim country and transnationally.

Esposito (1992, p. 100) stresses elements of the three preconditions for revolutions when he describes Islamic activism in Egypt as follows:

> The most important characteristic of Islamic revivalism in Egypt in the nineties is the extent to which revivalism has become part and parcel of moderate mainstream life and society, rather than a marginal phenomenon limited to small groups or organizations. No longer restricted to the lower middle class, renewed awareness and concern about leading a more Islamically informed way of life can also be found among the middle and upper class, educated and uneducated, peasants and professionals, young and old, women and men. They are active in Qur'an study groups (run by both women and men), Sufi gatherings, mosques, and private associations. As a

16. Hudson and Williams' articles were both published in *Islam and Development* (Esposito 1980). Both authors reflect the relatively less active period of IA, especially after Sadat's assassination in 1981 and the numerous assassinations and riots that followed in Egypt and the escalation of IA in Algeria, Tunisia, the Occupied Territories, and Jordan.

result, Islamic identity is expressed not only in formal religious practices but also in the social services offered by psychiatric and drug rehabilitation centers, dental clinics, day-care centers, legal aid societies, and organizations which provide subsidized housing and food distribution or run banks and investment houses.

Thus, as indicated in the literature on Islamic activism, the three conditions are more than evident in a number of Muslim societies. Fiscal distress as well as elite alienation and the mobilization of the populace are becoming increasingly evident indicators of change in Muslim societies. It is not surprising to find the masses relying on the services and institutions offered by the Muslim Brotherhood in Egypt, for example, where this phenomenon is indicative of both elite alienation and a high probability of potential mass-mobilization.

The logical question then about Islamic activism is: If there is change, what will this change entail? As Butterworth (1982, p. 110) notes in his article "Prudence versus Legitimacy," there are no progressive steps toward an understanding of how social institutions will function beyond rallying popular support, thus indicating the need for a "third wave of thinkers" to address particular details of justice according to the Divine Law (Shari'ah). Butterworth's call for clarity is later echoed by a number of researchers on Islamic activism such as Haddad (1991, p. 7) in her bibliographic survey of the literature on Islamic activism, where she stresses that "change [in Muslim nations] is imperative." She also indicates, however, that the challenging task is to understand "change to what?" (Haddad 1991, p. 7).

Esposito (1992, p. 99) also recognizes the lack of a "specific concrete alternative program" for the Islamic activists. He criticizes their focus on the failures of the incumbent government and religio-social issues rather than of "defining the nature of an Islamic state and its institutions.

Butterworth (1992, p. 36) also criticizes current Islamic political thought:

> Their rhetoric, addressed now more than ever to the unlearned masses of citizens, speaks only of what might be and ignores the practical, procedural issues of how these goals are to be reached without harming citizens along the way. It also ignores the major question of how to provide for prudent decisions once the goal of Islamic government has been reached . . . yet properly understood, it is against precisely this tendency to ignore procedural safeguards that Western criticism of political Islam is addressed.

Hence, using popular discontent to explain Islamic activism is plausible for a number of reasons:

(1) it avoids the analytical constraints that affect the modernization/economic development and cultural approaches,
(2) it is not confined to the idea that Islamic activism is a tangential, temporary state of malaise; rather, it allows for analyzing Islamic activism as a mainstream, grassroots movement,[17] and
(3) the popular discontent approach calls attention to the degree of alienation of the elite from the masses and helps explain the social forces leading to the formation of indigenous institutions, i.e., creating a state within a state.

In short, studying the scope and sources of mass mobilization in Muslim societies evaluates what Esposito calls "the quiet revolution" of Islamic activism.

On the other hand, Butterworth's, Haddad's, and Esposito's concern with a detailed, "concrete alternative program" or more bluntly "change to what?" remains to be addressed. This requires an understanding of the nature of change as a primary step.

Although Butterworth, Haddad, and Esposito justifiably demand "change to what?" all Islamic movements have stressed the necessity of implementing God's law on Earth (*Sharīʻat Allāh fi al 'arḍ*). Though the literature on Islamic activism recognizes the importance in those movements of implementing Islamic law, there has been little effort to decipher or understand the rudiments of that law and what it could entail for a Muslim community in terms of social justice. The state of the art literature on Islamic activism (Binder 1988, p. 131) indicates the importance of the Shariʻah as follows:

> A key doctrinal precondition for the contemporary reassertion of Islamic fundamentalism is whether under contemporary historical conditions, it is feasible to establish and maintain an ideal, Islamic government. An ideal Islamic government is one in which the law may be determined with absolute certainty so that Muslims are left in no doubt about what they must do and what they must not do.

17. Esposito underscores this in his book *The Islamic Threat: Myth or Reality?* (1992, pp. 199–200, 209–210).

Esposito (1992, p. 118) also draws attention to the importance of Islamic law:

> Is the implementation of Islam in state and society to be a restoration or a reformation, the resurrection of past doctrines and laws or the reconstruction of new models rooted in faith but appropriate to the changed circumstances of life today? The issue is clear when we look at the question of Islamic law. For many, the Islamic character of the state is determined by the implementation of Islamic law.

Haddad (1991, p. 15) criticizes the literature on Islamic activism for neglecting the issue of Islamic law:

> [I]n order to understand the dynamic of revival, we need more analysis of the issues being raised in the current debate over the reinstitution of the Shari'ah in countries such as Egypt, Jordan, Tunisia, Algeria, and Indonesia. Given the fact that the public discussion of these issues uses familiar Islamic language and themes, scholars have been tempted to dismiss the revivalists as seeking to return the Muslim community to the seventh century. It is clear that for most revivalist writers, however, this is not the case, and the exegetical and contextual analysis of the language they are using makes it clear that they are seeking a better understanding of the problems besetting their societies and of the ways in which traditional Islamic sources can be interpreted so as to help solve them.

Haddad emphasizes the importance of implementing Islamic law for Islamic activists, regardless of their differences. The "ideal blueprint for the good society" for Islamic activists is the Shari'ah. However, Haddad (1991, p. 53) notes that Islamic activists "differ in what they wish to implement. Conservatives tend to regard much of the corpus of the traditional Islamic law as binding. Reformers note that the law is subject to reinterpretation, ijtihād, and reform."

The latter (the reformers') stance lies at the crux of this research since it uses Islamic jurisprudential teachings (fiqh) to comprehend the rudiments of social justice in a Muslim society. Haddad and Dabashi both accentuate the grievances of Islamic activists, which are hypothesized to be causal to the rise of Islamic activism as a movement in several Muslim societies, as is proposed in this study. Consonant with Esposito's later work (Esposito, 1992), Haddad describes current Islamic activism:

> [T]he strength of contemporary revivalism remains with a growing moderate majority of Islamic activists whose activities have become part of mainstream Muslim life. Their vision of Islam is holistic. They believe that a faithful, righteous Islamic community is one that observes God's mandate to worship Him and to create a *socially just society*. This long-term process, which is weaving its way into political and social institutions, will have significance both for the development of Muslim societies and for their relationship with the West.

An understanding of what the basics of social justice entail under Islamic law might throw light on the inception of grievances in Muslim societies and could eventually help to explain current activism. Thus, the other side of the coin is injustice or, as Dabashi puts it, *ẓulm*, which according to Islamic activists is the cause of the current social/political phenomenon that is supposedly gaining momentum and popularity in Muslim societies.

Dabashi (1993, p. 506) captures the essence of the Iranian revolution[18] as follows:

> Perhaps the single most important theme in the mobilizing rhetoric of "the Islamic Ideology" was its insistence on the dichotomous battle between "justice" on the side of the revolutionaries and "injustice" on the part of the established regime. *Ẓulm*, Persian and Arabic for injustice, was the primary accusation against the monarch (the Shah of Iran) and his tyrannical rule. The Shah's government was *ipso facto* rendered illegitimate. This illegitimacy pronounced on moral, not primarily political grounds, the language of revolt then inevitably assumes an ethical posture that, in effect, renders any alternative invalid. Such a moral consolidation of revolutionary forces thus engages its enemies not only at the level of the established order but also at the level of its ideological competitors: the secular revolutionaries—radical or liberal.

It is precisely this concept of *ẓulm* that may be linked to Islamic activism. The separation between moral and political illegitimacy is built on the presupposition that the religious/moral and political arenas are separate. As Haddad notes, contemporary Islamic activists consider Islam a

18. In my opinion, it is reflective of Islamic activists' sentiments in other contemporary Muslim societies as well.

holistic order, so that the moral righteousness of the Islamic community is part and parcel of the politically and socially just society.

Thus, upon examination of the literature and in conjunction with previously discussed materials, this study will attempt to address Islamic activism as a mass movement that covers the spectrum from demonstrations of violence to nonviolent expressions of opposition. The study uses the popular discontent approach mentioned earlier to address the phenomenon without the value-laden assumptions of modernization versus traditionalism or rational versus irrational. As Haddad (1991, pp. 53–54) indicates, the Islamic activists call for creating a "socially just society," and this society's righteousness and sense of justice could only be upheld by the Shari'ah.

Conclusion

The current phenomenon of Islamic activism in many predominantly Muslim societies and societies that have Muslim minorities is not a recent or "new" ideological phase.[19] Historically, movements of different Muslim groups have been part of the ebb and flow of life in most Muslim societies.

As a student of the social sciences, I will study and examine the traditional legal aspects of Islamic social justice. The Islamic activists' insistence that the Shari'ah be reinstated as the supreme law of the land is a direct cause of my focus on *maqāṣid al sharī'ah* (the end goals of Islamic law), since the *maqāṣid al sharī'ah* represent the political, social, and economic ethos of Islamic jurisprudence.

The significance of my study lies in its effort to answer the following questions: What are the end goals for which Muslim societies strive? Could the lack of or decline in social rights according to *maqāṣid al sharī'ah* be the most important causal variable for the rise of Muslim militancy in many Muslim societies? What are the commonalities between the Western understanding of basic needs, social justice, and the Islamic perception of those values. Are the developmental paths of Muslim societies dependent on and related to Islamic law?

19. Therefore the words "revival" and "resurgence" are not used in this research.

To answer these questions, it is necessary to comprehend the frame of reference and the body of knowledge that Muslim activists draw upon. Chapter 2 will consequently aim at:

(1) understanding the importance of the Shari'ah to current Islamic movements,
(2) explaining the links between sources of the Shari'ah and the end goals of the Shari'ah (*maqāṣid al shari'ah*),
(3) explaining the four jurisprudential (*madhāhib* in fiqh) sources and how the *maqāṣid* relate to them,
(4) sketching the theoretical agreements and disagreements among the *fuqahā'* (legal scholars) on *maqāṣid al shari'ah*, and
(5) justifying the use of the *maqāṣid* in analyzing current Islamic activism.

Chapter 3 will focus on the methodological aspects of my research, including a theoretical specification of the *maqāṣid* and their operationalization in this study. Chapters 4 through 6 will then focus on each individual country, and chapter 7 will present my conclusion.

CHAPTER 2

Islamic Activism: The Relation between the Shari'ah and Muslim Peoples' Expectations

Chapter 1's literature review of the approaches that purport to explain Islamic activism has led to the development of this study. The three approaches—modernization/economic development, culture, and popular discontent—have in many ways failed to provide a comprehensive understanding of Islamic activism. The modernization approach has focused on Islamic activists' sentiments as a natural side-effect of development and growth, while the cultural approach has stressed the cultural differences (i.e., Islamic activism as a "counter-acculturation" movement) without taking into account the commonalities that Third World countries share, i.e., economic stress. Thus the development approach has generalized the common Third World dilemma and extended its explanations to Islamic activism, while the cultural approach has neglected the general and stressed the specific by focusing on culture as the unilateral cause of Islamic activism.

The third approach, which emphasizes popular discontent, is relatively neglected in studies of Islamic activism. It recognizes the intrinsic value of consolidating the general problems of Third World countries—all relating to the stresses of economic development—with the specificity of the Islamic culture's importance to Islamic activists. Therefore, I will attempt to explain Islamic activism through a more comprehensive model. I will try to combine cultural factors, economic factors, and other grievances of Islamic activists to understand the movement.

The term "mass mobilization" or "mass movement" usually implies violent conflict with an existing political structure. However, in current Islamic activist movements, the broad base of activists rely mainly on nonviolent actions that nonetheless affect the society. The "quiet revolution," as Esposito (1992, p. 199) terms it, has a potentially radical effect, even though the actions of Islamic activists considered here are not solely related to violence. My focus includes the nonviolent and quiescent change that is taking place in the Muslim societies under study. Thus the political as well as the social implications of Islamic activism are tested.

Islamic activists call for implementing the Shari'ah, and their expressed grievances are linked to the *maqāṣid*. This link manifests itself in two respects. First, Islamic activists write of the *maqāṣid* as a goal for rulership. Second, the spirit of the *maqāṣid* can be linked theoretically to the perceived state failure to observe the Shari'ah laws as propounded by Islamic activists. That is, their grievances are hypothetically related to state failures to uphold the *maqāṣid*.

This study will try to capture the meaning of the *maqāṣid* from a jurisprudential point of view. I will then attempt to match Islamic activists' grievances with the elements of the *maqāṣid*. State failure, judged by the principles of the *maqāṣid*, may be a major cause of the increase in Islamic activism.

In addition to understanding and explaining the elements of change in the Muslim societies under study, my intent in Chapter 2 and in this research in general is to focus on Islamic doctrines in order to comprehend the nature and origin of Islamic activist movements. As Masud (1977, p. 193) notes, there is

> a generally skeptical attitude of Islamicists[20] towards studies of Islamic doctrines on the formal level . . . Islamic doctrine thus presents an outer formulation (to Islamicists) rather than an inner function or reality. Hence Islamic doctrines, taken literally (according to Islamicists), are not of much help in understanding the inner religious attitudes of Muslims.

I hope to clarify the differences between most Third World revolutionary struggles and the imperatives of the revolutionary cultural change in current Muslim societies. Understanding the "quiet revolution" requires a closer analysis of the grievances of Islamic activists and an

20. Masud refers to scholars who write about Islam and Muslims as "Islamicists."

understanding of what they perceive as *ẓulm* (injustice) in their respective societies.

In this chapter I will lay out my approach to explain Islamic activism. First I will provide the rationale for my approach. I will quote some of the arguments made by Islamic activists that are linked to the theoretical framework of my proposed hypotheses.

In the first segment of this chapter I emphasize the need for different approaches in studying Islamic activism. That is, I include aspects of economic development, and cultural as well as popular discontent, in my analysis of Islamic activism. By understanding what Muslim activists assert, we may find answers to the cultural, economic and popular discontent question from within the movement.

In the second segment of this chapter, I will analyze the works of Muslim scholars who have renewed the academic interest in traditional legal thought. Scholarly interest in Muslim legal thought corresponds to the movement's interest in reviving Muslim law (Shari'ah), particularly the notion of the "public good" (*al maṣlaḥah/al maqāṣid*).

After stressing the Muslim scholars' current assessment of the public good, I will focus on defining Muslim law and its sources. I will also relate the public good to the differences among legal scholars and the historical development of the concept.

The Place of the Shari'ah in the Islamic Activists' Discourse and Their Expressed Grievances

Two issues ought to be considered when analyzing Islamic activist writings. First, like any underground anti-establishment movement, Islamic activists are not allowed to do research or conduct any scientific study that is suggestive of institutional change, or any other kind of change for that matter. As Ghanūshī, a well-known Islamic activist in Tunisia, notes:[21]

> We have tried more than once, whenever it was safe, to make up committees or even research centers for the study of the nature of the Islamic state, the rules of al Shari'ah and *maṣlaḥah*, economics . . . soon enough, however, our projects and research articles are

21. Ghanūshī notes this in a book that compiles numerous interviews done with him by Ṣāliḥ al Darwīsh (1992, p. 133).

> always taken against by the security apparatus to prove that we are involved in an anti-establishment movement. Then the questioning starts: Who wrote this research? Where was this research written? Who attended those lectures? That is to say, our research and effort are always handled as a threat to security.

Second, like many other anti-establishment movements, the more popular the movement gets, the more importance the leaders of the movement place on engaging all socioeconomic classes in their discourse. That is, with the increasing need for popular support, it is more likely that social and political jargon will be used to address the masses. A future Islamic government's shape and structure are not addressed with clarity and specificity when the movement is trying to acquire mass support for its cause.

With very few exceptions, Islamic activists have invoked the Shari'ah as the body of legal principles to which Muslims should adhere. The late Sayyid Quṭb, a widely read Islamic activist, describes the Shari'ah as an extensive body of knowledge that has a preset, general framework that branches off into details and applications, thus safeguarding the human being regardless of place and time (Quṭb, 1988, pp. 48–49). Qutb (1988, pp. 49–50) writes of the importance of fiqh as "the theoretical space allowing for change, however, within the constraints of a general framework of the Shari'ah." According to Quṭb, the Shari'ah is a constant body of rules that do not change, since they dictate God's word, derived from the Qur'an and Sunnah. Fiqh, however, is promulgated by the people, which makes it more flexible and inclusive of the changes and needs that take place in society (Quṭb 1988, p. 50).

Quṭb's *History: Thought and Discourse* (1983, pp. 32–33) stresses certain rights: "Every person is entitled to food, drink, clothes, transportation, housing, marriage, because those are necessities that preserve and provide the basics of life. Likewise, every person is entitled to medical care and treatment and to education, to work and to be trained."[22]

In *Implementing the Shari'ah*, Quṭb (1991, pp. 30–39) dedicated the chapter to the discussion of the importance of fiqh and the *maqāṣid* as they relate to Islam.[23] He draws on historical examples to illustrate and empha-

---

22. All those rights are part and parcel of the *maqāṣid*, the preservation of the end goals of the Shari'ah, as I will indicate further on.

23. Please refer to the glossary on page 199 for definitions of the Arabic terms used in this chapter.

size the practical aspects of the Shari'ah reinforcement in a Muslim society. He concludes the chapter by stating (Quṭb 1991, p. 39) that the

> entrusted ruler has to act in accordance with *al maṣāliḥ al mursalah* [*al maqāṣid*],[24] so that he does not disregard the end goals of the Shari'ah [*maqāṣid al Sharī'ah*] . . . He [the ruler] is also entitled to adapt to the various issues that change with time and place,[25] however he has to uphold the *maqāṣid* as a legal measure in his decision making.

In a dissertation about al Bannā (the founder of the Muslim Brotherhood in Egypt: 1928–1949),[26] al Baiyūmī (1992, p. 276) comments on al Bannā's perception of the responsibilities of governing: "The state derives its legitimacy from obeying the rules and end goals of the Shari'ah (*al maqāṣid*)."

The dissertation (al Baiyūmī 1992, pp. 37–41) also includes al Bannā's ideas for change:

> (1) Renewing Muslim self-confidence, (2) re-educating Muslims about their religion and their mores, (3) stressing the need to utilize an Islamic stance for development, (4) educating people about Sufism, some of its myths and its relation to Islam, (5) stressing the need to de-colonize all Muslim lands, (6) changing the educational system in Egypt, because education in Egypt (a) teaches religion as an extracurricular course, (b) the educational system has no particular objective, (c) there is a lot of stress being put on learning foreign languages whereby it is considered as a main course requirement (i.e., while religion is taught is an extracurricular course).

Tunisia's al Ghanūshī, a well-known contemporary Muslim activist, also indicates, in *A Collection of Dialogues* (al Darwīsh 1992, pp. 130–139) that the *maqāṣid* should provide a legal basis, the reasoning for future Muslim societies.

Al Turābī (1980, pp. 27–28), a well-known Islamic advocate in Sudan, writes:

---

24. The interchangeability of the two concepts will be further clarified in sections C and D of this chapter.

25. Quṭb dedicates the third chapter to how adaptable the Shari'ah is to issues that could change according to place and time.

26. The years indicate al Bannā's activity as a leader of the Muslim Brotherhood of Egypt as noted in the aforementioned dissertation (al Baiyūmī 1992, p. 336).

> Worship is the most inclusive of all end goals of the Shari'ah. The end goals of the Shari'ah are in agreement with another source of jurisprudential reasoning and that is *istiṣḥāb* (using precedence from other cases until different rules prove to be better for the common good). *Istiṣḥāb* promotes gradual change, i.e., it does not negate all that came before Islam and generate a totally new system; *istiṣḥāb* is a state of continuous change.

He adds (al Turābī 1980, pp. 27–28), "Therefore if we combine *istiṣḥāb* with *al maṣāliḥ*, we will find the essence of public life in Islam.

Al Qaraḍāwī (1981, p. 152), a contemporary member of the Muslim Brotherhood, states:

> If one takes a verse from the Qur'an or any particular *ḥadīth,* without going back to other *ḥadith* or to the Prophet's practice and without relating it to the *maqāṣid*, one is likely to misunderstand and misinterpret the Shari'ah . . . . This is why al Imām al Shāṭibī in his book *The Treatise* insisted that to understand the Shari'ah one has to comprehend and know its end goals (*al maqāṣid*). This only happens when one is knowledgeable about the verses of the Qur'an and the *ḥadīth*; why, how and when they were revealed, the reason behind the revelation, which *ḥadīth* are eternal and which were temporal . . . etc.

Al Qaraḍāwī (1981, pp. 60–61) states that the reasons for Islamic "extremism" were analyzed by several schools:

> One has to recognize that extremism is not caused by one factor or the other, i.e., it is not fair to reflect a partial explanation by stressing one factor or the other like many theorists have done. There are theorists who have focused on psychological factors that relate every human action to particular psychological elements; then there is the sociological explanation that takes the Durkheimian view that man is a puppet that is moved by society, i.e., it relates everything to society and its effect on the individual. Another explanation is historical materialism, which relates everything to economics: to them, economics creates history. Last but not least are the few who understand that extremism is not related to one cause or the other, i.e., that the phenomenon needs a balanced combination of all factors. Those factors could be religious, psychological, ideological, or all of the above.

From al Qaraḍāwī's writing, therefore, the assumption that development or culture is a unilateral cause of Islamic activism might not be fruitful. A multilateral explanation of the phenomenon might lead to better understanding.

Al Qaraḍāwī (1981, pp. 60–61) writes of his grievances:

> The reason for extremism could also be related to the corruption of the rulers, their tyranny, and their selfish desires and their neglect of the people's rights. Those rulers are the leaders who follow the corrupt at home and ally themselves with the opponents of Islam abroad. Thus a gap between the Qur'an and rulership was created, religion and state therefore became two parallel phenomena that do not intersect at any point.

He indicates the reasons for the grievances of young people (al Qaraḍāwī 1980, pp. 108–109):

> Young people are often witness to things that are against their mores, and corruption continues to grow, secularism and Marxism are presented as ideologies, and the media continually broadcast indecent programs. Young people see naked women, liquor drunk in public, and night clubs that turn night into day. They see the market for desire wide open: indecent songs, explicit photos, movies, soap operas and plays that stimulate the instincts and that act as a barrier against the young people's interest in their religion and beliefs. The young people see all this in their Muslim world, in their own land.
>
> They see flagrant social injustice: people who play with millions and others who don't have enough pennies. Mansions that are built with millions and others who do not have shelter from the heat of summer or the cold of winter.

Al Qaraḍāwī (1981, pp. 124–125) also stresses the importance of allowing Islamic activists to air their grievances:

> It is better for our society to let Muslim activists take their natural course in society: allow them to breathe freely, away from oppression. Otherwise they will find a way to express themselves that might not be appreciated by many. The appeal of Islam runs like a strong current of water; it has to find its way even between the rocks. If this appeal is not given its proper place, it will find its

> rocks. If this appeal is not given its proper place, it will find its place in the corridors underground where it is dark and foresight is not clear. This is when extremism finds its way to the souls and minds of men.

He also writes critically about the conditions of imprisonment for many Islamic activists (al Qaraḍāwī 1981, pp. 125–126):

> Many practicing Muslims have been exposed to various kinds of torture in prison. You (the reader) could ask about the 1945 or 1965 incidents of extreme torture in military prisons. People were burnt with metal rods, men and women were hung from their feet like animals . . . . Many died from torture. They were tortured by those who do not fear God, and have no compassion for their fellow humans. It is inside those prisons that extremism was born and the idea of repentance was founded.

To summarize, in the first paragraph quoted, al Qaraḍāwī stresses the injustice of the system in general. In the second paragraph, he expresses the cultural grievance of the lack of Islamic mores in Muslim society, and toward the end of the paragraph, he writes of the economic grievance of the discrepancy between the rich and the poor. The third and fourth paragraphs stress grievances about human rights abuses.

In another publication, al Qaraḍāwī (1973, pp. 108–109) also stresses the importance of the Shari'ah:

> First, we need to investigate and analyze our cultural heritage in fiqh literature with its different schools and at different ages, in order to choose what will ensure the enforcement of the *maqāṣid* and the resurrection of *al maṣlaḥah* in light of the changes taking place in contemporary life. Second, we need to go back to our roots: i.e., to the Qur'an and the Sunnah, to analyze it in light of the *maqāṣid*. Third, we need to make a greater effort to understand contemporary issues that were not part of our ancestors' life, i.e., where the old *fuqahā'* did not contribute to the issue as it relates to our modern times.

Al Huḍaybī (1973, pp. 11–12), another leader and thinker from the Muslim Brotherhood, writes of issues stressed in the Qur'an that relate to governance and rulership:

Shari'ah is a flexible body of law, (3) the Qur'an stresses the importance of educating men and women about the Islamic Shari'ah, (4) the Qur'an emphasizes the rights of all the poor, whereby they are provided with shelter, clothes and food, and (5) the Qur'an stresses the necessity of respecting other religions: the freedom of its believers, the protection of their lives and their property.

In al Huḍaybī's writing we find that the first grievance relates to equality among rulers and ruled; therefore it is a grievance that relates to human rights. The second grievance relates to the failure to reinstate the Shari'ah as the supreme law of the land. The third grievance is related to education, thus stressing the cultural issue. The fourth grievance relates to economic inequality, and the fifth point expresses al Huḍaybī's concern with protecting believers of other faiths.

Last, but not least, a booklet that was distributed at the Cairo University campus (1992?) by the Jamā'ah al Islāmīyah (a group that claimed responsibility for most violent attacks against foreigners and public figures in 1993–1994) indicates the group's grievances and its members' stress on reinforcing the Shari'ah by upholding the *maqāṣid*. Their grievances are expressed as follows (al Jamā'ah al Islāmīyah 1992?, pp. 16–17):

> In September 1981, in a few hours most of the leaders of the Islamic movement were imprisoned according to instructions from the President [Sadat]. The Pharaoh's soldiers were swarming everywhere: scaring the people, robbing the houses, and taking away men, women and children (there were 20 boys included in the roundups who were less than 15 years old). Most of the Muslim intelligentsia were in the prisons of Lumān, Istiqbāl, and Abū al Za'bal: in chains, with no knowledge of what would happen next, totally in the dark. Their hands were tied, their mouths were gagged. This is why it was necessary that swords, gunpowder and guns be used. The *mujāhidūn* had to rise to fight injustice and corruption, they had to respond . . . . At that point things became clear: either we confronted and fought our enemy, or we became prisoners, subject to humiliation. This is the truth that is not known, or was denied by many. The path has become very clear.

The description indicates a strong grievance against torture and human rights violations according to his group's account of what happened before President Sadat was shot in 1981. The author of the booklet (al Jamā'ah al Islāmīyah 1992?, p. 23) explains the necessity of confrontation by stressing that it is part of the Shari'ah.[27] "The first task is to overthrow the ruler who does not rule under the Shari'ah precepts, since by doing so he is an infidel."

The booklet then recounts the many instances where the Shari'ah is violated. After a discussion of how civil law violates the Shari'ah and how that could be changed by overthrowing the current government, the author goes on to explain the third step: "Nominating a *Khalīfah* [Ruler] and the Establishment of an Islamic Government." Under this title, the author goes on (al Jamā'ah al Islāmīyah 1992, p. 63) to explain the nature of the future Islamic government:

> As al Imām al Shāṭibī indicates in his book *al I'tiṣām*, all the ulama have agreed that the leading imam should know how to extrapolate from the Shari'ah's different fields. [Ideally] *khilāfah* [rulership] in an Islamic system entails two basic elements: justice and *shūrā* [consulting and accounting for the opinions of others].

In the first al Jamā'ah al Islāmīyah paragraph quoted, there is stress on torture and other human rights violations as sources of the group's grievances. Second, there is stress on implementing the Shari'ah. By implication, therefore, failure to implement the Shari'ah is a grievance. And third, even a violent group such as al Jamā'ah al Islāmīyah notes al Shāṭibī's work as a reference for rulership in an Islamic state. When they combine their expressed grievances in their writings, Islamic activists' call for the reinstatement of the Shari'ah, and their intermittent reference to the *maqāṣid*, become stronger and more clear.

Although there may be a discrepancy between expressed grievances and other motivations behind the movement, I will focus here on the Islamic activists' expressed grievances. Islamic activists' writings provide support for the central hypothesis in my study because through their writings their dialog is linked to the theoretical imperatives of reinstating the codes of Islamic law—to be more specific, to the observance of the end goals of the Shari'ah (*al maqāṣid*).

27. The booklet comes from one of the most violent Islamic activist groups. The idea of violence begetting violence, and the need for confrontation, is representative of the group's political stand.

It is essential to comprehend the weight and origins of Islamic jurisprudential thought in the Muslim culture to clarify further and explain the hypothesized link between state performance (i.e., the extent to which it falls short of Islamic activists' expectations) and the extent of Islamic activism. It is also necessary to examine the opinion of a number of authors about the roles played by fiqh and the Shari'ah in the cultural makeup of Muslim societies. That is, it is imperative to understand the significance of fiqh and the Shari'ah to the Muslim community at large as well as to Islamic activists in particular.

The Cultural Importance of Fiqh and Its Sources (*'Uṣūl al Fiqh*) in Islamic Discourse[28]

The Shari'ah is recognized by all Muslims as the set of rules and mores decreed by the Qur'an and the Prophet's Sunnah. Even though some Muslims might argue for secularism and a separation between religion and state, they would still recognize the Shari'ah as an embodiment of Islamic codes and regulations.

Islamic activists are not the sole nor the only principal proponents of the importance of the Shari'ah. However, their advocacy of the Shari'ah as the law of the land lies at the crux of this research: What is the ethos of the Shari'ah? What are the Islamic activists' expectations of their political system?

In describing the importance of the Shari'ah to Muslim society, Charnay (1971, pp. 77–78) states:

> In Islam, the law aims at providing guidance; but not as a mere instrument. It has a much more far-reaching vocation. It creates a mode of living and tends to regulate all human activity, or to qualify it with respect, if not to an ethics, at least to a law, transcending not only the individual, but all humanity. Furthermore, Muslem law is not only pragmatic. Over and above the striving for efficaciousness and security, *it [Muslim law] constitutes an act of piety in its application.* The general rule is absolute for the believer, who however modest his condition, must respect it. It is a blessing to strive continually for a better attainment of that end. In view of this

28. See Diagram 2 on page 40, which outlines the theoretical origins of Muslim legal concepts discussed in this study.

Diagram 2
Theoretical Origins of Muslim Legal Concepts

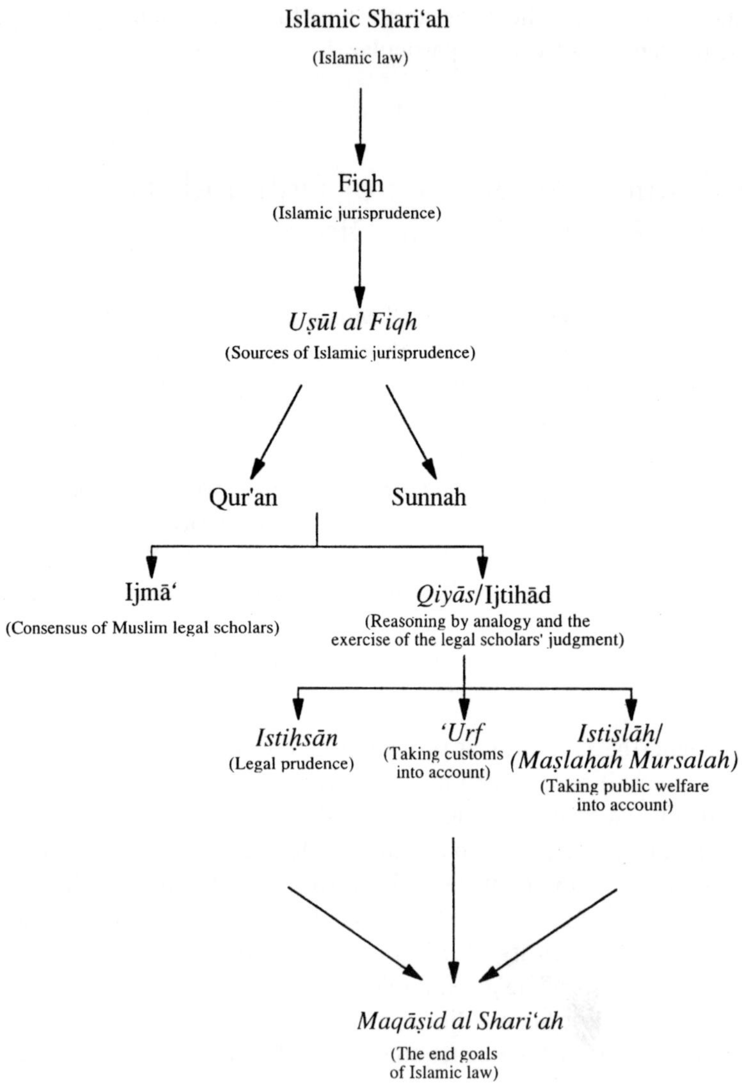

> moral purpose, the social desiderata on non-contradiction and legal efficaciousness shrink in importance.

Schacht (1964, p. 1) also describes the place of the Shari'ah and fiqh in Muslim societies:

> Islamic law is the epitome of Islamic thought, the most typical manifestation of the Islamic way of life, the core and kernel of Islam itself. The very term *al fiqh,* "knowledge," shows that early Islam regarded knowledge of the sacred law as knowledge par excellence . . . . But even at the present time the Law, including its (in the narrow sense) legal subject matter, remains an important, if not the most important, element in the struggle which is being fought in Islam between traditionalism and modernism under the impact of Western ideas. Apart from this, the whole life of the Muslims, Arabic literature, and the Arabic and Islamic disciplines of learning are deeply imbued with the ideas of Islamic law; it is impossible to understand Islam without understanding Islamic law.

In agreement with Schacht, on the role of the Shari'ah in prevailing discussions in Muslim countries, Noori (1987, p. 25) emphasizes:

> The ongoing discussion is now centered upon the type of approach to Islamic law which should be adopted by modern Islamic legislators and jurists who are required to find solutions to the problems facing modern Muslim societies by digging into the corpus of the classic works produced by jurists of the medieval time. This is the greatest challenge which faces the advocates of law reform on the one hand and the campaigners for the purification and de-colonization of law in Muslim countries on the other. They have to define their own relationship vis-à-vis the great masters of Islamic jurisprudence whose Institutional Writings have been accepted in respective schools of Islamic law without questioning for generations.

However, Noori (1987, pp. 25–27) goes a step further by distinguishing "three bodies of opinion" on the "approach of modern Muslim jurists" in interpreting Islamic law (Shari'ah/*al shari'ah*): (1) the conservative approach, (2) the liberal approach, and (3) the moderate approach. The moderate approach, in Noori's terms, exemplifies what this research intends to address. According to him (Noori 1987, p. 27), the moderate approach is:

> a middle of the road approach which acknowledges the due respect for the Institutional Writings of old masters [*fuqahā'*], but at the same time recognizes that if and when these old solutions conflict with public interests of the Muslim community, other legal solutions can be found under the doctrine of *istiṣlāḥ* or *maṣāliḥ mursalah,* i.e., public interest or public policy.

Muslim scholars have also emphasized the important role the Shari'ah and the *maqāṣid* will have in future Muslim societies. Thus, Muslim activists' writings are accompanied by a renewed interest in Muslim jurisprudential thought on the academic and theoretical level which reflects the weight given to the *maqāṣid.* This further justifies the choice of the *maqāṣid* as a baseline for evaluating the degree of activism in Muslim societies. The Shari'ah, and more specifically fiqh, are upheld by a number of Muslim academics as a "pure" form of Muslim thought. Al Fāsī (1972, pp. 94–95), for example, maintains that even though Roman, Greek, Persian, and Indian civilizations have affected Muslim culture in many ways, Muslim legal theory (fiqh) has retained its uniqueness. Therefore, according to al Fāsī (1972, p. 95), in order to restructure Muslim thought and utilize the Shari'ah in Muslim courts of law, the study of fiqh, its sources and end goals, is an indispensable necessity.

Another Muslim legal theorist, al 'Alwānī, writes that *al maṣlaḥah* (or the *maqāṣid* that ensure the implementation of public good) is extremely important in Muslim legal practice and thought. He believes that *al maṣlaḥah* is part of *qiyās* (analogical reasoning) which he in turn equates with ijtihād.[29] Al 'Alwānī (1988, p. 5) cites Prophet Muhammad's *ḥadīth,* "If the ruler practices ijtihād and his interpretation of the Shari'ah is accurate [i.e., in accordance with God's laws], he will gain double the rewards from God, and if he misinterprets, he will only gain a single reward." Thus, the importance of ijtihād and the exercise of reason is strongly encouraged by the Prophet, who implies that the judge could not go wrong if the public good or the *maqāṣid* (i.e., preserving religion, the self, the mind, posterity, and property) are taken into account when deciding a case.

Al 'Alwānī (1988, p. 33) concludes by classifying fiqh into three categories: (1) *waḥī*: the Qur'an and Sunnah, (2) *al 'aql*: reason, and (3) *al*

---

29. *Ijtihād,* as defined by Netton (1992, p. 117), is "the exercise of independent judgment unfettered by case law or past precedent."

tajārub wa al a'rāf wa al maṣāliḥ: experience, tradition, and public good. Thus he emphasizes the central role that the notion of the public good (or the preservation of the end goals of the Shari'ah) plays in a Muslim society.

Al Darīnī's *The Features of Islamic Law in Politics and Governorship* reinforces al 'Alwānī's stress on the importance of: (1) the Shari'ah in general as the law of the land and (2) *al maṣlaḥah* or the *maqāṣid* as guides for justice and rulership in Muslim societies. Al Darīnī (1982, p. 8) introduces his book by stating:

> The Shari'ah depends on the Islamic legal concept of *maṣāliḥ* (preservation of the *maqāṣid*) as a source of law. Therefore, the Shari'ah is capable of fulfilling the needs of the state and the Islamic ummah at large, regardless of time and place—this in itself constitutes the testimony for the Shari'ah's eternity.

Al Darīnī draws on old and contemporary literature on the *maṣlaḥah* and the *maqāṣid.* He clarifies the stance of other contemporaries when he comments (al Darīnī 1982, p. 275) on the work of Khallāf:[30]

> Contemporary *fuqahā'* have indicated that: All decisions are built upon the public good. Those decisions basically aim at preserving the good and prohibiting the evil in society. The Prophet used to prohibit a certain practice for a certain *maṣlaḥah* (public good), then he would allow the same practice for a certain *maṣlaḥah*—this testifies to the end goal of the Shari'ah: the preservation of *al maṣlaḥah.*

Al Darīnī (1982, p. 275) adds in a footnote:

> If we make *al maṣlaḥah* and the end goals of the Shari'ah the basis on which we make decisions, it would exemplify the realistic relation that exists between the Shari'ah and our everyday life, regardless of place and time. *Al maṣlaḥah* means the protection of the needs and the wants of individuals as well as states. Therefore building decisions upon *al maṣlaḥah* is the only solution for ensuring the protection and the realistic implementation of such needs.

30. Khallāf, *al Sīyasah al Shar'īyah* [Ruling According to Islamic Law], 1977.

It is necessary to define the terminology used in fiqh[31] in order to understand the cultural context of the words and their importance to Muslim societies.

Defining Shari'ah and Fiqh

A definition of Shari'ah provided by *The Concise Encyclopedia of Islam* (Glasse 1989, p. 361) is as follows:

> Revealed Law, also called al shari'ah. The canonical law of Islam as put forth in the Koran and the Sunna and elaborated by the analytical principles of the four orthodox schools (*madhhab*=pl. *madhāhib*), the Shāfi'ī, Hanbalī, Hanafī, and Mālikī, together with that of the Shi'ites, and the Ja'farī.

Although this definition is clear, it does not convey the social and political importance of the word to Muslim societies. Manzoor (1988, p. 1) provides this insight when he writes:

> The unity of Islam as a world civilization derives in large measure from its possession of a sacred law, the Shari'ah. This law is an essential expression of Islam that supplies the vital link between its faith and the socio-political order.

He further elaborates the role of the Shari'ah (Manzoor 1988, p. 1):

> Any revival of Islamic thought, it goes without saying, is contingent upon the Muslim effort to revive the methodological framework of the Shari'ah. Only a creative reinterpretation of the Shari'ah's legacy that enables it to work under modern conditions and yet be in consonance with the Islamic conscience, would lend meaning and cogency to the moral and civilizational aspirations of Muslims today. For submerged beneath all the cross-currents of political activism and resurgence lies the bedrock of Islamic conscience that serves as the moral foundation of the Muslim's historical search for justice and equity.

Esposito (1988, p. 75) in stressing the Shari'ah's role in society, reminds us:

> Islamic law has remained central to Muslim identity and practice, for it constitutes the ideal social blueprint for the good society. The

31. Which will also be briefly defined.

Shari'ah has been a source of law and moral guidance, the basis for both law and ethics.

In light of how important the Shari'ah is to Muslim society according to the previously mentioned arguments, the search for what constitutes the Shari'ah is of particular relevance. The Shari'ah is the law based on the Qur'an and the Prophet's teachings. Esposito (1988, p. 79) clarifies the relation between the Shari'ah and fiqh as follows:

> Fiqh "understanding," is that science or discipline that sought to ascertain, interpret, and apply God's will or guidance [al Shari'ah] as found in the Qur'an to all aspects of life. As a result of al Shāfi'ī's efforts, classical Islamic jurisprudence [*fiqh*] recognized four official sources, as well as other subsidiary sources.

Uṣūl al Fiqh: Sources of Islamic Law and Their Role in Theory and Practice in Muslim Societies

The sources of Islamic law, or *usūl al fiqh* in Islamic legal terminology, are divided into two categories. One category comprises *al naṣṣ* (the Text) i.e., the Qur'an and the Sunnah. The other constitutes human judgment in several forms, e.g., ijmā' (the consensus of the *fuqahā'*) and *qiyās* (analogical reasoning). Therefore, theoretically, there are two kinds of issues in the Shari'ah, as indicated in al Nādī's writing (1973, pp. 77–78). The first kind deals with *qaṭ'īyāt* or definitive-conclusive rules (i.e., rules that are not changeable in Islam, for example, times of prayer, fasting, alms-giving, etc.). The second type deals with *ẓanīyāt* or issues that allow for thought and speculation (i.e., issues that are open to ijtihād and that change with time and place—especially those pertaining to interpersonal relationships). Such interpersonal relationships include the relation between governments and peoples; therefore, ijtihād or the extrapolation of legal principles is admissible, if not encouraged.

Uṣūl al fiqh is, according to the *Concise Encyclopedia of Islam* (Glasse 1989, p. 411):

> literally the roots of jurisprudence. The bases of Islamic law. Among the Sunnis these are: the Koran, the Sunna (acts and statements of the Prophet), *al qiyās* (analogy), and *al ijmā'* (popular consensus or agreement). *Al ijtihād* (effort) is the extrapolation from these principles to specific cases.[32]

32. Glasse's definition is not altogether clear about ijtihād, since he does not tie *qiyās* (analogy) to ijtihād (extrapolation), and *qiyās* is by definition in need of ijtihād since the use of reasoning is central to compare and contrast issues for the sake of analogy.

Some of the more articulate definitions of *uṣūl al fiqh* are provided by Masud, Esposito, and Noori. Masud (1988, p. 24) says,

> *Usūl al fiqh* is the formal science in which Muslim jurists have dealt with legal theories, the principles and interpretations of legal texts, methods of reasoning and of deduction of rules and other such matters.

After defining the four bases of Islamic law (the Qur'an, Sunnah, *qiyās*, and ijmā'), Esposito (1988, p. 24) writes of other sources of law:

> While all [*fuqahā'*] came to accept the four sources of law, Islamic jurisprudence recognized other influences, designating them subsidiary principles of law. Among these were custom [*'urf*], public interest [*istiṣlāḥ*], and jurist preference or equity [*istiḥsān*]. In this way, some remnant of the inductive, human input that had characterized the actual methods of the law schools in their attempt to realize the Shari'ah's primary concern with human welfare, justice and equity were acknowledged.

After Noori's[33] description of the four basic courses of Islamic law, he names and defines supplementary sources of Sunni Islamic law as follows (Noori and Amin 1987, pp. 5–6): " 1. deviation [*istiḥsān*], 2. public interest [*istiṣlāḥ*], and 3. custom and usage [*'urf*]."

In commenting on supplementary sources of law in Islam, Sardar (1985, pp. 114–115) explains the reason for their importance as follows:

> Beyond these limited parameters, the Shari'ah is completely open: it can be developed and shaped according to the needs of society and time by any number of its other sources: *ijmā'*, *qiyās*, *ijtihād,* and *istiṣlāḥ*. The sources of the Shari'ah that supplement the Qur'an and the Sunnah are problem-solving tools; they provide a methodology for adjusting to change.

Thus, whether one considers the subsidiary sources of the law to be part of the Qur'an or part of human extrapolations (that observe the spirit of the law), one cannot help but observe the weight given to the subject matter by Islamic activists, Muslim academia, and intellectuals who write about Islam and its followers.

---

33. Ayatollah Yahya Noori's publication written with Sayed Hassan Amin is *Legal and Political Structure of an Islamic State: The Implications for Iran and Pakistan* (1987). The book provides a unique comparative on Sunni/Shi'i legal thought and practice.

The Public Good and the End Goals of Islamic Law: *al Maṣlaḥah* and *Maqāṣid al Sharī'ah*

In my research I take into account public interest (*istiṣlāḥ*), since the end goals of the Shari'ah are part and parcel of the public's welfare in a Muslim society. By public interest I mean the sociopolitical ethos of what Muslim societies expect from their respective governments. Thus, a clarification of *istiṣlāḥ* and the *maqāṣid*, and their theoretical weight among *fuqahā'* of different Sunni schools, needs to be addressed and brought to the forefront.

Istiṣlāḥ is a conjugated word that shares the same root with *maṣlaḥah*: *ṣaluḥa*, meaning to be good, suitable, or befitting.[34] In fiqh, *istiṣlāḥ* carries more weight since it is a notion that counts as a source of law. In Islamic terms, says Netton (1992, p. 130), *istiṣlāḥ* is:

> Taking into account the public good. This was a supplementary principle of Islamic law particularized by the Mālikīs (one of the four main schools of law). Since *istiṣlāḥ* in theory and effect seeks to discover the *maṣlaḥah* (public welfare) it is not surprising that the practice of *istiṣlāḥ* has not been confined to the Mālikīs.

Shalabī (1943, p. 281) of al Azhar University writes in a published dissertation that "*maṣlaḥah* could be dichotomized according to three issues: (1) whether it was considered or stressed by God, or not, (2) whether it is constant or not, and (3) the degree and need for *maṣlaḥah* for reasons of survival and well-being."

Shalabī (1943, p. 281) gives the different kinds of *maṣlaḥah* in accordance with the first issue as follows:

(a) Contemporary/Recognized *maṣlaḥah* (*maṣlaḥah mu'tabarah*): the *maṣlaḥah* that has been clearly stated in the Qur'an and Sunnah, or has gained the consensus of the *fuqahā'* (*ijmā'*).

(b) Nullified *maṣlaḥah* (*maṣlaḥah mulghā*): the *maṣlaḥah* that is in clear contradiction to the Qur'an, the Sunnah, and did not gain consensus from the *fuqahā'*.

(c) Conveyed *maṣlaḥah* (*maṣlaḥah mursalah*): the *maṣlaḥah* that has nothing directly related for or against it in terms of *ijmā'* or in the Qur'an and the Sunnah.

---

34. *Istiṣlāḥ* is conjugated on the pattern of *istif'āl* (to impose the act of doing on a verb), while *maṣlaḥah* is conjugated as *maf'ala;* therefore the root *fi'l* is *ṣ-l-ḥ*. For example, when the expression *istiṣlāḥ arāḍī* is used, it means the reclamation of land; therefore, *istiṣlāḥ* in general Arabic terms means bettering or making good.

The concept of nullified *maṣlaḥah* created a split between the different *madhhab*, or schools of fiqh. Some *fuqahā'* thought it was incorrect to give *maṣlaḥah* an equal rank with the primary sources of law: the Qur'an and the Sunnah.

The kind of *maṣlaḥah* considered here is *maṣlaḥah mursalah.* Some might argue that the notion of *maqāṣid al Sharī'ah* is part of the first kind of *maṣlaḥah, maṣlaḥah mu'tabarah* (recognized *maṣlaḥah*).[35]

Maṣlaḥah is an important notion in Muslim legal thought because it is the general formula that ties the different schools of Islamic jurisprudence together, as I will illustrate further on. As Sardar (1985, p. 113) indicates:

> Traditionally, Muslim scholars have focused not on *istiṣlāḥ,* but its more general form, *maṣlaḥah,* which means a cause, a means, an occasion, or a goal which is good . . . . Its [*maṣlaḥah*'s] use as a principal tool of promoting the Shari'ah is based on the argument that good is lawful and that lawful must be good.[36] On the basis of such reasoning, traditional Muslim scholars developed a whole array of *maṣlaḥah* categories, some of which required direct evidence from the Qur'an and the Sunnah while others could lead to binding legal sanctions on the basis that they clearly promote a noted ethical criterion such as preservation of life, property, promotion of Islamic mores and sound reasoning of the Shari'ah.

Sardar's definition of *maṣlaḥah* entails what is commonly addressed by the *fuqahā'* as *maqāṣid al Sharī'ah* (the end goals of al Shari'ah). Sardar's definition therefore equates *maṣlaḥah* with the *maqāṣid.*[37]

---

35. Some *fuqahā'* and other Muslim scholars have quoted verses from the Qur'an and Hadith to prove that *maṣlaḥah* is considered and recognized in the main two sources of legislation. Other *fuqahā'* might be more conservative in their arguments and prefer to view *maṣlaḥah* as a "conveyed" notion (i.e., an indirectly addressed notion).

36. Muslims in general, and Muslim activists in particular, adhere to this notion. However, they might stress that good is legal and that the Shari'ah must be good.

37. As will be discussed in more detail further on, most *fuqahā'* have defined five things to be preserved: religion, the self (life), the mind, property, and posterity.

The Differences between Schools of Islamic Jurisprudence on the Specifics of *Maṣlaḥah*: Their Genesis and Reason[38]

The differences that existed in early Islamic jurisprudential writings are almost impossible to discern in this day and age. However, for the purpose of this study, it is necessary to justify the choice of a certain legal notion (*maqāṣid*) by stressing its importance and commonality to the four different schools of early Muslim legal thought. The differences that existed between the *fuqahā'* were basically related to the degree of conservatism or liberalism of the interpreter of the *naṣṣ* (the Text, i.e., the Qur'an and Sunnah). Not only did *fuqahā'* differ in their perceptions of the Text, but they also had different methods of deducing and inducing law.

The four Sunni schools of law are the Mālikīs, the Ḥanafīs, the Shāfiʿīs, and the Ḥanbalīs. The Mālikīs and the Ḥanafīs were the founders of other fiqh schools in the later stages of the schools' development. Mālik was a contemporary of Abū Ḥanīfah. Mālik lived in the Ḥijāz (part of contemporary Saudi Arabia) from the year 93 A.H. to the year 179 A.H. Abū Ḥanīfah lived in what is now Iraq from the year 70 A.H. to 150 A.H. (al ʻAlwānī 1988, p. 31). Mālik and Abū Ḥanīfah did not write of their practices, but their students wrote later of their teachings and practices. Al Shāfiʿī (one of the leaders of the four *madhāhib*) was the first to write of *uṣūl al fiqh* in his books *al Risālah* (The Message), and later, *al Umm* (literally "mother," but in this context, "The Origin").

Mālik and Abū Ḥanīfah both left their marks on *fuqahā'* to come. Mālik was the founder of the Ahl al Ḥadīth school, which preached the practice and sayings of the Prophet Muhammad and his relatives who lived in the Ḥijāz. Meanwhile Abū Ḥanīfah in Iraq founded the Ahl al Ra'y school (People of Persuasion). The first school was more conservative in its interpretation of the Hadith, especially the practice of the Prophet's family. The latter school, led by Abū Ḥanīfah in Iraq, did not enjoy the privilege of having direct access to the relatives or friends of the Prophet. Therefore, their tendency was to discuss the traditions of the Prophet and his next of kin, which is why they are called "People of Persuasion" (al ʻAlwānī 1988, pp. 14–31).

As I will indicate further on, the difference between Ahl al Ḥadīth and Ahl al Ra'y is indicative of the first signs of divergence in the fiqh tradition

---

38. See Diagrams 3 and 4 on pages 55 and 56, respectively, for a graphical presentation of these differences.

because it laid the theoretical grounds for different *fuqahā*'s interpretations of what the Shari'ah is and how the *naṣṣ* should be interpreted.

Another difference, mentioned earlier, is the methodology used in analyzing the *naṣṣ*: there were the *mutakallimūn*, or the Shāfi'īs[39] and the Aḥnāf. The first school was generally followed by Shāfi'īs, Mālikīs, Ḥanbalīs, and Mu'tazilīs; the latter was followed mainly by Ḥanafīs. The Shāfi'ī (*mutakallimūn*) school went from the general rules in the Text to the specific, while the Ḥanafīs went from the specific to the general in interpreting the Text. Thus, the Shāfi'īs deduced the rules of the Shari'ah, while the Ḥanafīs induced them (al 'Alwānī 1988, p. 27). This general introduction to some of the differences between legal scholars in Islam will aid in focusing on how the four *madhāhib* conceptualized *maṣlaḥah*'s and, therefore, the *maqāṣid*'s role in the Shari'ah. As explained earlier, all four *madhāhib* agreed that there are four guides to the Shari'ah, two of them dependent on the others. That is, ijmā' and *qiyās* are dependent on the *Kitāb* (the Qur'an) and the Sunnah. The difference between *fuqahā'* (not the *madhāhib*), therefore, stemmed from their perception of the Shari'ah: (1) how conservative they were in interpreting the *naṣṣ* (i.e., whether they took into account the spirit of the law as well as its word), and (2) the degree to which they viewed the public good (*al maṣlaḥah*) as tantamount to the other sources of law.

In order to illustrate these points further, I will consult and analyze some secondary sources on *uṣūl al fiqh*.

First, in comparing Mālik and Abū Ḥanīfah, Abū Zahrā' (1952, p. 353) writes that both schools take *istiḥsān* as an equivalent alternative to *qiyās* (analogical reasoning). They both perceive *istiḥsān* as a strong source of law commensurate with *qiyās* (Abū Zahrā' 1952, p. 353). Abū Zahrā' stresses, however, that Mālik did not perceive *istiḥsān* to be, in itself, a legally binding rule. Abū Zahrā' proposes (1952, p. 353) that Mālik saw it as a legal principle used when needed to make exceptions to the rules of the Shari'ah.

The main second difference between Mālik and Abū Ḥanīfah is that Mālik used *istiḥsān* as a source of law when he found that *qiyās* rules (1) did not befit the culture or tradition of a society, (2) did not fit a preferred *maṣlaḥah*, and (3) did not help in avoiding hardships and providing basic needs. For Abū Ḥanīfah, *istiḥsān* meant that he had to choose from two competing analogical reasonings (*qiyās*) to decide an

39. Shāfi'ī, being the author of the first book on *uṣūl al fiqh*, was later followed methodologically by the Mālikīs and the Hanbalīs.

issue. That is, he treated *istiḥsān* as a part of *qiyās* (Abū Zahrā' 1952, p. 355).

Before comparing the rest of the legal schools, Abū Zahrā' (1952, p. 391) makes an important distinction concerning the individual *faqīh*'s perceptions of *maṣlaḥah*. He identifies four theoretical stands:

1. The Shāfi'īs took the public good (*maṣlaḥah*) into account when there was evidence in the Text to support it. *Maṣlaḥah* was dependent on analogical reasoning (*qiyās*).
2. The Ḥanifīs took public welfare into account, seeing *istiḥsān* (or more specifically *maṣlaḥah*) as an equivalent source of *qiyās*.
3. Some more radical *fuqahā'* claimed that *maṣlaḥah* (as a source of law) could override the Text. One of the famous *fuqahā'*, al Ṭūfī (a Ḥanbalī) was accused of being a Shi'i for subscribing to this opinion.
4. The moderate view was represented mostly by the Mālikīs, who considered *maṣlaḥah* only when it was *mursalah*, i.e., neither prohibited nor permitted in the Text.

The distinction Abū Zahrā' draws here is important, since it stresses that the differences of opinion regarding the weight given to *maṣlaḥah* was a theoretical issue rather than a sectarian issue. That is, it was not based upon the four legal schools' divisions. The differences were not tied to the *madhāhib,* but rather were directly related to how liberal or conservative *fuqahā'* were in interpreting the Shari'ah—(whether they were attached to the Text or whether they allowed for other subsidiary sources of law). Most Mālikīs and Ḥanbalīs weighed *maṣlaḥah* as an independent subsidiary source of law. However, this did not restrain al Ṭūfī from giving precedence to *maṣlaḥah* over the Text. This is viewed as heretical and is still unacceptable among modern Islamic scholars.[40]

Even though sectarian differences did not play an important role in the division of opinion on *maṣlaḥah, istiḥsān,* and *maqāsid*, al Shāfi'ī's strong negation of Mālik's *istiḥsān* is particularly relevant since he is the head of one of the four schools of Islamic jurisprudential thought.

Al Shāfi'ī, Mālik's student in the Hijāz,[41] was the first to write about *uṣūl al fiqh* and one of the few legal scholars who documented both his the-

40. Al Ṭūfī was an exception in the Ḥanbalī tradition. Most of the Ḥanbalīs were conservative in their legal interpretations.

41. Abū Ḥanīfah's teaching methods were strikingly different from Mālik's. Abū Ḥanīfah allowed his students to question his opinion and thought; thus he allowed his students some independence. Mālik illustrated the logical steps to his deductions, but did not allow his students (during his lifetime) to exercise their reason or to question his opinion (Abu Zahrā' 1952, pp. 433–434).

ory and practice in writing.[42] Al Shāfiʿī refused to take *istiḥsān* as an independent source of law because it did not restrain itself to the basic religious sources like the Qur'an, the Sunnah, ijmāʿ, or *qiyās*. Rather, *istiḥsān* seemed to al Shāfiʿī to be a concept totally dependent on human reasoning, which separated it from religion altogether (al Būṭī 1966, p. 377). In a primary source, al Shāfiʿī (n.d., p. 273) writes:

> Whoever gives his legal opinion (*fatwā*) with no restraint or *qiyās*, is in fact saying: I do what I please, even if it is against my belief—thus going against the Qur'an and the Sunnah . . . . I have not seen an incident where the people of knowledge [*fuqahā'*] allowed the people of reason to give their legal opinions, since the people of reason have no knowledge of *qiyās* from the Qur'an and Sunnah or *ijmāʿ* and the usage of analogical reasoning.

Further on, al Shāfiʿī (n.d., p. 303) writes: "The essence of *ijtihād* on an issue (exercising one's judgment) comes only after the consultation of the Qur'an, the Sunnah and issues of consensus. But if any of those sources provide an answer, their *ijtihād* is not called for."

Thus al Shāfiʿī was more conservative in his conception of *istiḥsān* and *maṣāliḥ* (plural of *maṣlaḥah*), for he feared its encroachment upon the importance of the basic sources of the law. The last quote, however, indicates that if there are no answers to a specific issue from the Text and the consensus of *fuqahā'*, one should exercise one's own judgment.

The classification of the kinds of *maṣlaḥah* mentioned earlier might shed light on the positions of the different legal scholars:[43] al Shāfiʿī, for example, equated "conveyed" *maṣlaḥah* with "recognized" *maṣlaḥah*, since he believed the Text to be all-inclusive of people's welfare. Therefore, al Shāfiʿī could not conceive of a legal issue that would transpire outside the boundaries of the Text (al Būṭī 1966, p. 375).

Mālik took *istiḥsān* as an exception to the rule. He took the conveyed *maṣlaḥah* as a cause to practice *istiḥsān*. Therefore, although he was misunderstood by many (especially his student al Shāfiʿī), he did not call for *istiḥsān* on the basis of the nullified *maṣlaḥah*. Mālik called for *istiḥsān* when there was no reference point in the Text concerning the issue at stake.

42. Neither Mālik nor Abū Ḥanīfah wrote of their theoretical arguments or practices. Their *madhāhib* were maintained by their respective students, who afterwards documented their theoretical views and practices.

43. See Diagram 3, page 55.

That is, Mālik took *istiḥsān* as an alternative only when the Text and ijmā' did not provide him with an answer. This agrees with al Shāfi'ī's teaching and leads al Ghazali (a Shāfi'ī) to define *istiḥsān* in terms of the conveyed *maṣlaḥah* (Hasan 1971, p. 387; and Abū Zahrā', 1952, p. 391).

Since the comparison of Abū Ḥanīfah and Mālik was presented earlier, the only school of jurisprudence that remains to be addressed is Ibn Ḥanbal's. Ibn Ḥanbal takes *maṣlaḥah* as a subsidiary source of law (branching from *qiyās* from the basic four sources) and as an extension of the aims and end goals of the Shari'ah (al Būṭī 1966, p. 369).

Many of Ibn Hanbal's followers wrote about *maṣlaḥah.* Al Shawkānī (*Irshād al Fuḥūl*, n.d., p. 242) writes, "We have no doubt that Mālik exercises the notion of *maṣlaḥah* more than other *fuqahā'* followed by Ibn Ḥanbal." Ibn Taymīyah (a Ḥanbalī) in *al Manār* (n.d., p. 679) writes,

> If one is in doubt as to whether an issue is prohibited or permissible, one should consider its consequences, aims and its harm. If the consequences are harmful (i.e., do not promote *maṣlaḥah*), it is impossible that such an issue is ordained by God, therefore, it becomes prohibited.

Ibn al Qayyim al Jawziyah (a Ḥanbalī) in *I'lām al Muwāqi'īn* (n.d., p. 288) writes, "Human interactions should be guided on the basis of necessity, need and *maṣlaḥah* so that the judge is always in need of such principles.

Last, al Ṭūfī (also a Ḥanbalī) took the extreme view that the Text could be overridden because of *maṣlaḥah* (see Abū Zahrā' 1952, p. 391).

The above citations are an indication of (1) Ibn Ḥanbal's more moderate acceptance and practice of the notion of *maṣlaḥah*, and (2) the degree of divergence within one school, which further proves that the difference of opinion on *maṣlaḥah* fell along a conservative-versus-liberal divide rather than a sectarian or school-of-fiqh dichotomy.

The Ḥanbali, like the other schools of Islamic jurisprudence, agreed on *maṣlaḥah* and more specifically on the *maqāṣid.* Abū Zahrā' (1952, p. 404) identifies the major theoretical issue that caused the previously mentioned differences. He writes:

> Their [the *fuqahā'*s] differences were not related to whether they accepted the *maṣlaḥah* as a source of law or not. Rather their differences stemmed from their degree of using reason alone to acknowledge the *maṣlaḥah* without considering the *nuṣūṣ* (plural

of *naṣṣ*: the Text), i.e., the basic Islamic sources: the Qur'an and Sunnah.

Al Būṭī also indicates three reasons for those differences: (1) The *fuqahā'* did not clearly define the reasons for considering or avoiding *istiṣlāh* in their discussions and arguments; (2) the *fuqahā'* did not verify and test the allegations made about Mālik's views and his account of what *maṣlaḥah* meant, to the degree that he was accused of heretically disregarding rules set forth by God (by overriding those rules with what he deemed to be good, or *ḥasin*); (3) Shāfi'ī totally rejected Mālik's *istiḥsān,* by paying little attention to Mālik's effort in keeping with the end goals of the Shari'ah and its Creator. This total rejection consequently led to the belief that Mālik is against *maṣlaḥah* (which is not true in his writing and practice). This perception of al Shāfi'ī is also related to the very fine line that distinguishes *maṣlaḥah* from *istiḥṣān* (al Būṭī 1966, pp. 401, 405).

The similarities and differences between the *fuqahā'* of the different *madhāhib* are summarized in Diagrams 3 and 4 on pages 55 and 56 of this chapter. Diagram 3 illustrates each *faqīh*'s view of conveyed *maṣlaḥah* and how it relates to the Text or the recognized *maṣlaḥah*, thus reflecting how conservative the legal scholar was. Diagram 4 illustrates how each *faqīh* utilized *maṣlaḥah* in his legal practice.

It is important to note that the differences of opinion in considering *maṣlaḥah* were related to the interpretative stance of the legal scholar rather than a ideology for the whole school. Al Shāfi'ī was Mālik's student, but this did not stop him from rebelling against his teacher. Meanwhile, al Ṭūfī, a Ḥanbalī (considered one of the most conservative schools), went to the extreme of writing that *maṣlaḥah* could supersede the Text.

Al Shāfi'ī is said to be the forefather of *uṣūl al fiqh* since he wrote the very first publication that relayed the practices of other *fuqahā'* and their analysis. Al Shāṭibī is the first legal scholar who dedicated his writing to the issue of *maṣāliḥ* in his book *al Muwāfaqāt* (The Treatise) (Masud 1977, p. 25). Even though the concept of *maṣlaḥah* was part and parcel of jurisprudential thought and practice, al Shāṭibī wrote four volumes of *The Treatise* to demonstrate the essence of the Shari'ah. Masud (1977, p. 225) notes that according to al Shāṭibī,

> The obligations in the Shari'ah concern the protection of the *maqāṣid* of the Shari'ah, which in turn aims to protect the *maṣāliḥ* of the people. Thus *maqāṣid* and *maṣlaḥah* become interchange-

Diagram 3

The Weight of Conveyed *Maṣlaḥah* (*Mursalah*) Versus Recognized *Maṣlaḥah* (*Maṣlaḥah Mu'tabarah*) According to the Four *Madhāhib*

Mālik

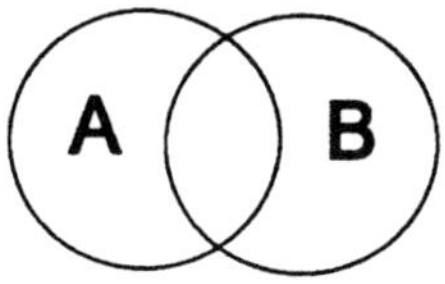

Maṣlaḥah mursalah is an independent instant where there is no *naṣṣ* for or against it, but there are logical reasons for its consideration as part of the intentions or end goals of the Creator.

Abū Ḥanīfah

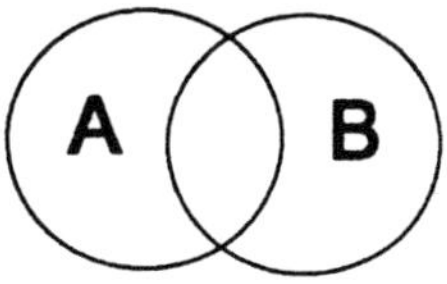

Theoretically, Abū Ḥanīfah defines *maṣlaḥah mursalah* in terms of *maṣlaḥah mu'tabarah* (like al Shāf'ī). However, in practice, he takes *maṣlaḥah mursalah* as an instant where there is no *naṣṣ* (like Mālik).

al Shāfi'ī

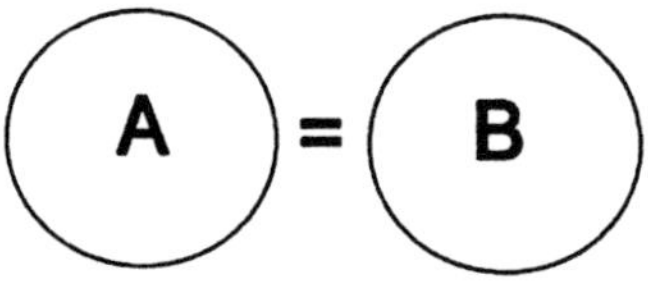

Al Shāfi'ī considers *maṣlaḥah mursalah* inclusive or equal to *maṣlaḥah mursalah.*

Ibn Ḥanbal

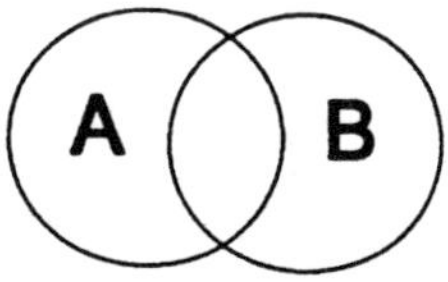

Ibn Ḥanbal, like Mālik, considers *maṣlaḥah mursalah* as an independent instant where there is no *naṣṣ* for or against the *maṣlaḥah.* However, it is in the spirit of the *naṣṣ* and the end goals of the Shari'a.

N.B: "A" represents *maṣlaḥah mursalah*
"B" represents *maṣlaḥah mu'tabarah*

Diagram 4

Uṣūl al Fiqh According to the Four *Madhāhib*

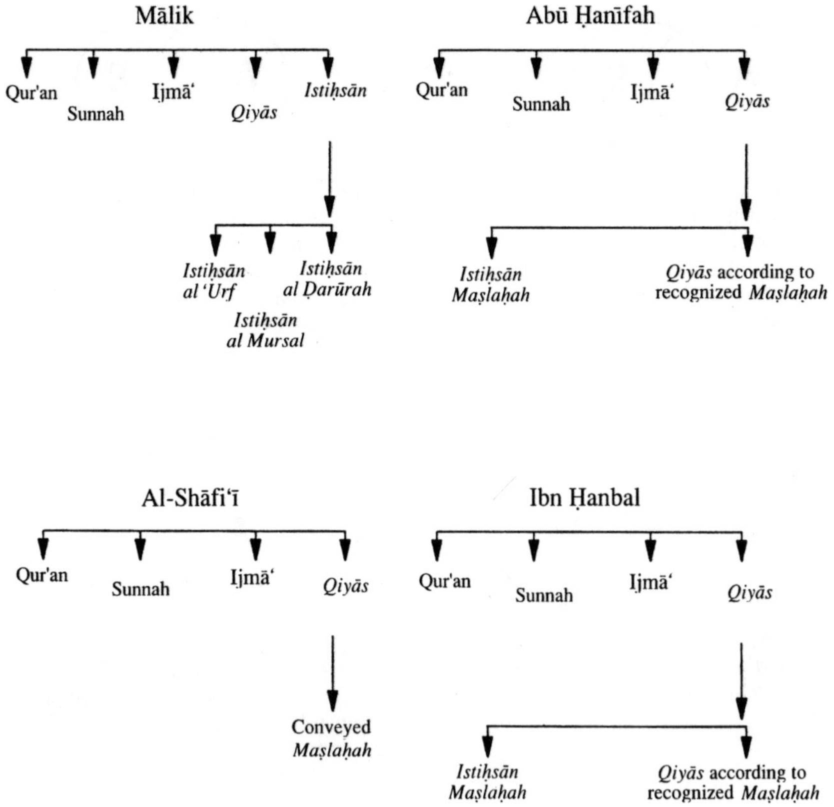

able terms in reference to obligation in Shāṭibī's discussion of *maṣlaḥah.*[44]

However, al Shāṭibī was not the only *faqīh* who observed the *maqāṣid*, even though he is considered to be an authority because he was the first to analyze thoroughly and expose the essence of the concept.

The Development of the *Maqāṣid* in Islamic Legal Thought

The differences separating the four main legal scholars mentioned earlier became less distinct with the passage of time, to the extent that scholars from the same school disagreed on certain issues. In order to clarify the understanding of later legal scholars and to verify their agreement on the *maqāṣid*, I will cite different works representative of each legal school. The agreement of the legal scholars on the *maqāṣid* is proof of the prevalence of the concept among them.[45]

Evidence in the *Origins of the Law* by Abu al Ma'ālī al Juwaynī (also known as Imām al Ḥaramayn), a Shāfi'ī who died in 478 A.H. (1085 C.E.):

> Our main consideration is to refer to their end goals and purposes. The person who dismisses the end goals from our practices could not apprehend the totality of the Shari'ah. (Part 1, pp. 294–295)

> The Shari'ah is composed of (1) what we are decreed to do which is mainly part of worship, and (2) what we are prohibited from doing. *Shar'* therefore preserves blood [meaning life] by punishing the killer, preserves posterity [and] property. (Part 2, pp. 1150–1151][46]

The Eclectic Source of the Origins of the Law by al Ghazālī, a Shāfi'ī who died in 505 A.H. (1111 C.E.):

> A matter that is not observed by the *shar'* through the Text, should be considered in light of *maṣlaḥah,* keeping in mind its degree of importance [whether it is a necessity, a need, or an amenity]. Let

44. Thus, *maṣlaḥah* and *maqāṣid* (the end goals of the Shari'ah) will be used interchangeably herein.

45. Since all the citations agree on the five *maqāsid* (to be mentioned), they will be arranged chronologically, by title, name of author, legal school, and the year the author died.

46. Most of the cited literature in this segment of the chapter is very old; publication dates and other bibliographic details are not available.

> me first explain *al maṣlaḥah. Al maṣlaḥah* originally means the protection of what is beneficial and the avoidance of all corruption, which in turn means the protection of those end goals. The way to protect the end goals could be summarized in five issues: the protection of religion, life, the mind, posterity, and property. (Part 1, pp. 286–287)
>
> Protecting those five elements is part of every faith and every legal statute that observes the well-being of humankind. (Part 1, p. 288)
>
> *Maṣlaḥah* is not a fifth source of law,[47] since *maṣlaḥah* is defined in terms of protecting the goals of *shara‘* and those end goals are observed in the Text and in consensus with other *fuqahā'*. Therefore, whoever practices *istiḥsān* is a heretic. *Maṣlaḥah* means the protection of the end goals of *shara‘*, which is well defined in the Qur'an, the Sunnah and the consensus of the *fuqahā'*. Thus if we equate *maṣlaḥah* with the end goals of *shara‘*, there should be consensus in observing it as a resource, when making a legal decision. (Part 1, pp. 310–311)

The Harvest of the Origins of the Law (recently published in 1992) by Fakhr al Dīn al Rāzī, a Shāfi‘ī who died in 606 A.H. (1209 C.E.):

> This [*maṣlaḥah*] has to be part of the Shari‘ah, because the end goal of all statutes ordained by God [*sharā'i‘*][48] is to preserve and protect the *maṣāliḥ*. (Part 6, p. 165)
>
> Whether we consider *maṣlaḥah* through reason or through the Text and *ijmā‘*, the end goal of all statutes of law is to preserve *maṣlaḥah*. (Part 6, p. 167)

Mastering the Origins of the Law by Sayf al Dīn al ‘Āmidī, a Shāfi‘ī who died in 631 A.H. (1233 C.E.):

> The five end goals that exist in all faiths and in all legal statutes ordained by God are: the preservation of religion, life, the mind, posterity, and property. (Part 3, p. 394)

47. Al Ghazālī is a Shāfi‘ī; in accordance with his teachings, he stresses the importance of the *nuṣūṣ* (the Text).

48. *Sharā'i‘* is plural of Shari‘ah.

The Rules for Perfecting the Interest of the People by 'Izz al Dīn al Salmī, a Shāfi'ī who died in 660 A.H. (1261 C.E.):

> The Shari'ah is composed of *maṣāliḥ*: it either prohibits corruption or encourages *maṣlaḥah*. If you listen closely to the Qur'an, whenever an *āyah* [verse] starts with "Ye who have faith," what follows is always the prohibition of evil and the encouragement of what is beneficial [*maṣlaḥah*]. (Part 1, p. 9)

Revising the Details of the Origins of the Law by al Qarāfī, a Mālikī who died in 684 A.H. (1285 C.E.):

> What is just and appropriate could be divided into: necessities, needs and their amendments. The necessities being the preservation of five elements: life, religion, lineage, the mind, property (and it is said that one could include chastity). (*A Collection of Original Works*, p. 66)
>
> Al Qarāfī also indicates:
>
> I consider *al maṣlaḥah* as a source of law, and if one is diligent one would find that it is common in all schools of law [*madhāhib*]. (*A Collection of Original Works,* p. 67)

A Collection of Legal Opinions by Ibn Taymīyah, a Ḥanbalī who died in 728 A.H. (1327 C.E.):

> The Shari'ah came to ensure the *maṣāliḥ* and to avoid corruption. (Vol. 20, p. 48)
>
> The main notion in this chapter is to know the best *maṣlaḥah* (*al aṣlaḥ*).[49] This knowledge could be gained through: (1) knowing the end goal of ruling, (2) knowing the means to the end goals. (Vol. 28, p. 260)
>
> Others who write about the origins of the law have considered *al maṣlaḥah* in two ways: (1) one is related to the afterlife which is connected to disciplining oneself, and (2) the other is related to this world which is in turn connected to the preservation of life, property, posterity, the mind and religion. (Vol. 32, p. 234)

---

49. *Al aṣlaḥ* is conjugated *al af'al,* therefore it comes from the root *ṣ-l-ḥ*. It is another word for *maṣlaḥah,* but it literally means "the best form of *maṣlaḥah*."

Seeking Sanctuary by Abū al Iṣḥāq al Shāṭibī,[50] a Mālikī who died in 790 A.H. (1388 C.E.):

> The conveyed *maṣlaḥah* means taking into account reasonable judgment that is not referred to in legal sources . . . . Mālik, as well as Shāfi'ī and the Ḥanafis, gave precedence to the spirit of the law; however, it has to be close to what the Text offers; this is what Imām Juwaynī wrote, too. (Part 2, p. 351)

The Treatise also by al Shāṭibī:

> The *ummah* [meaning the Muslim community of believers] and even all faiths have agreed that *sharā'i'* [legal statutes] are there to protect the necessary basics: religion, the soul [life], posterity, property and the mind. (Part 1, p. 15).[51]

Advice to the Ulamā' by Ibn Qayyim al Jawziyah, a Ḥanbalī:[52]

> The foundations of the Shari'ah are based upon the *maṣāliḥ* of its followers in this life and the afterlife: it is thoroughly just, thoroughly merciful, it thoroughly looks out for the *maṣāliḥ*, and it is full of wisdom. Therefore, what crosses the boundaries of what is just, merciful, wise and what leads to *maṣlaḥah* is not part of the Shari'ah. (Part 3, p. 5)

A Treatise on al Maṣāliḥ by Najm al Dīn al Ṭūfī, a Ḥanbalī:[53]

> Out of nineteen sources of law, the Text and consensus are the strongest sources, but they either agree or disagree with protecting *maṣlaḥah*. If they coincide with *maṣlaḥah*, then there is no conflict on the issue. If the Text and consensus are discordant to *maṣlaḥah*,

50. The first *faqīh* to write about the *maqāṣid* and the *maṣāliḥ* in depth; i.e., other *fuqahā'* mentioned it in their usage and understanding of the legal concept, but al Shāṭibī was the only *faqīh* who dedicated four volumes to *maṣlaḥah* as well as part of his second book: *Seeking Sanctuary*.

51. The specifics of which *maqṣad* should be given priority over the other and the citation of many legal cases where the notion of *maṣlaḥah* was used make up the body of al Shāṭibī's second part of *The Treatise*. This is why he is regarded as the forefather of the *maqāṣid*.

52. The author's date of death is unknown to the writer; therefore his contribution is placed at the end of the chronologically arranged citations.

53. Al Ṭūfī was accused of being a Shi'i imam owing to his extremity in taking *maṣlaḥah* as a legal source even if it was in direct contradiction to the Text.

> then *maṣlaḥah* should be given priority. (*A Collection of Essays on Original Legal Works*, pp. 46–47)
>
> The Text and consensus agree on the five basic necessities in need of protection: life, property, posterity, the mind, and so forth. But if there is disagreement between the Text/consensus and *maṣlaḥah, maṣlaḥah* should be given precedence, because *maṣlaḥah* is the end goal of governing, and since all decision making is a means to an end, the end goals of the Shari'ah should be give priority over the means. (*A Collection of Essays on Original Legal Works*, pp. 64–65)

The primary sources cited support my contention that despite some differences between legal schools, *maṣlaḥah/maqāṣid* is considered part of the public good recognized by the Text (*al maṣlaḥah al mū'tabarah*). In other words, there is substantial convergence whereby the applications of basic principles are similarly interpreted.

The importance of *maṣlaḥah* to the Shari'ah was emphasized in most of the quotations. The authors stressed that all faiths and statutes exist to provide humankind with their needs.

In order to comprehend all Islamic activist movements' emphasis on reinstating the Shari'ah, one has to understand what *maṣlaḥah* or the *maqāṣid* entail. If there are five end goals—preserving religion, life, the mind, posterity, and property—how does one comprehend their magnitude in relation to contemporary Muslim societal needs? Further clarification of what each *maqṣad* is and how it could be measured is necessary.

Conclusion

Arguments made by Islamic activist leaders and Muslim scholars increasingly emphasize the role of the Shari'ah in future Muslim societies. More specifically, they cite *maṣlaḥah* as a crucial element that underlies the ethos of the Shari'ah. This stress on the cultural importance of the Shari'ah, fiqh, and their sources justifies my choice of *maṣlaḥah* as a baseline against which to assess Muslim peoples' expectations of their respective governments.

The differences among *fuqahā'* on legal matters serve many purposes:

(1) they prove that different *madhāhib* agree on *maṣlaḥah*, thus allowing testing of the hypothesis, regardless of the Sunni *madhhab* followed in the country studied;
(2) they clarify the importance of the legal concept of *maṣlaḥah* in relation to the Shari'ah;
(3) they provide insight into the practice and expectations of Muslim peoples that were implemented until the collapse of the Ottoman Empire; and
(4) they allow for the extrapolation of what *maṣlaḥah* means in contemporary Muslim societies.[54]

The link between Islamic activist movements and upholding the Shari'ah is a necessary tool in understanding the causality of the phenomenon. The underlying argument is that the movements' call for implementing the Shari'ah is a reflection of Islamic activists' expectations about their respective governments as well as a foreshadowing of future Islamic societies. The study of *maṣlaḥah* therefore is significant in understanding the cause and direction of Islamic activist movements.

After the literature review in the first chapter and the discussion of the theoretical framework in the second chapter, it is necessary to explain how the research will be conducted. That is, it is necessary to explain what the *maqāṣid* mean and how they will be measured. I will discuss the countries under study, their similarities and differences. Chapter 3 will lay out the research design used in this study.

54 . I do not include Ja'farī thought in the comparison because: (1) the countries studied are Sunni (Egypt, Algeria, and Turkey) and (2) generally speaking, the Ja'farī school of fiqh was comparatively more liberal in its extrapolations of the Qur'an and the Sunnah and upheld public welfare as a legal principle in everyday practices.

CHAPTER 3

The Research Design: Developing the Link between Islamic Law and Islamic Activists' Grievances

The main hypothesis of this study is that Islamic activism is a function of the extent to which state performance in Muslim societies falls short of the principles of Islamic social justice. Since the study utilizes the *maqāṣid* as an embodiment of Islamic social justice, one needs to clarify what each *maqṣad* means legally and connect it to the current grievances raised by Islamic activists.

This links the general principle of the law to the Islamic activists' specific grievances in Muslim societies today. This chapter will also explain the sources of information used for coding and discuss the comparability of the countries studied.

Measuring the Independent Variables

Preserving Religion and the Mind: The Link between the Two Concepts

Preserving religion first of all entails faith in God and the Day of Judgment and abiding by the five pillars of Islam[55] ('Uthmān 1982, p. 41;

55. The five pillars of Islam are (a) the *shahādatayn:* to declare that there is no god but God and that Muhammad is His messenger; (b) *ṣalāḥ:* the five prayers of the day at sunrise

al 'Ālim 1981, pp. 227–247; 'Āṭīya 1988, p. 106; al Būṭī 1966, p. 119; al Zuḥaylī 1969, p. 50). It also entails jihād against a threat to Muslim societies and punishing the apostate (*murtadd*) and the heretic (*mubdi'*) (see al Būṭī 1966, p. 119; al Shīshānī 1980, p. 312; 'Uthmān 1982, p. 42). The preservation of religion, therefore, falls within a larger context based on two issues: faith (*'aqīdah*) and worship (*'ibādah*) (al Shīshānī 1980, p. 311).

Islamic activists feel that the *'aqīdah* is endangered in current Muslim societies. The right of practicing one's religion is restricted by current governments in many Muslim societies. For example, martial law in most of those societies restricts people from congregating for religious purposes, and the mosques are usually guarded by armed police at the Friday prayers. The curtailment of the religious ethos might have led to the current confused message that is sent by most Muslim governments to their peoples. The cultural importance of freely practicing one's religion[56] is therefore an important element in Islamic activist discourse and the first *maqṣad* of the Shari'ah.

Taking into consideration the grievances of Islamic activists and their call for reinstating the Shari'ah (and more specifically the *maqāṣid*), I hypothesize that one of the factors affecting Islamic activism is the state's restrictions on freedom to practice the religion, especially in public.

Preserving the mind means forbidding the consumption of alcohol and the punishment of its consumer and its seller. Another element that is forbidden by analogical reasoning (*qiyās*) is the consumption of narcotics. *Fiqhī* literature has often explained that a person's mind does not totally belong to him, because the society suffers if one person loses his rational capabilities. By association, therefore, not only is the drinking of alcohol forbidden, but also the consumption of narcotics (Abū Zahrā' 1982, pp. 278, 367–368; al Shīshānī 1980, p. 313; al Zuḥaylī 1969, p. 50).

A few of the more contemporary writings have developed the meaning of the preservation of the mind from the effect of alcohol and narcotics to include preserving it also in a nonmaterial sense. Education and the protection of the mind from anything that would ruin it are emphasized in more contemporary literature. For example, 'Āṭīya writes (1988, p. 106): "In

---

(*fajr*), noon (*ẓuhr*), evening (*'aṣr*), sunset (*maghrib*), and night (*'ishā'*): (c) *zakat:* giving out alms to the poor and the needy; (d) *ṣiyām:* fasting the month of Ramadan from dawn to sunset; and (e) *hajj:* performing the pilgrimage to Makkah for every able Muslim.

56. Preservation of religion and preservation of the mind are closely related. The first addresses the right to practice the religion, while the latter addresses the right to express one's religious beliefs in terms of publishing materials and freely summoning others to Islam.

order to preserve *'aq*l, the Shari'ah demands us to seek education, to speculate, to analyze, and to finally make decisions built upon our knowledge."

Aside from restricting inebriation in Islam, the necessity of observing one's mores stems from the continuous process of educating oneself and teaching others about practicing the religion. The freedom to express one's religious ideas, therefore, is part and parcel of preserving the mind (*ḥifẓ al 'aql*). It is practically impossible to separate them in the daily practice of religious norms. For example, when a woman wears a veil, is she preserving her religion as an individual, or is she also preserving her mind by publicly expressing her beliefs? When people congregate for Friday prayers, is each individual practicing his/her faith (acting to preserve his/her religion), or is the congregation a collective expression of the faith and its strength? The private versus the public practice of one's faith becomes increasingly difficult to discern. I combine both *maqāṣid* as a single concept: the practice and expression of the faith (*'aqīdah*). The variable property[57] of this concept is the degree to which the government protects the practice and the expression of the faith. The indicators for this variable are found in the government's reaction to a number of religious issues: for example, wearing headscarves in schools or universities, publishing religious articles and books, building mosques, congregating for prayers, or holding religious tutoring sessions. The scale used for scoring the regime's degree of protection of this *maqṣad* includes these categories, ranging from high protection (1) to low (3):

(1) The regime supports the Islamic activists' arguments or acts in favor of defending or representing Islam.
(2) The regime refers the issue to a third party (such as the Ministry of Religious Endowment).
(3) The regime clearly states its conflicting stand on the issue. (No information = 00).

The second category refers to incidents wherein religious authorities act or make statements that are congruent to governmental policies—in other words, religious authorities use the state's political ideas and language in addressing Islamic activists.

57. The methodology used to define the concepts, variable properties, and indicators is found in Barbara Harff's chapters (Gurr and Harff 1994).

Preserving the Self

The third *maqṣad* deems it necessary to observe the sanctity of the human body by not violating it or any of its organs ('Āṭiya 1988, p. 106; al Būṭi 1967, p. 119; 'Uthmān 1982, p. 42). *Ḥifẓ al nafs*, therefore, considers it essential to maintain the dignity of people by not harming their bodies and by providing a basic level of subsistence. If a person's life is violated, punishment for manslaughter (*ḥadd al qatl*) has to be observed according to the Islamic Shari'ah. The respect of the sanctity of the body is also exemplified in notions such as freedom of movement and travel and freedom of expression.

The judicial authority bears a large responsibility for preserving the self, according to the Shari'ah. The authorities have to be absolutely convinced of the evidence before indicting a suspect. Therefore arresting—let alone torturing—suspects is a far cry from Islamic mores and the elementary principles of the Shari'ah.

Contemporary fiqh literature cites the practice of the four rightly guided caliphs (the four immediate political successors of the Prophet) to indicate the importance of human rights as a cornerstone of Muslim practice. In 'Umar's time, for example, beating a subordinate was prohibited. A soldier was said to have handed his superior fewer arrows than required. His superior responded by beating him and shaving his hair. When 'Umar came to know about this, he wrote to the military commander: "If you have acted toward your subordinate in public, let him do unto you the same act in public. If you have punished him in private, let him do unto you the same in private." It is said that when the military commander followed 'Umar's rules, his subordinate forgave him (al Fāsī 1963, p. 236).

Another historical incident that also sets strong precedence in preserving human integrity took place when 'Amr ibn al 'Āṣ (one of the leading military commanders during the conquests [*futūḥāt*] in Caliph 'Umar's time) conquered Egypt. After a squabble with a Jewish native, 'Amr hit him, claiming that he ('Amr) was the "son of an honorable creed." When 'Umar learned of the story, he reprimanded 'Amr and uttered his famous quote: "Since when did you take people as slaves, when their mothers have borne them free?" (al Fāsī 1963, p. 236).

In light of those exemplary citations, the sanctity of a person's being is respected and observed according to Muslim practice. Even if security forces seek indictment of a person implicated in a crime, they do not have the right to violate him, because in doing so they are taking a minute chance of harming a possibly innocent soul. Observing human dignity is an inherent part of Islamic beliefs and practice. Violating the due process of law is a strong indicator of violating the variable of preserving the self.

Respect for human dignity also corresponds to the Muslim activists' call for restricting arbitrary arrests and the necessity of recognizing the due process of law. Another of their grievances is the torture to which Islamic activists are subjected after their arrest and during their trial by military courts.

The importance of preserving the self, according to Islamic mores and the grievances of Islamic activists, suggests a relationship between Islamic activism and current human rights violations in each of the countries studied. In analyzing this concept, the variable property is the degree to which the government preserves or protects the self.

The indicators developed to examine this variable property are the preservation of human dignity, the period of incarceration without trial, the right of defense in the court of law, the trial of political prisoners in military courts, the practice of torture during incarceration, using torture to implicate the prisoner, violating the human rights of the prisoner's family members, hunger strikes by the prisoners, and the sudden death of prisoners during incarceration. The scale developed will be as follows:

The preservation of human dignity before and during imprisonment. A five-category scale is used to score the regime's preservation of human dignity in a given year:

(1) 1–20 incidents of human dignity violations
(2) 21–40 incidents
(3) 41–60 incidents
(4) 61–80 incidents
(5) More than 81 incidents
(00) No information

Incidents of torture and death during imprisonment. A ten-category scale is used:

(1) 1–20 incidents of torture and death
(2) 21–40 cases
(3) 41–60 cases
(4) 61–80 cases
(5) 81–100 cases
(6) 101–300 cases
(7) 301–500 cases
(8) 501–700 cases
(9) 701–800 cases
(10) 801–900 cases
(00) No information

Use of police brutality to disperse and deter Islamic activists. A four-category scale is used, in addition to a two-category subscale that qualifies the reason for police brutality:

(1) The crowds were harmless, but police used brutal force (killing or wounding people). The number of people killed or wounded:
 (a) Less than or equal to 50
 (b) 51–100
 (c) 101–500
 (d) 501–1,000

(2) The crowds were harmful (i.e., armed) and therefore the police used brutal force (killing or wounding people). The number of people killed or wounded:
 (a) Less than or equal to 50
 (b) 51–100
 (c) 101–500
 (d) 501–1,000

Since the Foreign Broadcast Information Service (FBIS: the main source for coding all the variables) usually has a number of reports on the same incident, and sometimes the number of people is not specified, I have used scale categories to record the information. Then I used category midpoints for purposes of aggregation. Thus the approximate numbers in the tables in Appendices 1, 2, and 3 are based on the summation of category midpoints.

Preserving Posterity/Youth

The concept of preserving posterity is an important one, according to the *maqāṣid.* Part of preserving posterity is the religious emphasis on the role of parents in bringing up their offspring. The conservation of the family unit according to Islam is a basic part of religious mores. The family unit creates the social setting required for healthy offspring. Abū Zahrā' (1982, p. 278) writes:

> Preserving posterity is preserving the human qualities so that [humans] grow strong in body, talent, feelings, behavior, and religion. This entails the preservation of the family so that children are granted the care of their mother and father, which nourishes their feelings and their reasoning [rationality].

Another element of preserving posterity/youth is educating young people about their religion and its mores. Islamic activists have repeatedly criticized their respective political systems for reinforcing "secular" methods of teaching, whereby children are not taught religion as a basic part of the curriculum. Religion, therefore, becomes secondary in the education of children and youth. This grievance of Islamic activists is a measure of the government's contradicting the spirit of preserving offspring.

The variable property of preserving posterity is the extent to which the government encourages or discourages religious education and religious practice in schools and universities. Some indicators used for measurement are the availability of religious classes, the allowance of religious expression by wearing a headscarf or growing a beard at school, and permission to pray at school. The scale for scoring this variable includes two categories:

(1) The regime encourages religious education and practice.
(2) The regime openly discourages religious education and practice.
(00) No information

Preserving Property/Wealth

The last end goal (*maqṣad*) is described by Abū Zahrā' (1952, pp. 368–369) as follows:

> Preserving property is upheld by prohibiting theft and extortion, distributing wealth in a just and equitable manner, protecting produce from spoiling, aiding the growth of public resources, and prohibiting the control of the peoples' wealth by way of deceit and treachery. Preserving wealth also includes all transactions between people like buying, selling, renting, and all other consensual contracts.

Preserving property is also observed by prohibiting usury (*ribā*). Prohibiting usury is part of an economic conception that underlies all dealings in Islam. It is clearly stated in the Qur'an that *ribā* is forbidden (*ḥarām*). Therefore, in order to preserve property, *ribā* is prohibited whether it is practiced on the international, national, or personal level ('Uthmān 1982, p. 42; 'Āṭiya 1988, p. 107; al Shīshānī 1980, p. 313).

Preserving property is concerned with four main principles: circulation of assets (*tadāwul*), clarity/frankness (*wuḍūḥ*) in all dealings, justice (*'adl*), and protection from transgression (*al muḥāfaẓah 'alā al māl*) ('Ālim 1991, pp. 495–568). *Tadāwul* is sought by prohibiting (1) hoarding one's money, (2) usury, and (3) the monopoly of the market. *Wuḍūḥ* is ascertained by having clear, plain contracts in all market dealings, whether this is through a written contract or through witnesses to the agreement. Justice is sought by (1) seeking middle ground between overspending and being extremely thrifty, and (2) giving alms (*zakah*)[58] to the needy. Preserving property is also realized by punishing theft or any transgression on one's property ('Ālim 1991, pp. 495–568).

The concept of preserving property will vary according to the extent to which the government maintains the country's economy: that is, controls economic instability and inflation. The indicator for this variable will focus on price inflation and the government's response to it. The indicator consists of a scale with two categories:

(1) Inflation varies (that is, it increases and decreases over time, thus reflecting waves of economic revival).
(2) Inflation is continually increasing.
(00) No Information.

Measuring the Dependent Variable: Activism

The concept that concerns this research is Islamic activism. The variable property accordingly is the degree of Islamic activism. Although a number of studies have focused on violent elements of Islamic activist movements, I examine the violent as well as the nonviolent components of the movements. Thus the events examined will include peaceful demonstrations, public lectures (especially on Fridays), violent clashes with police forces, armed attacks, bombings, and assassination attempts. Four indicators of the annual extent of Islamic activism are used. Three of those categories variable V. A., B., and C. (like variable II. A., B., and C.) are measured on the basis of the Foreign Broadcast Information Service (FBIS) reports. Since the FBIS often has several reports of the same incident, and sometimes the number of people is not specified, I have used scale categories to record the information. Then I used category midpoints for purposes of aggregation. Thus the approximate numbers in the tables are based on the summation of category midpoints.

The first indicator has a four-category scale of regime response, the number of Islamic activists arrested each year:

58. *Zakah* is one of the five pillars of Islam.

(1) Less than or equal to 50 activists arrested.
(2) 51–100 arrested
(3) 101–900 arrested
(4) More than 901 arrested
(00) No information

The second indicator of Islamic activism is the number of attacks against public figures, secularists, and tourists. Threats of attacks are also counted, since they reflect the potential for violent acts against public figures and secularists. For example, the number of assassination attempts (whether they are successful or not), the number of incidents of killing or assassinating policemen,[59] the number of threats to use violence or the use of violence against other religious minorities, and the number of attacks on tourists.[60] The scale used for this indicator is a three-category scale of the number of attempted attacks/threats against public figures, police forces, secularists, and tourists:

(1) 1–10 attempted attacks/threats
(2) 11–20 attempted attacks/threats
(3) 21–40 attempted attacks/threats
(00) No information

The third indicator of Islamic activism is a five-category scale of the number of Islamic activists who join public demonstrations/rallies in a given year:

(1) Less than or equal to 50 demonstrators
(2) 51–100 demonstrators
(3) 101–500 demonstrators
(4) 501–1,000 demonstrators
(5) More than 1,000 demonstrators
(00) No information

Those demonstrations will also be coded in terms of their degree of violence using a four-category scale:

(1) Peaceful
(2) Harmed property
(3) Entangled in a clash with the police forces, military, or any other state agency
(4) Harmed individuals not related to the state

59. Killing or assassinating policemen is different from armed massive clashes coded in variable II. C. or in variable V. D. Those assassinations are usually sporadic and enacted by a small number of individuals (usually 1–5 individuals), whereas II. C. and V. D. are more massive acts of violence (i.e., more people are involved in assaulting the police).

60. Targeting tourists has been used by Islamic activists in recent years to embarrass the ruling regime and to reflect the inability of the regime to provide efficient security.

The fourth indicator of Islamic activism concerns the extent to which activists gain influence in certain provinces or professional organizations (for example, professional syndicates)[61] by way of elections. A three-category scale is used to measure this indicator:

(1) Winning an election or gaining acceptance in one or two provinces
(2) Winning an election in a certain syndicate
(3) Losing elections in a certain province/syndicate owing to the regime's interference
(00) No information

The four indicators mentioned above are assumed to reflect the degree of Islamic activism in the countries under study (Egypt, Algeria, and Turkey) in a given year.

Not all variables are operationally independent. For example, events used to code the violation of preserving religion and the self are also coded in the violation of preserving posterity if they relate to the student body or youth in general. If students are arrested, the event is coded in the preservation of posterity and in the approximate number of Islamic activists arrested. The third incidence of overlap in coding is in variable II. C.: the use of police brutality to disperse/deter Islamic activism and variable V. D.: the demonstrations that involved clashes with police forces.

Sources of Information for Coding the Dependent and Independent Variables

The main source of information used for coding in this study is the *Foreign Broadcast Information Service—Daily Reports from October 1988 to September 1993*. The FBIS is utilized in this study for a number of reasons. First, human rights sources like the country reports provided by the U.S. State Department proved useless in reflecting a realistic image of human rights abuses. The inadequacy of such reports is discussed at length in a study by Human Rights Watch (Helsinki Watch, 1985).[62]

61. Winning elections in certain professional syndicates might have serious political implications. The qualitative aspect of this variable will be discussed in the data analysis section for each country.

62. *Critique: Review of the Department of State's Country Reports on Human Rights Practices for 1984* (Americas Watch Committee, Helsinki Watch Committee, and Lawyers Committee for International Human Rights, 1985).

Second, Amnesty International and Human Rights Watch reports were not adequate for the purposes of this research. Since I am trying to explain the variance in degree of Islamic activism, it is important, for example, to get as accurate an account as possible of the number of Islamic activists arrested, tortured, and killed. The information provided by both Amnesty International and Human Rights Watch was not that specific. It provided the total number of people arrested, tortured, and killed, regardless of the charges against the detainees.[63]

The third issue of concern is that Amnesty International and Human Rights Watch report human rights abuses according to the international definition of human rights violations, which also lacks the specific information needed to assess Islamic activists' grievances.

The FBIS daily reports, on the other hand, provide a general account of incidents which allows for the flexibility needed to code the variables used in this research. The large number of daily articles in FBIS usually provides a diversity of information for coding, and the information provided is "raw" (i.e., it is not qualified); thus it allows the researcher the flexibility to interpret events according to the cultural issues under study.

Having defined each *maqṣad* and its indicators, as well as the indicators for the dependent variable, we need only a methodological note on the countries studied to complete the broad outline for this research.

The Methodological Aspects of Comparing the Countries under Study

In light of the literature review and the theoretical arguments presented, it is necessary to restate the basic hypothesis proposed for research: The extent of Islamic activism is a function of the extent to which state performance in Muslim societies falls short of the principles of Islamic social justice. The implication of this assumption is that changes in each country over the last five years in state performance are associated

63. For example, in Turkey a number of offenses were considered a threat to the state. Legal codes like law 142 and 163 were enacted to arrest and try anyone associated with leftist or Islamic political organizations. As a result, Amnesty International and Human Rights Watch report that X number of people were arrested for violating law 142 and law 163. This lacks the specificity needed to indicate the variance of Islamic activism.

with changes in the extent and intensity of Islamic activism. This study focuses on intercountry and intracountry comparisons.

I will compare three countries over the past five years in order to test the proposed hypothesis. Algeria, Egypt, and Turkey were selected because (1) they share some similarities and (2) the differences or variance between them are significant to the hypothesis proposed. Thus, as Collier (1991, pp. 10–11) suggests, this study will attempt to

> focus on comparable cases, cases that: (1) are matched on many variables, that are not central to the study, thus in effect "controlling" for these variables, and (2) differ in terms of the key variables that are the focus of analysis, thereby allowing a more adequate assessment of their influence. Hence the selection of cases acts as a partial substitute for statistical or experimental control.

The three countries selected for this study are similar in several of the following respects.

In the *World Development Report 1992,* Algeria and Turkey are both listed as middle-income economies. The World Bank defines low-income countries and middle-income countries as follows: Low-income economies had a GNP per capita of $610 or less in 1990, whereas middle-income economies are those with a GNP per capita of more than $610 but less than $7,620 in 1990. A further division—at GNP per capita of $2,465 in 1990—is made between lower-middle-income and upper-middle-income economies (*World Bank Report 1992*, p. xi). The GNP per capita in dollars for Egypt, Turkey, and Algeria was, respectively, $600, $1,630, and $2,060.

Algeria, Egypt, and Turkey are also mostly composed of Sunni Muslims. In Egypt, 90 percent of the population are Sunni Muslim and 10 percent are Coptic Christian, Protestant, Greek Orthodox, and Jewish (Slugett and Farouk-Slugett 1991, p. 33). In Algeria, the population is composed almost entirely of Sunni Muslims (Slugett and Farouk-Slugett 1991, p. 197) Turkey comprises 90 percent Sunni Muslims and 10 percent Alevi Shi'ites (Slugett and Farouk-Slugett 1991, p. 269).

The three countries are similar with respect to ideological and institutional change from Islamic legal precepts to what are characterized as "secular" or "modernized" institutions. They are also similar in the degree of exposure of their respective elites and masses to westernization.

Algeria, Egypt, and Turkey were all part of the Ottoman Empire—from 1517 to the late nineteenth century in Egypt (1882 is the date of the British conquest of Egypt), and from 1520 in Algeria till the early nineteenth century (1830 is the date of the French conquest of Algeria) (Ageron 1991, p. v; Hourani 1991, pp. 472–475; and Yapp 1991, p. 52). Ottoman rule in the three countries is characterized thus by the late Albert Hourani (1991, p. 223):

> The most fundamental duty of a Muslim ruler, and that which both expressed and strengthened his alliance with the Muslim population, was to maintain the Shari'ah. In the Ottoman period, the institutions through which the Shari'ah was preserved were drawn into closer union with the ruler than before. The school of law favored by the Ottomans was the Ḥanafi, and the judges who administered it were appointed and paid by the government.

Hourani (1991, p. 224) further emphasizes the role of the sultan and the elites.

> The sultan used his power to uphold the Shari'ah, and it was an expression of this that those who administered the law were regarded as *asker,* members of the ruling elite.

Peretz (1988, pp. 55–56) describes the religious establishment of the Ottoman Empire:

> The religious or Muslim establishment paralleled the government. In theory, the *sheikh ul-Islam* held more power than the sultans since he was authorized to veto any decision by the sultans that was contrary to the Shari'ah. In fact, the *sheikh ul-Islam* was appointed by the sultan and could be dismissed by him at any time. Even so, the *sheikh ul-Islam fetvas*[64] generally were always respected. No sultan could issue a *kanun* (law) before obtaining a *fetva* from the *sheikh ul-Islam* stating that the intended *kanun* was compatible with the Shari'ah. The *sheikh ul-Islam* was always a free-born Muslim, as indeed were all members of the religious establishment. All members of the government as well as all Ottoman Muslim citizens came under the jurisdiction of the Shari'ah. The Shari'ah was administered by *kadi*s.

These descriptions of the Ottoman system clarify the role of Islam and particularly Islamic law in decision making and maintaining order in the countries under Ottoman rule. In Turkey, for example, the authority of reli-

64. In Arabic, *fatāwī* (plural), fatwa (singular) means "legal opinion."

gious teachers and legal experts has diminished, leaving the way open for government nonreligious officials and civil law to replace the Shari'ah (Peretz 1988, p. 169). As Peretz (1988, p. 171) notes:

> The experiment of the fervent secularists did not achieve the result Atatürk had envisioned. His religious reforms never received genuine popular support. Nor, for that matter, did they ever succeed in retaining their hold over the intellectual elite. Beneath the surface of Turkish life attachment to Islam remains one of the binding social forces. Indeed, many intellectuals have now come to feel that a reformed and modified Islam fills a vital need in their nation. Islam has returned, not as the state religion, but as the religion of the state's people, and it is again acknowledged as such by the government.

Among Atatürk's reforms, "there was nothing more devastating than [the reform] which abolished the Shari'ah and replaced it with civil, penal, and commercial codes borrowed wholesale from Swiss, Italian, and German models" (Sharabi 1987, p. 41). Atatürk abolished the fez, encouraged Western attire, adopted the Gregorian calendar, and declared Sunday as the day of rest, and replaced the Arabic alphabet with the Latin (Sharabi 1987, pp. 41–42; Slugett and Farouk-Slugett 1991, pp. 268, 272; Yapp 1991, pp. 157–158).

Although by comparison Egypt did not undergo such radical cultural change, it still experienced "Westernization" and "Secularism." As in many other accounts, Yapp (1991, p. 63) describes Egypt of the 1920s as follows:

> The tone of Egyptian intellectual life had been set by the small secular elite which dominated politics and the press. This elite had played down the Islamic element in the Egyptian past, denied that Islam had a role in politics, and even questioned the nature of the Qur'an. Islam had been excluded from developments in education and legal reform also reducing its scope. Instead the elite had stressed the geographical, historical, and cultural identity of Egyptians and Egypt's continuity from ancient times when it was the standard bearer of world civilization. There grew up a romantic image of the Egyptian peasant who was held to exemplify the true immemorial Egyptian virtues of endurance, pragmatism, realism and humor. Egyptians also looked more and more to Europe for

> ideas . . . . Socialism, social Darwinism, and positivism were only some of the ideas which fascinated Egyptian writers of the period.

For its part, Algeria is still experiencing an ongoing cultural crisis that divides Arabophones and Francophones. As Tlemcani (1986, p. 190) indicates, the differences between Berbers and Arabs, and between Francophones and Arabophones, still create a "cultural crisis that splits the Algerian intelligentsia." Tlemcani (1986, p. 191) argues that those differences became more clear in the 1960s when

> the Arabophones moved to favor a prompt and total Arabization of schooling, education and the public services in general. On the other side, the Francophones, the proponents of the neo-culture, labeled the sympathizers of "Algérie Française," advocated the status quo, i.e., French as the main tool of communication in an independent Algeria. They were thus regarded as a residuum of French colonialism or [as] communists.

Tlemcani (1986, pp. 194–203) also observes that the split between Arabophones and Francophones intensified owing to the influence of religious revival in Algerian and the Muslim world in general.

Egypt, Algeria, and Turkey share four characteristics:

(1) the three countries share a common Islamic cultural heritage;
(2) they are all "lower-middle income countries" in the 1990s, which means that economically, their performance and their needs are similar;
(3) the peoples of each country are mostly Sunnis; and
(4) the three countries share a history of Ottoman rule.

Algeria and Egypt experienced Ottoman rule followed by European conquest, while Turkey was the center of the Ottoman Empire.

There are important differences among them. One is that the three countries experienced different degrees of exposure to "Westernization," ranging from Turkey's abrupt severance of ties with cultural history to Algeria's ongoing cultural tension, where the lines of cultural identity are still evolving. Egypt is an intermediate case between Algeria and Turkey; its "Westernization" has been more gradual.

The second important difference between each country is the degree of Islamic activism. Turkey's Islamic movement is less active than the Egyptian and Algerian movements. Moreover, Islamic activism in Turkey is nonviolent in its political expression. Algeria's Islamic activist movement was nonviolent and engaged directly in the political process, until January 1992 when the elections were canceled and the Islamic activist party was dissolved. Egypt's movement, meanwhile, remains on the periphery of the electoral process since it is not a legally recognized party, but both its violent and nonviolent wings have become more active in the late 1990s.

Conclusion

This chapter has described the concepts and indicators used for the dependent and independent variables and clarified the reason for choosing the FBIS daily reports as the main source of information for coding. The remainder of this research reports and analyzes the data from the three countries studied.

CHAPTER 4

The Place of Religious Discourse in Modern Egypt

The Historical Background of Islamic Activism in Egypt in the 1980s and 1990s

The Egyptian variant of Islamic activism is said to be the trigger of many other Islamic activist movements across the Middle East. The main group that represents Islamic activism in Egypt is known as the Muslim Brotherhood. The Muslim Brotherhood was established in the late 1920s, but its strength as a mass movement did not become evident until the 1940s. In a time of turbulence in Egypt due to World War II and the ongoing British occupation, the Muslim Brotherhood tried to meet the needs of the poor through its social network of mosques, schools, hospitals, and clinics (Baker 1990, p. 251). Baker (1990, p. 252) describes the rivalry between the government and the Muslim Brotherhood in the 1950s and 1960s:

> The regime treated the Brotherhood as its most dangerous opponent. Major Muslim Brother thinkers and activists, including Sayyid Quṭb, were assassinated or executed. Thousands of followers were held in political detention camps.

The Muslim Brotherhood existed in Egypt before the 1952 Free Officers revolution. Nasser, as leader of the Free Officers, crushed the Muslim Brotherhood's movement in support of socialism and its proponents. Even though the leftist trend attracted laborers in industrial zones such as Ḥalwān and al Maḥalā during Nasser's time, the Muslim Brotherhood still held a wide base of appeal.

After Nasser's death, Sadat came into power and changed his predecessor's policies 180 degrees. Sadat was both fearful of the leftist opposition he inherited from his predecessor and eager to establish a new basis for legitimacy. As a result he started releasing the Muslim Brotherhood members from prison, and by 1976 the Muslim Brotherhood was

> formally allowed to function once again and to publish its periodicals . . . . Sadat used the Brotherhood very effectively as a counterweight to the left, which he had neutralized by the time of his visit to Israel in November 1977. (Davis 1984, p. 152)

The Islamic activist movement in Egypt, however, sustained two important changes. First, it underwent an ideological shift; second, it splintered into groups that varied from moderate to radical. Membership in such groups could shift and/or overlap.

Davis (1984, p. 154) comments on the ideological shift in the Islamic movement:

> The fact that the ideology changed between the 1940s and the 1970s from an emphasis on socio-economic variables to those emphasizing cultural issues relates in large measure to Egypt's relationship to the world market and its domestic class structure. Whereas members of the urban middle class saw the causes of Egypt's ills as stemming from British imperialism during the 1940s and 1950s, the expulsion of the British from the Suez Canal in 1956 signified the end of formal colonial control over Egypt. Increasingly, during the 1960s and 1970s, Islamic radicals came to see Egypt's problems as stemming from domestic rather than foreign sources.

Along with the focus on domestic issues, Islamic activism therefore became more concerned with cultural issues in addition to the socio-economic concerns that the movement dealt with in the 1940s.

The second change in Egypt's Islamic activist movement, its fractionalization, was in part due to the spread of Islamic activist groups in universities. The new groups "were not part of the traditional Muslim Brotherhood" (Davis 1984, p. 152). The number of such identifiable groups vary from one source to another. Zubaida (1989, p. 53) identifies the two major groups:

> The "Military Academy" (*al fanīyah al 'askarīyah*) group, deriving this name from the attack on the military academy in 1974 (as a prelude to a failed coup d'état), and the so-called *takfīr wa al hijrah* (inadequately translated as "repentance and holy flight") . . . which referred to itself as Jamā'at al Muslimīn (the Society of Muslims). This group came into prominence with the kidnapping and then the assassination of the Minister of Religious Foundations in 1977. The so-called al Jihād (holy war) group, some of whose members were responsible for the assassination of President Sadat in 1981, is reckoned to be a continuation of the "military academy" group.

The engagement of Islamic activist groups in violent activities during Sadat's time signifies an ideological shift as well as a "generational split"[65] between the main Islamic activist movement, the Muslim Brotherhood, and the numerous university Islamic activist groups. The generational split became increasingly obvious after the Camp David Accords of 1977 (Baker 1990, p. 246):

> Radical Islamic groups such as the Jihād, the Takfīr wa al Hijrah, and Shabāb Muḥammad spearheaded active opposition to the state through radicalized student unions, direct and at times spectacular militant actions, and participation in sectarian strife. The actions of the radicals culminated in the murder of the president and the uprising of Islamic militants in Assiut in 1981. State repression eroded the power of the militants, while the centrist Brothers gathered strength.

Even though the Muslim Brotherhood was gaining a larger following, its members vehemently opposed the peace agreement. The Muslim Brotherhood's opinion became distinctly clear in its journal *The Call* (*al Da'wah*): "Palestine is an Islamic question" an article states, implying that Sadat was not in a position to negotiate and/or compromise with Israel—that is, Sadat could not express the Muslim point of view (Ibrahim 1987, p. 132).

Sadat's support of the Islamic activists (whether the Muslim Brotherhood or other factional groups); his focus on international issues, especially the peace agreement with Israel in 1977; and the lack of adequate economic progression (an element that was especially felt in the

65. Davis (1984, p. 153) writes of this generational split.

January 1977 bread riots) all contributed to his assassination on October 6, 1981.

The escalation of violence and the mushrooming of Islamic activist groups was a reaction to several issues. First, the implementation of the Shari'ah was important to the Muslim Brotherhood as well as to other factions. Telmecany, a Muslim Brotherhood leader, addressed Sadat as follows, "You hear from *The Call* [*al Da'wah*],[66] demands that are only the demands of the whole nation. We have no private interests. God's law must be applied. It is only when you do this that the masses will be with you" (Baker 1990, p. 244).

In defining a true Islamic society, the Muslim Brotherhood stated that "freedom of organization and expression would be guaranteed to all groups." These rights would not depend on the character of the regime in power; Islamic law and custom would guarantee them (Baker 1990, p. 257). This point raised by the Muslim Brotherhood is taken as an indicator in this study of preserving religion and the mind. In another comment (Baker 1990, p. 259), one member of the Muslim Brotherhood[67] stressed that:

> [t]he new materialist values invaded social spheres such as education, where they had no proper place, according to the standards of a good Islamic society. In the seventies the practice of teachers offering supplemental "private lessons" to their students for a fee became widespread. Such payments for preferential treatment effectively undermined the social ideal of equality and tarnished the proper role of a teacher. Education became a consumer commodity like cooking oil or soap, whose "price" is determined by the laws of the market.

The Muslim Brotherhood, which represents the moderate side of Islamic activism, stressed the need for freedom of expression and organization (preserving religion and the mind) and emphasized its dissatisfaction with services provided by the state, such as education (preserving posterity).

A second factor that has affected Islamic activism in Egypt is the lack of government accountability, adequately described by Ibrahim (1987, p. 121) as:

66. *Al Da'wah* is the Muslim Brotherhood journal that was published at the time.

67. Baker does not indicate the name of the Muslim Brotherhood member in his writing: "Thus one Brother pointed out..." (Baker 1990, p. 259).

> the state's inability to assimilate and integrate the body politic; its exclusion of the masses from the political process; its failure to eliminate inequality or its toleration of social injustice; and, finally, its impotence in defending the nation, its national honor, and dignity. At this point, the crisis may be defined as a decline in the status and power and the ruling class, which results in lessening its claim to legitimacy.

Ibrahim further on notes the effect of Sadat's "open-door" (*infitāḥ*) economic policy on Islamic activism. A policy that resulted in a gross increase in the gap between the rich and the poor, he writes (Ibrahim 1987, p. 129): "[led] militant Islamic groups [to intensify] their denunciation of social injustice and their attacks on the excessive enrichment and corruption among the privileged few."

The legacy of Islamic activism left by Sadat to his successor, Hosni Mubarak, remains the most organized political group in Egypt today.

The strength of Islamic activism as an oppositional force became more distinct in the 1980s, as Baker (1990, pp. 246-247) notes:

> The Brothers reaped handsome rewards for their decision to move toward acceptance of democratic rule. They participated in national elections in shifting alliances with major opposition parties, played a leading role in the doctors' and the engineers' syndicates, achieved a substantial presence in parliament, and created an economic base of Islamic companies and banks. Thus, while the eyes of the outside world focused on the Islamic militants and radicals with their violent means, the Muslim Brother centrists achieved the greatest successes for the Islamic current since the forties by accepting the concept of working through government. In the Sadat years they began the tactical elaboration of an approach that transformed the face of civil society in the eighties.

The success of the Muslim Brotherhood in gaining political control is also emphasized by el-Sayed (1990, p. 228):

> The Brotherhood's presence in the People's Assembly jumped from 8 members after the election of 1984, which the Brotherhood contested on the slate of the Wafd Party, to 38 after the legislative elections of 1987, in which the Brotherhood was the senior partner in an alliance with two smaller parties, the Socialist Labor Party and the Socialist Liberal Party. It is estimated that the Brotherhood

polled 9 percent of the vote, receiving more than half a million votes, despite the heavy-handed methods of the Ministry of the Interior, which supervised the election. The Alliance, led effectively by the Muslim Brotherhood, emerged as the largest opposition bloc of about 60 deputies, with the Wafd coming in second place. Moreover, the lists of candidates of the Islamic movement won the majority of seats in the elections of the executive councils of major professional associations in the country, such as the Councils of Administration in Clubs of University Professors in Cairo, Alexandria, and Assiut.[68]

After the 1984 elections, in June of 1985, a march was planned by Islamic activists (Springborg 1989, p. 216):

> A Green March (green being the favorite color in Islam) on Mubarak's Cairo office scheduled for mid-June and promoted by the radical Shaikh Hafiz Salama was intended to force the President to decree the implementation of the Shari'ah. The march did not occur because the Muslim Brotherhood ordered its members not to participate in a demonstration for which the government had refused to issue a permit and because security forces detained more than 500 activists prior to the scheduled commencement of the march and sealed off al Nur mosque, from which the parade was to have commenced. On 5 July the government moved to curtail the influence of Hafiz Salama, Omar Abd al Rahman, and other radical imams who had attracted large followings at various mosques in Cairo, Alexandria, Fayyum, and Upper Egypt.

The skirmishes between security forces and Islamic activists were on the increase; Muslim attacks on Christians in the South and on campus police were also on the rise (Springborg 1989, pp. 217–218). However, alongside the violence, the 1986 parliamentary election campaigns were in full gear, as previously cited by el-Sayed and Springborg. Not only did Islamic activists manage to gain a stranglehold in parliamentary elections and professional syndicates, they also managed to change the political discourse of other political parties and the mass media, so that they began including Islamic issues and themes in addressing the government and the public (el-Sayed 1990, p. 234; Springborg 1989, p. 218). El Sayed (1990, pp. 235–236) also stresses that part of the Islamic activists' success politi-

68. Springborg (1989, pp. 184, 215, 218) writes of Islamicist activity in elections, too.

cally was due to the failure of other parties to provide an alternative model for the Egyptian people.

Aside from the Islamic activist gains in the political arena, one of the most important factors affecting the movement's popularity among the masses was its ability to provide public services. Sheikh Kishk, a popular preacher who was sympathetic to Islamic activism, stated that "the mosque performs the task of several ministries." Baker (1990, pp. 261–262) further explains Kishk's statement:

> It [the mosque] was a ministry of culture that provided Qur'anic commentaries on Fridays and after evening prayers. The distribution of clothes and medicines at the mosque made it a ministry of social affairs. Doctors volunteered their services to the needy from the mosque and thereby transformed it into a ministry of health. Finally, the mosque served as a ministry of education when volunteer teachers gave private lessons without charge to needy pupils.

Springborg (1989, p. 225) further stresses Sheikh Kishk's point:

> Currently the proliferation of organizations providing social services is extremely impressive. The Islamic Medical Society, for example, operates seven clinics in Cairo, at one of which alone some 50,000 patients were treated in 1986. Like other Islamic-run clinics, those of the Islamic Medical Society are clean, well provisioned, and able to provide medical services virtually free of charge . . . . A related phenomenon has been the proliferation of social, health, and educational facilities in association with private mosques.[69]

From this review of the 1980s and 1990s in Egypt it is clear that, along with Sadat's encouragement of Islamic activism, there was already a process of disaffection with the government's performance. The disaffection of Islamic activism continued to accumulate in opposition to economic issues as well as to political-cultural issues. The organization of skills and strength of Islamic activists is also evident from the detailed accounts of the social and economic services that they provide to society. The politi-

69. In agreement with Kishk and Springborg, el-Sayed (1990, p. 232) notes that such services affect the Egyptian population: "The movement is already replacing the state in such areas, by rendering services which the state was expected to provide, and in some cases doing so much better and at a lower cost."

cal and social vacuum that prevails in current Egyptian society is well characterized by Springborg (1989, p. 225): "In providing alternative social, health, and educational facilities the Islamicist movement is challenging the state structure, hence the credibility and even legitimacy of the government.

An important issue is the ethic with which those services are provided: "Concern about social justice is, after all, at the very heart of religious militant movements" (Ibrahim 1987, p. 129). However, this study is an attempt to prove that seeking social justice is "at the heart of" both militant and nonmilitant Islamic movements as discussed in the following section.

The Analysis of the Data on Islamic Activism in Egypt for November 1988 to October 1993[70]

The hypothesis of this study is that Islamic activism is a function of the extent to which state performance in Islamic societies falls short of Islamic social justice as embodied in the *maqāṣid*. Accordingly, for each country, starting with Egypt, each independent variable's relation to nonviolent and violent Islamic activism will be analyzed for a given year. Then the analysis will focus on comparing the relationship between violent and nonviolent Islamic activism and the independent variable for a given year; that is, the analysis will attempt to establish whether there is a relationship between changes in the independent variable and changes in the type and extent of Islamic activism.

The third step in the analysis of the data will compare the relationship between the independent variable and Islamic activism over the five years. That is, I will attempt to comprehend the effect of each independent variable on Islamic activism over the five years to detect whether there is a general correlation between the two variables. The last step in analyzing the data will focus on the relative weight or importance of each independent variable in explaining Islamic activism for the five years.

70. The data on preserving religion, the mind, the self, posterity, property, and Islamic activism are all listed in Appendix 1 at the end of this study.

Preserving Religion and the Mind

November 1988–October 1989

The first dependent variable, preserving religion and the mind,[71] was measured by coding FBIS daily reports. The indicators used are the frequency and direction of government actions with regard to preserving religion and the mind.

In the year from November 1988 to October 1989, the regime supported Islamic activist arguments once. Three times the regime referred the Islamic issue being discussed to a third party, usually the Ministry of Religious Endowment. The regime clearly stated its conflicting position on Islamic issues eleven times. Thus, in the first year the regime typically rejected or conflicted with Islamic activist arguments, and on a few occasions referred the issues to a third party to deflect conflict.

The nonviolent aspects of Islamic activism are measured through a number of dependent variables:[72] the estimated number of Islamic activists who rally/demonstrate during a given year, the frequency of the kind of demonstration Islamic activists were involved in (i.e., whether the demonstrations were peaceful or involved clashes with police forces), and the election patterns during a given year.

The approximate number of Islamic activists who rallied or demonstrated in Egypt during the first year was 1,255 individuals. The frequencies of the kinds of demonstrations are as follows: seven demonstrations were peaceful, four involved entanglement with police forces, and one harmed individuals not related to the state.

The election patterns for the period from November 1988 to October 1989 show that Islamic activists won elections or gained more political influence in one or two provinces. Although most of the regime's response to issues raised by Islamic activists concerning preserving religion and the mind was negative, the pattern of demonstrations shows that Islamic activists were not engaged in direct, violent confrontations with the regime.

The latter point is amplified when the violent element of Islamic activism (the approximate number of attempted attacks on state officials, tourists, secularists) is analyzed. The first year of analysis witnessed thirty-five attempted attacks carried out by Islamic activists, one of them an attempted assassination of the minister of the interior. The estimated number of Islamic activists arrested was 2,340 individuals.

---

71. The reason for combining the two *maqāṣid* is discussed in chapter 3.

72. A summary of Islamic activism data is displayed in Table 1 on page 99.

November 1989–October 1990

In the second year, the preservation of religion and the mind shows the following: The regime referred one issue to the Ministry of Religious Endowment, and there were three incidents in which the regime was in direct conflict with Islamic issues. Thus, although the number of recorded incidents is few, most of the regime's decisions were in conflict with the Islamic activist stand.

The nonviolent aspects of Islamic activism in that year indicate that an estimated 2,220 Islamic activists rallied/demonstrated: six demonstrations were peaceful, six harmed private/public property, three demonstrations involved entanglement with police forces, and four harmed individuals not related to the state. The election patterns reported indicate that Islamic activists gained elections or more influence in two syndicates/professions, while the regime twice intervened to overturn the Islamic activists' gains.

Thus, although the total number of issues dealing with preservation of religion and the mind were fewer than in the preceding year, nonviolent Islamic activism increased. It is also important to note that some 3,660 Islamic activists were arrested that year, both a reflection of the spread of Islamic activism and a catalyst for its increase.

Violent Islamic activism measured by the number of attacks against public officials, tourists, and secularists rose to forty-four. The forty-four people attacked included the speaker of the Assembly, who was assassinated. Thus the increase in the number of demonstrators and the wider variance in the kind of demonstrations indicate that the movement was expanding and becoming increasingly violent in the second year of analysis.

November 1990–October 1991

During the third year of analysis, the independent variable measuring the preservation of religion and the mind indicates that the regime referred religious issues to a third party once,[73] while it stated its disagreement with Islamic activists on twelve different issues.

Meanwhile, nonviolent Islamic activism showed the following pattern for the third year of analysis: approximately 3,890 people joined rallies; ten of those rallies were peaceful, four involved entanglement with police forces, and two harmed individuals not related to the state. In terms of election patterns, the regime prevented the Islamic activists from gaining ground in a professional syndicate. About 3,710 Islamic activists were arrested.

73. In this case it was al Azhar, an Islamic institution of higher learning.

The data show that although the number of demonstrations was fewer in comparison with the first two years, the approximate number of demonstrators almost tripled during this year of analysis. The violent aspect of Islamic activism, reflected in the number of attempted attacks, increased slightly to forty-seven attempts (one of which was an attempt on the interior minister's life). Therefore, in the third year of analysis, most Islamic activists actions were nonviolent, but violent attacks remained relatively numerous.

November 1991–October 1992

During the fourth year of analysis, the regime's response to issues raised by Islamic activists was as follows: there were two instances in which the regime referred the issue to a third party, but in sixteen other issues the government rejected or was in conflict with Islamic activists on religious issues. The nonviolent aspects of Islamic activism were reflected in the following changes: The approximate number of demonstrators decreased to 190, and the kinds of demonstrations varied as follows: there was one peaceful demonstration, five demonstrations harmed property, two demonstrations involved entanglement with police forces, and seven demonstrations affected individuals not related to the state. Meanwhile, Islamic activists were gaining influence in elections held by one professional syndicate. The approximate number of Islamic activists arrested during this year was 2,800 people.

The government's clear conflicting stand on religious issues, combined with a strong crackdown on militants as well as civilians in terms of imprisonment, killing, and torture[74] affected the nonviolent aspect of Islamic activism. Although the demonstrators were fewer in number, there was a dramatic increase in their violence toward the police forces and individuals not related to the state. The violent aspect of Islamic activism, reflected in the number of attacks, rose to more than double of what it was during the last three years of analysis. During the fourth year of analysis (November 1991 to October 1992), the number of attacks was 124 in all.[75] Those attacks included the killing of a number of tourists and the assassination of a secular writer named Faraj Fūdah. The violent aspect of Islamic activism was gaining momentum for the fourth year of analysis.

---

74. An issue which will be discussed in the analysis of the second independent variable related to preserving the self.

75. Compare the number of attacks in the first year of analysis (35), the second year of analysis (44), and the third year of analysis (47).

November 1992–October 1993

In the last year of the analysis, the following patterns in the government's response to religious issues were noted: There were four instances where the government supported the Islamic activist views or appeared to compromise its secular position. There were seven instances where the government involved a third party to comment or act on a religious issue, and there were thirty-four instances where the government clearly stated its opposition to religious issues of concern to Islamic activists.

The nonviolent aspects of Islamic activism also increased; the estimated number of demonstrators rose to 7,110 individuals. Nine demonstrations were peaceful, eleven harmed property, one involved a clash with the police forces, and seven involved the harm of individuals not related to the state.

The election patterns also reflected the growing strength of the movement: Islamic activists won elections in three provinces and professional syndicates. The Islamic activists lost twice because of government interference.

The approximate number of people arrested that year was 10,450—almost triple the number of people arrested two years before, in November 1990–October 1991. The government was shifting tactics in its fight against Islamic activism. Its policies on religious issues seemed to fuel its increase, and the arrests reflected the inability of the government to control Islamic activism by other means.

The violent aspect of Islamic activism, i.e., the attempted number of attacks on public figures and tourists, also sustained a sharp increase, to 668 attempts. These included attacks on Copts and policemen, an attempt to assassinate the information minister, an attempt to assassinate President Mubarak, and an attempt to assassinate Chairman Arafat during his visit to Cairo.

The numbers and facts in the last year of analysis reflect

(1) a sharp increase in the government's rejection of religious issues of concern to Islamic activists,
(2) its inability to control the movement, reflected in the sharp increase in arrests, and
(3) the Islamic activists' growing influence in elections on the provincial as well as the professional level.

The evidence also shows a sharp increase in violent actions against the state and its security apparatus. Islamic activism was escalating rapidly in both its violent and its nonviolent aspects.

Preserving the Self

The second independent variable is measured using a number of indicators. First, the approximate number of *habeas corpus* violations is accounted for by checking the number of people rounded up in a short span of time,[76] and the length of time it takes for the person imprisoned to have access to a lawyer and a judge in a civilian court.[77] Another indicator for preserving the self is the approximate number of people reportedly tortured and estimates of the number of people who die during imprisonment. The fourth indicator for preserving the self is not related to the legal aspects of imprisonment or trial, but deals instead with the security forces' actions toward Islamic activism in demonstrations.

November 1988–October 1989

The indicators for violations of the preservation of the self during the first year of analysis reflect the following: *Habeas corpus* violations numbered about 260, the approximate number of people tortured or killed during imprisonment was fifty, and the approximate number of people wounded or killed by police during demonstrations was 180 in all. The crowd actions that triggered police brutality varied: There were three peaceful demonstrations in which the police used force to disperse people and four demonstrations in which the police reacted forcefully to violence instigated by the crowds.

Meanwhile, the independent variable, Islamic activism, was an estimated thirty-five attacks on public officials, tourists, and secularists. Approximately 1,255 Islamic activists were involved in demonstrations, most of which were peaceful. Islamic activists also won several provincial elections.

---

76. In instances when there is an assassination attempt, it is reported that several people were involved in the attack. However, the police round up hundreds of Islamic activists to capture the attackers. Thus the government gives the public a confused message because in many instances the only incriminating evidence is the person's appearance, that is, way of dress, long beards, . . . etc.

77. In many cases Islamic activists are tried in military courts where defending a criminal is more difficult and the sentences are much harsher than in civilian courts. The public is shut off from the trial process, which creates doubts with regard to the fairness of the trial.

November 1989–October 1990

In the second year of analysis, there were approximately 120 *habeas corpus* violations (about half of the violations reported during the preceding year), the number of people tortured/killed during imprisonment rose to 1,410, and the estimate of people killed or wounded in demonstrations was 330 (also double the figure of the preceding year). The crowds were peacefully demonstrating in five out of the eleven incidents where police brutality was reported.

The violent aspect of Islamic activism involved forty-four attacks on public figures, including the assassination of the speaker of the Assembly. Approximately 2,220 Islamic activists joined demonstrations. Six demonstrations were peaceful, six harmed property, three involved a clash with police forces, and four harmed individuals not related to the state. Electorally, Islamic activists won twice in professional syndicates. There were also reports that the government interfered twice to alter elections in its favor.

Although the number of people tortured or killed during imprisonment showed a dramatic increase and the number of people wounded or killed during demonstrations almost doubled, the violent aspect of Islamic activism (the number of attempted attacks) did not increase proportionally. However, demonstrations for the second year do reflect more violent tendencies in comparison with the preceding year.[78]

November 1990–October 1991

The third year of analysis reflected the following patterns: *Habeas corpus* violations increased to 390 cases, the number of people tortured or killed during imprisonment decreased to 945, and the estimates of people killed or wounded during riots showed a slight decrease to 300 individuals. However, the police were repeatedly more aggressive in their treatment of demonstrators, since in nine out of ten demonstrations they used force against Islamic activists.

With regard to the dependent variable, the number of Islamic activists arrested rose slightly to about 3,710 and the number of attacks on public officials increased to an estimated 47 attempts. The approximate number of demonstrators rose to 3,890, an increase of more than 1,000 from the preceding year. The kinds of demonstrations varied: ten were peaceful, none harmed property, four involved clashes with the

78. We also observe a slight increase in the estimated number of Islamic activists arrested during the second year of analysis in comparison with the first year: 3,600 and 2,340, respectively.

police, and two harmed individuals not related to the state. In terms of electoral activity, there was one reported incident of government interference in local elections.

In this third year, the government's actions concerning the preservation of the self (i.e., the three previously cited indicators) remained stable. Likewise, the violent aspects of Islamic activism did not increase dramatically. The nonviolent aspect of Islamic activism increased, as indicated by the number of demonstrators.

November 1991–October 1992

In the fourth year of analysis, the number of *habeas corpus* violations decreased to an estimated 280 cases, the approximate number of people tortured or killed during imprisonment increased to 1,323, and approximately 300 people were wounded or killed by police in demonstrations. In comparison with the preceding year, Islamic activists were more likely to initiate clashes with the police: seven out of ten demonstrations involved aggression by the rioters.

As for Islamic activism, the following patterns were noted: The number of Islamic activists arrested decreased relatively, and the approximate number of Islamic demonstrators decreased to 190 individuals. The demonstrations turned more violent: five harmed property, two involved clashes with the police, seven harmed individuals not related to the state, and only one was peaceful. Attacks numbered an estimated 124 cases, double the numbers for the three preceding years.

Meanwhile, there was little Islamic activist involvement in elections for the year; they won in a single professional election. Islamic activists were increasingly involved in violent and indirect attacks on the government during the fourth year. Though the violations against Islamic activists were fewer than in preceding years, the Islamic activists were more likely to choose violent means to express their opposition to the government's policies.

November 1992–October 1993

In the last year of analysis, the estimated number of *habeas corpus* violations increased to 1,310, almost three times the highest previous number of violations reported (in the third year of analysis). The number of people tortured or killed during imprisonment rose to an all-time high, an estimated 1,610 cases, and the number of people killed or wounded by the police also rose sharply to an estimated 998 individuals. Eleven of these incidents involved peaceful crowds of protestors and twenty involved violent crowds. The violation of the preservation of the self is starkly obvious in the last year of analysis.

Islamic activism reflected the following patterns: An estimated 10,450 Islamic activists were arrested. Attacks rose sharply to 668, and the approximate number of demonstrators also rose sharply to 7,110 people. The kinds of demonstrations varied: nine demonstrations were peaceful, eleven harmed property, one involved a clash with police, and seven harmed individuals not related to the state. This year also witnessed the highest degree of Islamic activist involvement in the election process: A number of provinces were won by Islamic activists, and they also won in two professional syndicate elections. The government interfered twice to annul syndicate elections. The data reflect a sharp increase in the last year of analysis in both the dependent and the independent variables.

In the last three years, violations of the self and violent Islamic activism seemed to increase. The increase in the last three years does not reflect a cause-and-effect relationship only. The increase also signifies an escalation in the conflict spiral between the government and Islamic activists. That is, the duration of violations and the Islamic activists' reaction seemed to entangle both parties in a continuous cycle of violence—an issue that is referred to in Algeria and discussed at length in the conclusion.

Preserving Posterity/Youth

The independent variable measuring the preservation of posterity/youth focuses on the government's reaction to religious education and practice in public and private schools and in universities. The preservation of posterity/youth is of particular importance to Islamic activism because one of the activists' main grievances is deliberate government policies to dissuade young people from observing their religion, especially at an impressionable age. This variable is measured as follows:

(1) the regime encourages religious education and practice
(2) the regime does not take an explicit stand for or against religious education and practice
(3) the regime openly discourages religious education and practice

November 1988–October 1989

In the first year of analysis, there were three instances where the government openly discouraged religious education and practice. The first incident involved banning Islamic group activities and investigating Islamic activism inside and outside campuses; the second involved the arrest of children aged ten through sixteen because of their participation in an education trip with Islamic activists; and the third involved the arrest of a number of people because they were allegedly instilling youths with extremist ideas.

Islamic activism during this year of analysis reflected moderate trends in both violent and nonviolent aspects of the movement. As described above, 35 attacks and approximately 1,255 activists demonstrated, mainly in peaceful demonstrations (seven out of ten were peaceful). There was minimal involvement of Islamic activists in elections.

November 1989–October 1990

There were two incidents that reflected the government's opposition to religious education during the second year of analysis: both incidents involved interference with and arrest of Islamic activist students owing to their participation in campus elections.

Islamic activism reflected moderate changes in comparison with the previous year: There was a slight increase in the number of attacks to forty-four, and an estimated 3,660 Islamic activists were arrested. Numbers of Islamic activist demonstrators rose to 2,220, with a shift toward more violence: six of the demonstrations were peaceful, six harmed property, three involved clashes with the police, and four harmed individuals not related to the state. In the two elections in which Islamic activists gained influence in professional syndicates, the government intervened.

November 1990–October 1991

The third year of analysis reflected an increase in the regime's opposition to religious education and practice. There were eight events in which the security forces cracked down on Islamic activists, mainly those involved in student elections. Police forces also cracked down on Islamic activists involved in rallying against the police's use of force and students involved in rallying against the Gulf War. In one rally, 185 Islamic activist students were arrested for protesting against the Peace Conference in Madrid.

Islamic activism reflected the following patterns for the third year: The number of Islamic activists arrested increased for the second consecutive year to 3,710 individuals. There was also a further increase in the approximate number of attacks to forty-seven, including an attempt on the life of the interior minister. The number of Islamic demonstrators increased to 3,890 individuals. There was virtually no electoral activity.

The pattern for the third year reflects a measurable increase in nonviolent Islamic activism and a slight increase in violent Islamic activism, corresponding to a significant increase in incidents of governmental opposition to issues pertaining to religious education and practice.

November 1991–October 1992

There were three reports of issues that the government rejected concerning Islamic education and practice for the fourth year of analysis. Two of those issues involved restrictions on campus Islamic activities, and the third involved a statement by the Sheikh of al Azhar[79] noting the inadequacy of religious curricula in schools and universities.

The fourth year reflected the following in Islamic activism patterns: Arrests of Islamic activists decreased to 2,800 people, and the nonviolent aspects of Islamic activism decreased to 190 demonstrators. Some demonstrations harmed property (five out of fifteen) or individuals not related to the state (seven out of fifteen). Islamic activists' involvement in elections was also nil. The violent aspect of Islamic activism, reflected in the number of attacks on public officials, tourists, and secularists, increased sharply to 124 individuals. The sharp increase in violent Islamic activism in the fourth year of analysis indicates that there is a link between the duration of violating posterity/youth and violent Islamic activism. However, the relationship between prolonged violations is not simply cause-and-effect; rather it indicates a conflict spiral that the governments and the activists get entangled in at later stages of the conflict.[80]

November 1992–October 1993

The last year of analysis showed a dramatic increase in the number of events where the regime opposed reforms or change in the religious education and practice of children and youth. The government's opposition was reflected in twenty events that ranged from the restriction of Islamic activist students and professors on campus to the minister of education's discouragement of schoolgirls from wearing the veil. Other incidents involved the dismissal of high school students and the

79. An internationally recognized Islamic institute of higher education.

80. The effects of conflict escalation are addressed in Algeria, especially after the December 1991 elections. The theoretical impact of conflict escalation will be discussed in the final chapter.

removal of hundreds of Islamic activist educators from their teaching posts.

This sharp increase in opposition to Islamic education of children and youth was dramatically reflected in Islamic activist trends during this year. The estimated number of Islamic activists arrested jumped to 10,450, and the number of Islamic activists who demonstrated also increased dramatically to some 7,110 individuals. Nine out of twenty-eight demonstrations were peaceful, eleven harmed property, one involved a clash with the police, and seven harmed individuals not related to the state. Islamic activist involvement in elections also increased in comparison with the preceding four years of analysis.

The violent aspect of Islamic activism, i.e., attacks on public officials, tourists, and secularists, rose to an all-time high of 668 attacks. The increase in governmental opposition to religious education issues was accompanied by increases in both violent and nonviolent Islamic activism throughout the five years of analysis. The parallel increases were especially evident in the last year of analysis.

Preserving Property/Wealth

The last independent variable is intended to reflect economic stability and is measured by the yearly increase or stability in inflation rates according to articles reported by FBIS. Inflation rates in Egypt show a steady increase for the five years (with the exception of the third year, where there was not enough information for coding).

Since both inflation and Islamic activism, violent and nonviolent, tended to increase over the five years, we may infer that the eroding effect of continual inflation on the preservation of property contributed to cumulative grievances.

Conclusion

Violent Islamic activism, measured by the number of attempted attacks on public officials, tourists, and secularists, shows a steady increase over the five years. That is, the violent element of Islamic activism has a tendency to grow over time in response to violations of the four independent variables (the *maqāṣid*) defined in this study.

However, there is a difference between the violent and the nonviolent patterns of Islamic activism, which brings us to a second observation. The nonviolent aspects of Islamic activism, reflected in the number of demonstrators, kinds of demonstrations, and electoral activities, tend to vary more closely with the government's responses to the four independent variables.

A third observation is that the independent variables of the preservation of religion, the mind, and the preservation of posterity are the strongest explanatory variables out of the four variables under study in Egypt. Their explanatory weight is relatively higher than the preservation of self and the preservation of property.

The preservation of self is only secondary in its explanatory strength and relates more closely to the violent aspects of Islamic activism. In the years that the government cracked down on Islamic activists by violating *habeas corpus*, killing or torturing prisoners, and wounding or killing Islamic activist demonstrators, the nonviolent aspects of Islamic activism decreased, whereas the violent aspects continued to increase. However, as indicated previously, one should not overlook the effect of prolonged conflict on the escalation of reactions that involve the government and Islamic activists in violent confrontations.

The least powerful explanatory variable out of the four defined in this study is the preservation of property. The increase in inflation rates reflected a constant pattern that may have a cumulative effect on Islamic activism.

The results of the five-year analysis (see Table 1 below) show that there are relative increases in both violent and nonviolent Islamic activism which correspond to increases in government violations of the preservation of religion, the mind, the self, posterity, and property, in varying degrees. The data reflect a pattern that supports the hypothesized relation between preserving the end goals of the Shari'ah (the *maqāṣid*) and Islamic activism.

Table 1
Summary of Data on Islamic Activism in Egypt*

Year	Nov 1988 - Oct 1989				Nov 1989 - Oct 1990				Nov 1990 - Oct 1991				Nov 1991 - Oct 1992				Nov 1992 - Oct 1993			
Approximate number of Islamic activists arrested	2,340				3,660				3,710				2,800				10,450			
Approximate number of attempted attacks	35				44				47				124				668			
Approximate number of Islamic activists who rally/ demonstrate	1,255				2,220				3,890				190				7,110			
Categories of kinds of demonstration	1	2	3	4	1	2	3	4	1	2	3	4	1	2	3	4	1	2	3	4
Frequency of kinds of demonstrations	7	-	4	1	6	6	3	4	10	-	4	2	1	5	2	7	9	11	1	7
Categories of election patterns	1	2	3	00	1	2	3	00	1	2	3	00	1	2	3	00	1	2	3	00
Frequency reflecting election patterns	1	-	-	-	-	2	2	-	-	-	1	-	-	1	-	-	3	2	2	-

* See Appendix 1 for information on the categories and scales used to code the data.

CHAPTER 5

The Place of Religious Discourse in Modern Algeria

The Historical Background of Islamic Activism in Algeria during the 1980s and 1990s

In the wake of the Algerian elections in 1991, the violence that overcame the country continues till this day (1999). Some factions in the Front Islam-ique du Salut (FIS) movement have grown more violent after cancellation of the elections in which they made a strong showing.

Adherence to Islam is not a new phenomenon in Algerian society. One of the main thrusts behind the Algerian war of independence from France was Islam, and the two concepts of nationalism and Islam were combined to provide the new rulers with legitimacy when Algeria become independent in 1962. In Entelis's (1981, p. 195) words, one of the main contradictory elements in Algerian political culture is the

> support for total Arabization and for the practice and perhaps imposition of ascetic, rigid and austere Islamic orthodoxy coexisting with a nationalist ethic which seeks to implement rapid and sweeping economic and social modernization, that is, Westernization, at the expense of Arabization.

Entelis's insight into the contradictory elements of Algerian culture is unique because he mentions "social modernization" as a factor affecting the struggle between Arabization and Westernization. He believes that it is not technological modernization that contradicts the Arab/Islamic cultural make-up of Algeria, but rather "social modernization" that transgresses the cultural boundaries of Algerian society.

Entelis (1981, p. 196) also states that the contradiction in cultural elements spills over to public policy making: "within a cultural environment in which the Arabic and Islamic components of national identity continue to be emphasized, Algeria pursues a practical policy of bilingualism."

According to Vatin (1982, p. 234)

> What is striking about most of the historical literature devoted to Islam in Algeria is the permanence of disputes between religious groups and the central power. A main characteristic has been the lasting opposition to central administration either based almost directly on religious arguments or using Islam at least as a means to contest the legitimacy of government authorities. It would thus be extraordinary not to have any form of Islamic protest now.

The disparities between Arabic/Islamic and Western culture still play an important role in separating the elite from the masses. The examination of the 1980s and 1990s in Algerian history sheds some light on this situation.

After independence, Ben Bella led the country until 1965 and was then put under house arrest and denounced by Boumedienne, who led the 1965 coup. Boumedienne's revolution failed to deliver on its promises to the masses, as Knauss (1980, pp. 91–92) notes:

> The Democratic and Popular Republic under thirteen years of Colonel Boumedienne was neither democratic nor popular. Boumedienne's authoritarian style and his secrecy never made him a popular leader with the majority of the people. His regime was widely known to be corrupt and at times brutal. Algeria under Boumedienne was really *sui generis*. It was the result of an alliance of expedience between petit-bourgeois national soldiers and bourgeois technocrats. Algeria between 1965 and 1978 was an excellent example of a country caught in the "throes" of a mythical revolution.

Boumedienne's years of rulership were regarded by many specialists as stable. The masses seldom participated in the political arena. Entelis (1982, p. 93) notes, "Algerian politics in the Boumedienne period (1965–1978) were dominated by a relatively small yet stable civil military oligarchy with remarkably little participation on the part of the masses."

In agreement with Entelis, Ruedy (1992, p. 209) states:

> With the streamlining and homogenization of the government, the growing authority of the technocracy, the bureaucratization of the party, and the harnessing of the labor, student, youth, and women's organizations, Algeria by the 1970s had become increasingly depoliticized. The professional bureaucrats, technocrats, and military officers who made policy functioned in increasing isolation from public opinion.

Entelis (1982, p. 99) also stresses the bureaucratization of the party during Boumedienne's rule:

> The FLN has not been a very credible force in stimulating political activity or in mobilizing the masses. The heavy hands of the state and the army have not allowed it any independent political activity. It is unattractive to young people with an educated and intelligent interest in politics because they are required, as members, to be more conformist than nonmembers.

Toward the last years of his rule, on June 19, 1975, which marked the tenth anniversary of his revolution, Boumedienne declared a plan to draft a new charter (Ruedy 1992, p. 209):

> The draft charter was published in 1976, and the public was invited to a wide-ranging national debate on its content. With a degree of freedom unparalleled in Algerian political life since the first year of independence, Algerians discussed and criticized the document over a period of months. After numerous amendments, of which none was particularly substantive, the 80,000 word National Charter was put to a referendum on June 27, 1976, from which it emerged with overwhelming approval.

After the approval of the charter in June 1976, the Islamic activists emerged in the political arena in Algeria. Although there are conflicting opinions of when Islamic activity began to affect Algerian political life, there is a general consensus that the late 1970s witnessed its emergence. For example, Burgat (1993, p. 262) quotes one of the Algerian Islamic activists: "Starting in 1976 and 1977, there started to be some Islamic activity in the mosques in general, and in the Bayt al Arqām mosque, where Mohammed

Sahnoun and Sheikh Abdellatif Soltani preached," Burgat (1993, p. 261) writes: "It was in 1978 that the first internal expressions of the Islamist current began to appear in the mosques of certain urban centers (Algiers, Oran, Sidi Bel Abbes, Laghouat, etc.)."

Ruedy (1992, pp. 241–242) states:

> As early as 1979, militant Muslims clearly distinguishable from mere Arabizers clashed with "Berberists" and "Marxists" on university campuses. Female students were intimidated for failure to abide by Muslim standards of dress or propriety. Soon, student and non-student fundamentalists undertook campaigns to ransack cafes, restaurants, and other establishments that served alcoholic beverages. Among the leaders of the emerging fundamentalists were Sheikh Abdelatif Sultani and Sheikh Ahmed Sahnoun, organizers and theoreticians of the Islamic *da'wah* movement. One of their understudies was Abbassi Madani, a former FLN loyalist who had broken with them after independence, eventually had gone off to London to earn a Ph.D., and had come back to teach sociology at the University of Algiers.

Although sources do not agree on an exact date, it is clear that the 1976 drafting and approval of the National Charter invigorated the public's interest in political life and contributed to the reemergence of Islamic activism in modern Algeria.

Boumedienne died in January 1979, and Chadli Benjedid was chosen in a national election in February of that year. Islamic activists' political weight become more obvious in the 1980s during Benjedid's rule. The 1976 changes in the National Charter were not the sole cause. As Mortimer (1991, p. 577) explains: "During the 1980s, as the regime's capacity to distribute services became constricted, dissatisfaction with the government's performance began to grow in various sectors of the society."

The voice of Islamic activists became more clear in 1982, when a direct confrontation between students of the University of Algiers took place (Burgat 1993, p. 263):

> In November, 1982, the second major strike by Arabic speaking students, in which Madani[81] played a key role, led to violent incidents inside the walls of the University of Algiers. On November 2, on the campus of Ben Aknoun, Fehallah Lassouli, a 28-year old

81. Madani later on became the leader of the FIS.

> former sailor, knifed Kamel Amzal, a student from Algiers, during a series of confrontations between "progressives" (who generally belonged to the French-speaking sections) and the Islamist "M.B." (Muslim Brothers). The clashes led to repression that the Islamist movement considered to be very one-sided. A public prayer, held ten days later, was attended by 5,000 people in the courtyard of the central campus in Algiers. A petition drafted by the old Sheikh Ahmed Sahnoun and Abbasi Madani calling for a more intransigent Arabization, including a ban on alcohol and a personal code closer to Sharia Law as well as other demands, was sent to the government. During the following days, other tracts were distributed calling notably for the constitution of an Islamic state in Algeria.

Madani as well as others were arrested and later released. This event marked the beginning of the Islamic activist confrontation with the regime. As Ruedy (1992, p. 242) notes:

> The government began to parole convicted fundamentalists in 1983 and 1984 and gradually to release those irregularly detained. Most militants were sufficiently impressed by the crack-down to keep activity within legal bounds for the next several years. Nevertheless, the continuing vitality of the movement was demonstrated by the turnout for the funeral of Sheikh Abdellatif Sultani in March 1984. Militants claimed 400,000 faithful participated in the emotional funeral and rally to honor him.

The next social upheaval was the 1988 uprising, which had no direct link to Islamic activism or any other specific political group. The October 5, 1988 uprising began with a number of strikes in the industrial areas of Algeria and the postal service. Ruedy (1992, p. 249) describes the episode:

> October 5 saw young men by the thousands storming through the center of Algiers and many residential quarters, destroying government and party property as well as property associated with profiteers and the lifestyle of the well-off. At least two ministries were sacked the first day. In the next two days, the movement was spreading like wildfire; rioting spread to Oran, Mostaganem, Blida, Annaba, and many other cities and towns. With little initial organization, it seems that the movement came soon to involve student groups, unionists, leftists of the PAGS,[82] and a large number of

82. Parti de l'Avant-Garde Socialiste, a Labor party.

fundamentalists. On October 6, the government declared a state of siege and the repression began in earnest. In addition to billy clubs and tear gas, the security forces began using live fire and, ultimately, resorted to several kinds of automatic weapons. Before order was more or less restored on October 10, hundreds of Algerians, mostly young men, had died; and thousands had been taken into custody, where many were tortured.

Following the 1988 upheavals, President Chadli Benjedid proposed a new constitution that was largely supported by the voters in February 1989[83] (Ruedy 1992, p. 250). While the 1976 constitution had guaranteed the basic human rights of the people, the 1989 constitution allowed freedom of expression and association in addition to basic human rights (Ruedy 1992, p. 251). The 1989 constitution differed in another important way that affected the Islamic activist movement and the elections later on in 1990 and 1991. Burgat (1993, p. 274) describes this dramatic change as follows:

> The real thunderbolt would come only a few months later on September 14, 1989. To the great surprise of a part of the local political class and against the advice of nearly all his Arab counterparts, Chadli, without even waiting for the dispositions included in the constitution against religious political parties to be modified, took the unprecedented step for the Maghreb of opening the gates of the political scene to the Islamist party.

This constitutional modification was to a great extent responsible for guiding the Islamist dialog in modern Algeria into conventional political channels (allowing Islamists to form a party and enter national elections). According to Ruedy (1992, p. 252), "the majority of the secular parties represented very narrow personal or regional interests." Out of thirty secular parties, only four had a relatively broader appeal than others (Ruedy 1992, p. 252): (1) the Front des Forces Socialistes, whose leader, Hocine Ahmed, advocated "cultural pluralism"; (2) the Rassemblement pour la Culture et la Democratie (RCD), led by Said Saadi of the Kabyle movement, who defended cultural Berber as well as individual human rights; (3) the Parti Social Democrate, comprised of entrepreneurs and academics and led by Abderrahmane Adjerid; and (4) the Parti de l'Avant-Garde Socialiste (PAGS), supported largely by labor unions and led by Sadek Hadjeres.

83. To be more exact, the new constitution was publicized on February 4, 1989, and accepted by referendum on February 23, 1989 (Burgat 1993, p. 271).

Ruedy (1992, p. 252) writes:

> more important than any secular opposition parties was the Front Islamique du Salut (FIS). It was founded in February 1989, by Abbassi Madani and Ali Belhadj, *imām* of al Sunnah mosque in the popular Bab el-Oued quarter of Algiers, who, during the 1980s, was the most popular preacher in the city.

He also notes (Ruedy 1992, pp. 252–253) that

> none of the secular parties was able to develop a nationwide grass-roots organization in preparation for these elections. Both Ahmed and Ben Bella called on Algerians to boycott elections they claimed were rigged against them. The FLN, after its years of power, maintained in effect a very impressive political organization. But the FIS, with linkages to 9,000 mosques, large and small, benefited from instant and extraordinarily effective organization.

FIS and its supporters called for the annulment of the law and launched mass demonstrations that called for new presidential elections and the establishment of an Islamic republic. Near the end of June, the army attempted to control the crisis by arresting hundreds of Islamic activists including the two most prominent leaders of FIS, Abbassi Madani and Ali Belhadj (Ruedy 1992, pp. 253–254).

The parliamentary elections took place in late December 1991, and on December 26 the results of FIS winning 188 out of 430 electoral districts sent shock waves through Algerian elite circles, the West, and other Arab countries. Key military leaders, along with President Chadli's opponents, forced him to dissolve the parliament and abdicate his presidency. Chadli resigned on January 11, 1992. The elections were canceled, and a "High Council of State" composed of five men and headed by Mohammed Boudiaf was to perform presidential duties. Boudiaf assumed his responsibilities on January 16, 1992 (Ruedy 1992, p. 255; Burgat 1993, p. 303).

Sid Ahmed Ghozali, the Algerian foreign minister, issued an edict prohibiting the use of mosques for political purposes. When the activists ignored the rules, the police matched this defiance with a massive wave of arrests. Violence spread throughout Algeria. The Islamic activists denounced the government's actions as "political piracy" and urged the people to "protect the popular choice." The police arrested thousands of militants (including AbdelKader Hachani, one of the FIS leaders), killing and wounding hundreds in the process. A state of emergency was declared in February, and the FIS was legally dissolved in March. Violent clashes ensued between Islamic activists and the police forces, culminating in the assassination of Boudiaf on June 29, 1992 (Ruedy 1992, p. 255; Burgat 1993, pp. 304–305).

As Ruedy (1992, p. 256) states:

> Early in 1992 the Algerian nation stood divided. One the one side was the largely secularized minority who were the principal beneficiaries of the existing Algerian system. On the other side stood a militant Islam calling for renewal of society through implementation of the Shari'ah and return to authentic Muslim values.

A number of hypotheses have been formed as to the causes of the rise in Islamic activism in Algeria. Ruedy (1992, p. 239), for instance, comments on "the regime's inability to deliver to most citizens the better life it promised" as a cause of Islamic activist opposition. The Islamic activist movement was trying to establish some guidelines for accountability.

More in line with the theoretical framework of my research, Burgat (1993, p. 100) emphasizes that "[the Islamist phenomenon's] social geography cannot be considered as being limited to economic victims of modernization." Rather than depending on the modernization/economic development approach to explain Islamic activism, Burgat (1993, p. 4) states at the beginning of his book that

> The South, after having undertaken to disconnect its political future from the West, and then to win more autonomy in the management of its material resources, has now turned towards the terrains of culture and ideology, domains previously conquered by the North, and which it now seeks to reappropriate. Even if it is very far from representing the outcome, Islamism, "the rocket of decolonization's third stage," manifests the acceleration of this process of repositioning the South in relation to the North. And it is an essential step.

Thus recent research on Algeria reinforces my theoretical argument by stressing the importance of accountability to Islamic activism and by underscoring the role of culture as a factor affecting the movement's discourse.

The Analysis of the Data on Islamic Activism in Algeria for November 1988 to October 1993[84]

Preserving Religion and the Mind

November 1988–October 1989

Coded events for the first year of analysis show that the Algerian government either referred Islamic issues raised to a third party or acted in opposition to Islamic interests. The first action, for instance, reflects the regime's opposition to Islamic activism: it ordered military tanks to surround a mosque in Chevalley in Algeria and to disperse the crowds after prayers. During this year of analysis, the regime opposed an Islamic issue once and referred such issues twice to a third party (the Islamic Higher Council and the Ministry of Religious Affairs).

The degree of Islamic activism[85] from November 1988 to October 1989 reflected the following patterns: First, there were no reported incidents of attacks on public officials, tourists, or secularists. Approximately 725 Islamic activists were arrested, and an estimated 3,300 Islamic activists demonstrated. All three demonstrations were peaceful, and there were no reports of Islamic activists winning elections for that year. Thus the data show a low level of nonviolent Islamic activism.

November 1989–October 1990

The patterns of preserving the mind and religion by the regime in the second year were as follows. The regime opposed Islamic activist views twice, referred an issue to a third party once, and acted once in favor of the Islamic issue raised. There was a slight shift in comparison with the preceding year, because the regime allowed the FIS, after it won the elections in Constantine, to make changes in education.

The dependent variable reflected a sharp decrease in the approximate number of Islamic activists arrested in comparison with the preceding year, only 120 people. There were no reported attacks on public figures, tourists, or secularists; demonstrators increased slightly to an estimated total of 4,340 people. Two demonstrations were peaceful; one damaged property, and one involved an entanglement with police. The election patterns for November 1989–October 1990 reflected a sharp increase in the involve-

84. The data on preserving religion, the mind, the self, posterity, property, and Islamic activism are all listed in Appendix 2.

85. A summary of the data on Islamic activism is displayed in Table 2 on page 120.

ment of Islamic activists (FIS) in elections, including victories in a number of provinces.

Though there was little change in government actions affecting the preservation of religion and the mind for the second year of analysis, nonviolent Islamic activism was gaining ground in Algeria. Violent manifestations of Islamic activism were totally absent.

November 1990–October 1991

The third year of analysis reflected a larger number of actions concerning the preservation of religion and the mind. In fifteen out of twenty issues the regime opposed the Islamic activist stand, the regime supported the activists in two out of twenty issues, and it referred two issues to a third party. Thus the regime mostly opposed the issues of concern to Islamic activists.

Islamic activism reflected the following patterns: the approximate number of Islamic activists increased dramatically to 4,720 people, there were sixty-eight reports of attacks, and the approximate number of Islamic activists who demonstrated rose sharply to 12,850 people. Fewer than half the demonstrations were peaceful (sixteen out of thirty-six), and the number of demonstrations involving police clashes was eleven out of thirty-six. Seven of those demonstrations harmed property, and four harmed individuals not related to the state. Thus there was a dramatic increase in both the number of peaceful demonstrations and the total number of demonstrations for the third year of analysis. The election patterns reflected minimal change, though the FIS was reportedly gaining ground in a number of municipalities.

It is evident that with the increase in the frequency of governmental opposition to Islamic issues, there was a corresponding increase in nonviolent Islamic activism for the third year of analysis.

November 1991–October 1992

The evidence for preserving religion and the mind in the fourth year shows that the Algerian government supported Islamic issues once, opposed Islamists on thirty-seven out of forty-one issues during the year, and referred an issue to a third party three times.

Parallel to the strong opposition by the government to Islamic issues, Islamic activism shifted toward violent forms. The approximate number of Islamic activists arrested decreased dramatically, in comparison with the preceding year, to 1,820 people, whereas attacks quadrupled to an estimated 272. Among these attacks was the assassination of Acting President

Boudiaf. About 141 people were wounded in this incident alone. Demonstrators dropped to an estimated 6,550 Islamic activists. The majority of demonstrations were violent: There were fourteen peaceful demonstrations, twelve that harmed property, sixteen that involved clashes with the police, and two that harmed individuals not related to the state.

The FIS won the first round of elections on December 30–31, 1991. Most of the turmoil associated with Islamic activism was caused by the government's canceling the second round of elections and dissolving the FIS party. Not only did the government increasingly oppose Islamic issues related to preserving the mind and religion, it also chose to crush the Islamic activist movement after the elections.

The increase in both violent and nonviolent Islamic activism is directly linked to the cancellation of the elections and the violation of preserving religion and the mind (as well as the other variables discussed in this study).

November 1992–October 1993

The preservation of religion and the mind was the subject of fewer government actions than in the preceding year. The government acted in favor of Islamic issues nine times out of a total of twelve issues.

Islamic activism reflected the following patterns for the fifth year of analysis: The estimated number of Islamic activists arrested remained constant at 1,800 people from the preceding year. The approximate number of attempted attacks increased slightly to 300 incidents. The political elite was increasingly targeted: the former prime minister and members of his family were assassinated, the former minister of education and the public prosecutor were assassinated, the labor and sports ministers were attacked, and the minister of equipment was targeted for attack.

There were no reports of demonstrations for the fifth year of analysis. There was also very limited electoral activity, reflected in a slight increase in the Islamic activists' influence in professional organizations. With the suppression of Islamic activism even before the elections of December 1991, the Islamic activist movement went underground and resorted to more violent means of expressing its grievances. The government's continued opposition to religious issues, together with the suppression of Islamic activism in general, led to an increase in violent Islamic activism and a virtual end to nonviolent activism.

Preserving the Self

The preservation of the self is measured by three indicators: the approximate number of *habeas corpus* violations, the approximate number of people killed and tortured during imprisonment, and the approximate number of people killed/wounded in confrontation with police forces (with a subindicator of the kind of Islamic activist action that caused police brutality).

November 1988–October 1989

In the first year, approximately 160 *habeas corpus* violations were reported, approximately 220 people were killed/tortured during imprisonment, and about sixty were killed or wounded by police during riots.

About 725 Islamic activists were arrested for that year. There were no reported attacks on public figures, tourists, and secularists. Some 3,300 Islamic activists demonstrated; all reported demonstrations were peaceful. There were no reports of Islamic electoral activity. Therefore, the major indicator of Islamic activism for the first year of analysis is the approximate number of Islamic activists who joined demonstrations. Despite the high level of government violence, Islamic activism followed a nonviolent course.

November 1989–October 1990

There are no reports regarding the preservation of the self during this year. That is, no *habeas corpus* violations were reported nor people killed/tortured during imprisonment. Neither were there any reports of people killed/wounded in clashes with the police.

The approximate number of Islamic activists arrested decreased sharply from the previous year (725) to 120 people. There were no reports of attempted attacks. However, there were reports of approximately 4,340 Islamic activists who joined demonstrations during this year. Two out of four demonstrations were peaceful, one harmed property, and one involved a clash with the police forces. The Islamic activists were more active in the political arena, with the FIS gaining strength in provincial elections.

Nonviolent Islamic activism was gaining ground in Algeria, even in the absence of government actions reflecting the violation of the preservation of the self.

November 1990–October 1991

These are the data on preserving the self for the third year of analysis: approximately 280 *habeas corpus* violations, an estimated thirty people killed/ tortured during imprisonment, and about 645 people killed/wounded in demonstrations. Almost half of those demonstrations were peaceful.

The dependent variable, Islamic activism, reflected the following patterns: Approximately 4,720 Islamic activists were arrested, 12,850 Islamic activists joined demonstrations, and the FIS was becoming more influential in public elections. Of thirty-eight demonstrations for the third year of analysis, sixteen were peaceful, seven harmed property, eleven involved clashes with the police, and four harmed individuals not related to the state. The violent aspect of Islamic activism was reflected in an estimated sixty-eight attacks on public officials, tourists, and secularists.

Thus with the increase in the number of *habeas corpus* violations and the drastic increase in numbers of people killed/wounded in confrontations with the police, there was a corresponding increase in both violent and nonviolent aspects of Islamic activism from November 1990 to October 1991.

November 1991–October 1992

The fourth year of analysis reflected the following for the preservation of the self: *Habeas corpus* violations almost quadrupled to an estimated 280 cases, the number of people reported tortured/killed during imprisonment increased dramatically to 1,930 cases, and the number of people killed/ wounded in demonstrations doubled, to an estimated 1,350 individuals. Seventeen demonstrations were nonviolent, and twenty-three were violent.

Indicators of Islamic activism reflect the following for the fourth year of analysis: The approximate number of Islamic activists arrested decreased to 1,820, and the approximate number of attempted attacks increased four-fold to 272, in comparison with the preceding year. The approximate number of Islamic activists who joined demonstrations decreased to 6,550 individuals. Demonstrations were mostly peaceful or, at most, involved clashes with the police (i.e., they did not harm property or individuals not related to the state).

The elections of December 1991 in which the FIS won the first round were the main reason for the increase in the government's violations of preserving the self. The increase in the government's violation of the self was accompanied by an increase in violent Islamic activism, represented by large numbers of attacks on public officials, tourists, and secularists, and by the kinds of demonstrations carried out by Islamic activists.

The relation between preserving the self and Islamic activism at this stage in Algeria is not a simple case of cause and effect. Owing to the massive arrests before the December 1991 elections (the estimated number of Islamic activists arrested from November 1990 to October 1991 was

4,720), and the cancellation of the December elections afterwards, the government created a conflict spiral that continues in 1999. Even though the FIS was involved in nonviolent activities prior to the massive arrests in 1990 to 1991, factions of the party engaged increasingly in violent activities, especially after the cancellation of the December 1991 elections. The government started out by arresting FIS members and canceling the elections; then the Islamic activists reacted by resorting to violence; meanwhile, the government increased its violation of the self by disregarding *habeas corpus* and torturing and killing imprisoned Islamic activists. Based on the Algerian government's initiative, the conflict spiral was escalating.

November 1992–October 1993

The last year of analysis reflects the following patterns for preserving the self: the estimated number of *habeas corpus* violations decreased to almost half of the preceding year:[86] 450 cases. The approximate number of people killed/tortured during imprisonment decreased slightly (though still high) to 1,8456 cases. Numbers of Islamic activists killed/wounded by police forces increased to an all-time high of an estimated 1,620 individuals. However, the Islamic activists were not engaged in outright demonstrations. There were many episodes of violent Islamic activism, but police forces attacked Muslim civilians indiscriminately.

Islamic activism reflected the following patterns: An estimated 1,800 Islamic activists were arrested, and there were approximately 300 attacks, mainly on public officials. There were no reports of Islamic activists who demonstrated, but there was some evidence of Islamic activism in professional elections. Therefore, similar to the preceding year, the fifth year of analysis reflects an increase in the government's violation of the self in the context of its direct confrontation with Islamic activism, which corresponds to an increase in specifically violent Islamic activism.

The patterns reflected by the preservation of the self variable, therefore, were linked to the increase in violent Islamic activism and decreased the possibilities for nonviolent Islamic activist participation. As indicated above, the causal relation between Islamic activism and the violation of the self becomes increasingly complex in the last two years of analysis owing to the spiraling effect of the government's actions and the violent response of Islamic activists. Therefore, it is important to note that violent Islamic activism in the later stages of conflict is not simply an effect of violating the self. Instead the escalation of violations and violent Islamic activism are

86. It was 1,030 for the fourth year of analysis.

part of an action/reaction chain: As tensions escalated between Islamic activists and the government after the December 1991 elections were canceled, both parties engaged in violent confrontations whereby the government increased violations against the self and the Islamic activists engaged in retaliatory attacks against public officials, tourists, and secularists.

Preserving Posterity/Youth

The independent variable for preserving posterity is measured by a method similar to that used to measure the preservation of religion and the mind variable. However, it focuses on Islamic issues that relate to children, youth, and college students. The government's actions are coded as either encouraging or discouraging Islamic education and practice for children, youth, and college students.

November 1988–October 1989

There were no reports in the first year of Algerian governmental actions concerning Islamic education and practice. As observed above, the dependent variable of Islamic activism reflects the prevalence of nonviolent participation through peaceful demonstrations (3,300 Islamic activists demonstrated). There were no reports of attacks on public officials and no noticeable participation by Islamic activists in any reported elections. This year's data thus are consistent with the hypotheses (i.e., because there were no violations, Islamic activism was low and nonviolent).

November 1989–October 1990

The second year of analysis saw the strength of the FIS demonstrated in provincial elections, as a result of which the activists were able to act on religious education issues. For example, the only reported issue for this year was an incident where the FIS banned mixed schooling in the city of Constantine.

The patterns of Islamic activism for the second year of analysis reflected the following: There were approximately 120 Islamic activists arrested, a decrease in comparison with the preceding year. There were no reports of attacks on public officials, and the estimated number of Islamic activist demonstrators rose slightly, to 4,340 individuals. Most demonstrations were peaceful. The FIS was also gaining ground in provincial elections.

November 1990–October 1991

There were two incidents in which the Algerian government discouraged Islamic education and practice during the third year. The first incident took place with the city council of Bab el-Oued and the Algerian Popular Council were denied a request to cancel performances during Ramadan by the Algerian Cultural Center. The second incident involved shutting down Annaba University in response to a strike by Islamic activist students and professors.

As for Islamic activism, the following patterns were reported: about 4,720 Islamic activists were arrested, and there were approximately sixty-eight attacks on public officials, tourists, and secularists. The number of Islamic activists who demonstrated increased drastically, to an estimated 12,850 people. The demonstrations were mostly peaceful (sixteen out of thirty-six demonstrations); however, there were seven demonstrations that harmed property, eleven that involved clashes with the police, and four that harmed individuals not related to the state. The election patterns show a slight increase in favor of the FIS, the leading Islamic party in Algeria. This reflects the preoccupation of the FIS with the coming elections of December 1991.

Thus in the run-up to the December 1991 elections, the nonviolent as well as the violent aspects of Islamic activism were on the rise. The nonviolent aspects were on the ascendant, so that activists were able to change successfully public policy relating to religious education in the city of Constantine.

November 1991–October 1992

The fourth year of analysis reflected strong opposition from the government to Islamic issues related to education and practice. All twenty reported incidents reflect this opposition. The government's opposition was demonstrated in its constant violation of religious observances on campus grounds and in mosques. Most governmental actions took place on college campuses. The police repeatedly dispersed students by force and shut down campuses to dissuade Islamic activist students from organizing demonstrations or, in some instances, from praying.

Islamic activism reflected the following patterns. Approximately 1,820 Islamic activists were arrested, and there was a sharp increase in violent Islamic activism: The estimated number of attacks rose to 272 incidents. The number of Islamic demonstrators decreased to 6,550 individuals. Of the demonstrations, fourteen were peaceful, twelve harmed property, sixteen involved clashes with police forces, and two harmed individuals not related to the state. The election patterns reflect the strength of the Islamic activist movement in Algeria: Activists won the first round of elections in December 1991. However, subsequent rounds of elections were canceled, and the FIS party, representing Islamic activism in Algeria, was dissolved.

Therefore, in correspondence to the increase of governmental opposition to religious education and practice, there was an increase in both violent and nonviolent Islamic activism.

November 1992–October 1993

There were no reported incidents of government action toward religious education issues for the fifth year, but violent Islamic activism seemed to increase.

Changes in the third independent variable, preserving posterity, are more closely related to nonviolent Islamic activism than to violent Islamic activism through the five years of analysis. The increase of government actions that violate preserving posterity, especially in the fourth year of analysis, seems to lead to a corresponding increase in the strength of nonviolent Islamic activism. During the same year there was a surge in violent Islamic activism, but the violence was mainly a reaction to the suppression of the FIS. My conclusion is that the third variable seems to have a relatively strong effect on nonviolent Islamic activism than on violent Islamic activism.

Preserving Property/Wealth

The fourth independent variable concerns the effect of economic welfare on Islamic activism. Economic welfare is measured in terms of the ability of the government's economic policies to maintain or stabilize inflation rates. In Algeria there was a sustained increase in the cost of living from November 1988 to October 1993, except that there were no reports on inflation rates for November 1990–October 1991.

The weight of violating the preservation of property is thus difficult to estimate. If inflation and other sources of economic grievance affect Islamic activism, the effects are cumulative rather than short-term. My findings are not inconsistent with the hypothesis that the more inflation rates continue to rise, the greater the long-term increase in Islamic activism.

Conclusion

Analysis of the data for Algeria suggests a number of observations about the relationship between the independent variables and Islamic activism (see Table 2 below). The fourth year of analysis marked the greatest increase in violations of the preservation of religion and the mind, the preservation of the self,[87] and the preservation of posterity. There was also a steady increase in violent Islamic activism that reached its highest levels in the fifth year of analysis.

In the third year, there were parallel increases in the number of Islamic activists arrested, the number of demonstrators, and the number of demonstrations involving clashes with the police. The second observation is directly linked to the first because it explains the dramatic increase in government violation of the four independent variables in the fourth year of analysis. That is, the government reacted to the increase in Islamic activism by increasing its violations of the independent variables (the *maqāṣid*). The government also imprisoned a great many Islamic activists during the third year of analysis before the December 1991 elections. Thus the regime tried to preempt the December elections, though the FIS still managed to win in the primaries.

After the elections were canceled and the FIS dismantled, the party went underground. As a result there was a decrease in government actions affecting all the independent variables (the *maqāṣid*) and an accompanying decrease in nonviolent Islamic activism. But all variables linked to violent Islamic activism continued to rise: The number of attacks by Islamic activists increased, and so did the number of violent clashes between the police and Islamic activists.[88]

The preservation of posterity and the preservation of property did not affect Islamic activism as the preservation of religion, the mind, and the self did. Violent Islamic activism seemed to respond to all violations but in particular the violation of the self. Thus with the increase in violating all the *maqāṣid* there was also an increase in violent Islamic activism. That is, the cumulative effect of *maqāṣid* violations affects the degree of violence of Islamic activism. Meanwhile, the nonviolent aspects of Islamic activism

87. The increase in self violation was noted in all three indicators of this variable: *habeas corpus* violation, killing and torturing during imprisonment, and police brutality.

88. The categories of variable II. C., which measures police brutality, also show an increase in the fifth year of analysis.

were relatively responsive to all violations of the *maqāṣid*, but most responsive to the violations of religion and the mind.

The data after December 1991 indicate that the cause-and-effect relation between the *maqāṣid* and Islamic activism was affected by the escalation in conflict between the government and Islamic activists. That is, the intensity of reactions to the other party affected the causal relation between government violations (especially the preservation of the self) and Islamic activists' violence.

The escalation in violations of the four independent variables (the *maqāṣid*) corresponds to increases in violent and nonviolent Islamic activism. After the December 1991 primary elections and their repercussions, the violations seemed to decrease, as did the nonviolent aspects of Islamic activism. Thus, whether Islamic activism is violent or nonviolent, the violation of the *maqāṣid* seems to have an effect on the strength and popularity of the movement. My hypothesis is supported by the findings of the five-year study of Algerian society.

Table 2
Summary of Data on Islamic Activism in Algeria*

Year	Nov 1988 - Oct 1989				Nov 1989 - Oct 1990				Nov 1990 - Oct 1991				Nov 1991 - Oct 1992				Nov 1992 - Oct 1993			
Approximate number of Islamic activists arrested	725				120				4,720				1,820				1,800			
Approximate number of attempted attacks	0				0				68				272				300			
Approximate number of Islamic activists who rallied/ demonstrated	3,300				4,340				12,850				6,550				0			
Categories of kinds of demonstration	1	2	3	4	1	2	3	4	1	2	3	4	1	2	3	4	1	2	3	4
Frequency of kinds of demonstrations	3				2	1	1		16	7	11	4	14	12	16	2		6		1
Categories of election patterns	1	2	3	00	1	2	3	00	1	2	3	00	1	2	3	00	1	2	3	00
Frequency reflecting election patterns					4				1				1		1			1		

*See Appendix 2 for information on the categories and scales used to code the data.

Chapter 6

The Place of Religious Discourse in Modern Turkey

The Historical Background of Islamic Activism in Turkey in the 1980s and 1990s

The role of religion in Turkish politics has been a subject of contention since the beginning of the twentieth century. Atatürk's rule in the 1920s and his "secularization" of Turkish society has, to a large extent, affected the nature of Islam in present-day Turkey.

There are several trends of Islamic activism in Turkey; these vary in their degree of "politicization." As Mehmet (1990) notes in *Islamic Identity and Development*, some groups have joined the current government. They participate through existing political channels (e.g., parties like the Motherland Party, the National Salvation Party, or the True Path Party), all of which participate in elections. Other groups, however, are more militant, and their participation in the political process takes place outside the system. They do not utilize the current political channels for expression.[89] The third type, *tarikats* (religious orders), are

> Religious orders [that] have been organized along the standard Anatolian patron–client basis providing charity in return for total obedience to the leader (*sheikh*). They have experienced the fastest

89. The militant groups are suspected to have "outside connections and funding" as Mehmet (1990, pp. 50–51) notes.

growth in the recent past, as a sort of underground Islam, since they are officially banned.[90]

The groups that have attracted many analysts' attention, however, are those that participate through the political channels that exist in current Turkish society, especially the NSP (National Salvation Party) and its predecessor, the NOP (National Order Party).

The NOP was a short-lived party that became active in 1969. During the establishment of the party in 1970, its spokesman Necmettin Erbakan promoted religion and attacked freemasonry and communism (Geyikdagi 1984, p. 120). The party was careful not to address Islam directly, since political parties are prohibited by law from using the word "Islam" (Geyikdagi 1981, p. 120). Geyikdagi (1981, pp. 120–121) explains that NOP got around the legal prohibition by

> using more indirect words like morals and virtue *ahlak ve fazilet* [both Arabic terms with strong Islamic connotations] to make its purpose clear. The party also stressed elements like social justice and the necessity of religious education. (Geyikdagi 1981, p. 121)

In the aftermath of the 1960s' turmoil and the numerous student riots, the military intervened on March 12, 1971 (Ozbudun 1987, p. 145; Reinhardt 1987, p. 65). The Supreme Commander of the military, General Gurler, demanded that the new government "suppress political violence" (Reinhardt 1988, p. 65). The enactment of martial law in eleven provinces (including Ankara, Istanbul, and Izmir) led to mass arrests of political activists, journalists, teachers, students, labor organizers, and a number of deputies. The NOP was dissolved (Reinhardt 1988, p. 65) and banned by the Constitutional Court on May 20, 1971 (Ozbudun 1987, p. 145). The court accused the leaders of NOP of "violating articles 2, 19 and 57 of the 1961 Constitution related to secularism as well as the Law on Political Parties (Geyikdagi 1984, p. 121). The party was also banned for seeking "to restore a theocratic order in Turkey (Ozbudun 1987, p. 145).

After the NOP was dismantled, Necmettin Erbakan sought refuge abroad, only to return and reestablish his party as the National Salvation Party (NSP) in October 1972 (Geyikdagi 1984, p. 121; Ozbudun 1987, p. 145; Sunar and Toprak 1983, p. 432).[91] In the 1973 elections, the NSP

90. Mehmet cites a number of sources to support his argument, including Kiray (1982), Saylan (1987), Dumont (1987), and the *Middle East Report* (1988).

91. The NSP's rebirth and the chronology of events in Turkish politics is discussed by many, including Feroz Ahmad (1977) and Richard Tapper (1991, pp. 8–9).

attracted attention as an Islamic party that could sway the elections to the right or left of center in Turkey. The NSP got 48 seats in the Turkish National Assembly out of 450—10.7 percent of the total. The relevance of this party to my study lies in its ability to attract voters to its platform and its representation of the growing influence of religion in Turkey.[92]

In agreement with Toprak,[93] Ozbudun clarifies that NSP party members are "well educated, of middle or upper-middle class." Ozbudun (1987, pp. 150–151) concludes,

> The elite culture is no longer as monolithic as it was for the past four and a half decades since the establishment of the Turkish Republic. For the first time in the history of the Republic, there has emerged a counter-elite with a different cultural orientation than that of Kemalist Westernists. In other words, the elite–mass gap is being supplemented by an elite–elite gap.

Geyikdagi (1984, pp. 11–12) argues that Turkey's "rapid change from an agricultural to an industrialized economy" led to a "state of anomie" which caused "many people to try to find a haven in religion and become devout believers until they adapt themselves to the new circumstances. Subsequently, they regain their self-confidence and become more flexible in their ideas.[94]

The traits of voters for NSP and the causes of their support have been interpreted differently. While a number of social scientists agree that the cultural homogeneity of the upper classes is fragmenting, others, like Tapper and Geyikdagi, argue that modernization is causal to the rise of Islamic activism in Turkey.

---

92. As Ozbudun notes (1987, p. 145), "the political influence of the religious factor in Turkey cannot be reduced to this party alone. Since the NSP has been the most important manifestation of political Islam in modern Turkey, however, an analysis of its ideology, appeal, leadership, social bases, and governmental performance will hopefully shed light on the overall influence of Islam in contemporary Turkish politics."

93. In Toprak's earlier writings, especially in a paper presented to the Berlin Institute for Comparative Social Research (1989), he stresses that Islamic activism in Turkey is part of the modernization process and that the religious phenomenon is related to the emigration of villagers to the metropolis.

94. The idea of anomie is also indicated in Tapper (1991, p. 18):

> Like other countries in the process of modernization, Turkey is experiencing the passage from *Gemeinschaft* to *Gesellschaft* and the consequent identity void . . . . Islam is a social discourse which represents an alternative to the Western and secular *Gesellschaft* in contemporary Turkey, one which would be free of the emptiness and injustice they attribute to modern society.

The emergence of a counter-elite, or at least an "elite–elite gap," indicates that the influence of Islamic activism extends beyond structural issues such as modernization. The NSP not only succeeded in attracting elites to join and lead its cadres, it also succeeded in influencing public policy. Mehmet and Landau (1990, p. 123) note:

> Several Islamic measures were enacted, including compulsory religious instruction in all primary and middle schools, anti-pornography laws, more religious broadcasts on state radio and television, and a major expansion in the size of the religious bureaucracy.

Toprak also discusses in detail the NSP's role in reasserting Islamic mores:

> The sculpture of a nude in an Istanbul square was lifted by the order of the Minister of Interior, an NSP member, on the grounds that it was a piece of pornographic material. A television documentary about the Amazon tribes, which included shots of naked bodies, prompted the Minister of Justice, again an NSP member, to take legal action against the General Director of the state-owned television with the charge of encouraging obscenity. An application for government credit to construct a tourist resort was rejected by the Ministry of Commerce, then under NSP control, on the basis that tourists corrupt the morality of Turkish people. Restaurants and sandwich stands without a permit for sale of alcoholic beverages were forbidden to sell beer . . . . The NSP's Minister of Justice started on a nationwide campaign against pornography which was much publicized in the party press. The wives of NSP leaders started a new fashion which the party apparently saw fit for Moslem women: maxi skirts, long sleeves, and scarved heads. NSP parliamentarians with a background in law took up the defense of a woman lawyer who had been expelled from the Ankara Bar Association for dressing in the NSP fashion. One of her lawyers in the lawsuit that she filed against the Bar, a leading MP of the NSP, issued a statement in the party press in which he pointed out that "the scarf of the Turkish woman is as sacred as the Turkish flag." The NSP-controlled ministries and government officers became famous for their special rooms which were reserved as places of worship for the personnel who performed the *namaz* (daily prayers).

Such measures will be analyzed further in coding and describing the responsiveness of the regime to the public; they are mentioned here to emphasize the effect of the party and its followers on Turkish society in the early 1970s.

In 1977, Turkey's left-of-center party, the Republican People's Party (RPP), attracted some NSP followers, to the extent that both the RPP and NSP weakened over time owing to their interparty divisions and ideological disputes[95] (Mehmet 1990, p. 123). The political instability of the late 1970s finally came to an end with the third military coup d'état in September 1980. Just before this coup, the NSP organized a large rally on September 6, 1980, in the city of Konya (Geyikdagi 1984, pp. 135–136): "One group was clamoring for the establishment of an Islamic state. Some were wearing turbans and fezes and did not stand up while the Turkish National Anthem was being played." General Kenan Everan, the leader of the coup, declared that the latter disrespect for the National Anthem was "the straw that broke the camel's back" (Geyikdagi 1984, p. 136).

Even though the coup d'état provided some degree of political stability in Turkish society after the 1970s unrest, it did not check the growing influence of religion on Turkish society in the 1980s (Mehmet 1990, pp. 123–124):

> *Tarikats* became bigger and more prosperous, their publications multiplied, and the Islamic extremists' call for a sheri'at regime in Turkey became louder, though not more popular. During 1984-7, the number of people tried by the state for attempting to change the character of the secular Turkish republic rose from 2 to 128. A new and significant trend in the Turkish *tarikats* was the fact that they began to go international, developing funding and ideological links with like-minded organizations in Saudi Arabia and Iran as well as with the Turkish guest-workers in Western Europe.

After the coup in September 1980,

> more than 40,000 were reported arrested in the first few weeks after the coup because of their [i.e., the leftists and religious oriented activists] political activities. A year later in 1981, 25,000 were still being held, and, after 2 years (1982), an estimated 10,000 remained in custody, some without having been formally charged. (Pitman 1988, p. 82).

95. The NSP's weakness was evident in the 1977 elections where it only got 8.6 percent of the total vote (Toprak 1984, p. 129; Weiker 1981, p. 139).

NSP leaders and members were tried in February 1981 for their attempt to overthrow the government in order to establish a theocratic government in its stead.

However, after the first few years of the coup, the religious "revival" adapted (Tapper 1991, p. 22):

> In the new circumstances of the 1980s in Turkey, Islamic revival has taken on quite new forms, which are socially and ideologically not necessarily the same as any previous version; they are even more varied than before, both in their manifestations, and in their differences from revivalism elsewhere.

According to Tapper (1991, p. 10), the excessive focus on political parties in earlier writings "failed to recognize how far religious revival was already moving from these geographically and socially peripheral locations into the center." He further described those changes as follows:

> There has been a massive increase in Islamic publishing activity, including both intellectual treatises and popular prayer-manuals, *tarikat* journals, and other literature. Media attention has been particularly drawn to visible symptoms of Islamic activity and identity, such as women's headscarves and men's facial hair, mosque-building and formation of Islamic communities, and the growth of religious education. Some of these phenomena, notably the last, have received government support.

From readings on the 1980s in Turkey, we might deduce that there are two forms of Islamic activism. The first form consists of the religious cults (*tarikat*) like Nurcus, the Suleymancis, and the Isikcis that existed since the Ottoman times.[96] The second form of Islamic activism is the academic movements such as the Intellectuals' Hearth (IH [Aydinlar Ocagi]) and the Turkish-Islamic Synthesis (TIS) (Norton 1990, p. 8; Tapper 1991, p. 11).

> The religious orders (*tarikats*) are representative of the popular appeal of Islam that has remained more or less constant throughout the years (Suleyman Efendi, the leader of Suleymancis, started this religious order in 1836). However, the IH and TIS movements

96. A lengthy account of the *tarikats* in the late 1970s and early 1980s is provided in Marguiles and Yildizoglu's article in the *Middle East Report* (August 1988): 12-18.

indicate a shift in the elite's ideological stance from secularism to religiosity.[97]

It is important to note that *tarikat* all have similar aims: "[they] all call for the re-establishment of Islamic rule in Turkey."

The Islamist trend is said to have five aims (Norton 1990, p. 8):

> (1) To reject all sources of authority other than Allah and His Prophet, (2) To unite all Muslims in a world-wide Islamic state, but until that goal is achieved to establish the rule of the Shari'ah in individual Islamic communities, (3) To reject utterly all the political, economic and cultural influences of the West upon the Islamic world, and continue to accept only its technology and science, (4) To reject nationalism and nation states since these conflict with the concept of a universal Islamic state, [thus the Islamist trend differs markedly from the Intellectuals Hearth that attempts to reconcile Islam and Turkish nationalism in a "Turkish-Islamic Synthesis"], and (5) To regulate all human relations in the Islamic community in accordance with Islamic principles of justice.

The elitist movements, like the IH and TIS, are interested in synthesizing Islam with Turkish nationalism to maintain the political system and avoid its fragmentation by political parties or the Kurdish separatists. Thus, says Tapper (1991, p. 11), IH and TIS

> wished to bring traditional values to the surface, to peel away the false Western veneer . . . and to recognize a national synthesis of fundamental values. Proponents of the TIS wanted an authoritarian but not an Islamic state: religion, the essence of culture and social control, must be fostered in schools, but it must not be politicized.

TIS was challenged intellectually by secularists in the late 1980s.

Although most parties were incorporating religious ideals into their platforms to absorb what was viewed as an "Islamic threat," religious violence increased when key secularists were assassinated in the late 1980s (Tapper 1991, p. 11).

---

97. The *tarikats* also attract some of the upper class in Turkey. Prime Minister Özal's brother Korkut held an important position in the Nakhshbandi order (Marguiles and Yildizoglu 1988, p. 16).

In addition to noting the political elite's motives and directions in the Islamic discourse of the 1980s, it is important to look at the more popular dimension of Islamic activism, especially in 1987. Erbakan[98] was carried on his supporters' shoulders in Istanbul after Friday prayers on January 16, 1987. Some imams who joined the demonstrations denounced the 1982 Constitution as a violation of the Holy Qur'an (Ahmad 1988, p. 751). In sum, as Marguiles and Yildizoglu (1988, p. 17) note, "the Islamicist movement is definitely stronger today than it was six years ago, but how much so is difficult to quantify."

Thus, in reviewing recent Turkish history concerning Islamic activism, one notes two issues:

First, Islamic activism in the 1970s and 1980s was supported by a mixture of the masses and elite. In the 1970s the *tarikat*s, as well as the NOP and NSP, represented the popular appeal of religion to the people. In the 1980s and early 1990s, the political elite became more involved in the religious realm as they discovered that religion could be the cement that would hold Turkish society together and a source of authority that would attract the loyalty of the people. The elites sought to establish stability and maintain the status quo by using religious appeals.

Second, and more important to this research (since it ties in with the schools of analysis presented in the first chapter), are the elements used to explain the phenomenon of Islamic activism in Turkey. Numerous social scientists relate Islamic activism in Turkey to "structural" elements, i.e., the modernization/development link to Islamic activism discussed in the literature review (Chapter 1). The structural explanation maintains that the Turkish people's attachment to religion is a consequence of industrialization and development (Geyikdagi 1984, p. 12):

> When Turkey becomes an industrialized state that can provide a decent job and future to all its citizens, religion is likely to become a private matter between man and God and to lose much of its political importance. Turkey is now in the midst of this painful process which is a necessary phase of modernization.

98. Erbakan was the President of the NP in 1971 when it was disbanded, only to reappear as the NSP in 1973 and dissolve in the 1980 coup. Erbakan emerged again as the President of the Welfare Party in 1983, when the restrictions on political parties were lifted (Ahmad 1988, pp. 759–760). The Welfare Party won the mayoral elections in some of the largest Turkish cities, like Ankara and Istanbul on March 29, 1994 (*The Boston Globe*, March 30, 1994: p. 84).

Geyikdagi believes that religion will carry less importance in the public realm once Turkey passes through the bottleneck of development. Like other analysts of Turkish modern history, he relates Islamic activism to structural issues.

Tapper (1991, p. 21) writes of the "new adherence to Islamic values" as "evidence of a renewed ability of Islamic discourses to articulate structural conflicts, attitudes to the state and the process of change." Tapper offers a unilateral explanation of Islamic activism by relating it to "structural conflicts."

In agreement with Heper, Toprak and Mehmet, this research assumes the existence of a link between cultural and structural issues, which supports my argument that mass mobilization offers a valid general explanation of Islamic activism. Heper (1980, pp. 373–374), writes:

> The cultural cleavage of Westernization versus Islamism and/or "Turkish" has persistently been the major cleavage in the Turkish polity. The recent rise to significance of socioeconomic problems in Turkey led to the superimposing of functional cleavages upon the persisting cultural cleavages.

In agreement with Heper, Toprak (1984, p. 10) stresses that

> There are, of course, both structural and cultural reasons behind Islam's increasing role in Turkish society. However, given the general process of depoliticization by the military and the reorganization of political life along non-participatory precepts after 1980, it seems paradoxical that the Islamic movement managed to become more politicized.

Mehmet's argument is necessary to note because not only does he agree with Toprak and Heper, he also recognizes a theoretical cornerstone of the hypothesis under study. After comparing Malaysian and Turkish polities, he writes (Mehmet 1990, p. 52):

> The growth process pursued in a top-down manner, with little accountability of the leaders to the masses, violated the Islamic ideal of social justice. The secularist leaders in charge of post-war modernization promised the followers tangible benefits. When, after several decades of patience and sacrifice, the mass of followers only saw poverty and injustice, they joined the Islamic resurgence.

Mehmet (1990, p. 73) defines his line of argument as follows:

> [T]he Muslim dilemma today is a question of accountability of the rulers to the ruled in social, political and economic terms. Spiritual needs, as matters of conscience, deserve to be respected as fundamental human rights. The proper domain of people and the major criterion of good government must be the degree to which these needs are satisfied. When the policies and performance of rulers satisfy the needs of the ruled, and such satisfaction is popularly and freely confirmed, then the accountability test is duly met.

Mehmet concludes his research by stressing the differences between *'ibādah* (worship) and *mu'āmalāt* (social relations). He indicates that practicing *'ibādah* individually is a human right related to freedom of belief. If one desires to join a congregation to practice *'ibādah*, one is then concerned with the human right of freedom of association. Mehmet (1990, p. 227) ends his paragraph:

> Inevitably, there will be cases of abuses of these religious freedoms, but it would be unreasonable to equate every case of fanaticism and extremism as a political conspiracy justifying total suppression of religious freedoms.

The rights Mehmet mentions lead to an analysis of the rights hypothesized to cause an increase in Islamic activism. In agreement with Mehmet, we examine the protection and violation of a few of those rights to assess the accountability of each government to its people and their resulting socio-political reactions as manifested in Islamic activism.

Analysis of the Data on Islamic Activism in Turkey for November 1988 to 1993[99]

Preserving Religion and the Mind

November 1988–October 1989

The violation of preserving the mind and religion is measured by the analysis of government actions toward general Islamic issues, including issues raised by Islamic activists. In the first year of analysis the government rejected nine Islamic issues, referred one issue to a third party (in this case the Religious Affairs Department), and supported the Islamic stance on three issues. The main issues that were raised revolved around government opposition to the proposed "turban" bill, which would have allowed female students to wear a veil on college campuses. Other issues pertained to the laws restricting religious freedom of expression (Law 163). The government imprisoned an imam for speaking against the state in his sermon and put an Islamic activist mayor under arrest and seized 287 of his books because he stated his allegiance to Islam. Thus the preservation of religion and the mind was substantially restricted by the Turkish government.

Islamic activism[100] reflected the following patterns: There were approximately eighty Islamic activists arrested, and four attempted activist attacks. The approximate number of Islamic activist demonstrators was 790, and all four demonstrations were peaceful. The election patterns for this year suggest that Islamic activists were gaining ground in provincial as well as professional elections. Although Law 163 restricts the freedom of Muslims to express their religion and also restricts the formation of any political party based on religion, Islamic activists in Turkey were given a limited amount of political space with respect to elections.

November 1989–October 1990

In the second year of analysis, there were only three rejections of Islamic issues and three issues that the government encouraged. Among the issues that reflected the government's opposition to Islamic issues was suspension of a pro-Islamic magazine and the investigation of 15,000 Muslims who gathered for burial prayers for an Islamic activist in Anatolia. The main Islamic issue that the government acted on during the second year of

99. The data on preserving religion, the mind, the self, posterity, property, and Islamic activism are all listed in Appendix 3.

100. Islamic activism data is summarized in Table 3 on page 142.

analysis was the annulment of the turban bill, an issue that had created a controversial religio-political climate in Turkey the preceding year of analysis.

Islamic activism reflected the following patterns for the second year of analysis: approximately eighty activists were arrested, and activists made an estimated fifty attempted attacks. The approximate number of Islamic activists who joined demonstrations rose to 2,310 demonstrators; all seven demonstrations were peaceful. The elections for 1989–1990 showed that Islamic activists continued to gain, especially in professional organizations/syndicates.

The violence reflected in the number of attempted attacks is due largely to attacks on secular lawyers, professors, and journalists who were opposed to the turban bill during the first year of analysis. The violence was a delayed reaction to government policy during the preceding year.

November 1990–October 1991

The third year of data on Turkey shows that the government rejected five Islamic issues, referred one issue to a third party, and supported one Islamic issue. The main controversial issues raised during this year were related to demonstrations against the Gulf War. Also equally important was the dismissal of a large number of bureaucrats for praying, keeping copies of the Qur'an in their desks, and carrying prayer beads. The Grand National Assembly passed a bill that abolished Article 163, which restricted religious freedom. Thus the government simultaneously sought to accommodate an Islamic issue while in practice it discouraged the observance of religious customs.

The pattern of Islamic activism was as follows: 100 Islamic activists were arrested, and the approximate number of attempted activist attacks decreased dramatically to twelve. Most attacks targeted foreign embassy officials and foreign businessmen. The approximate number of Islamic activists who joined in demonstrations decreased dramatically, in comparison with the last year of analysis, to 420 demonstrators. Most of those demonstrations were peaceful, with the exception of one demonstration against the Gulf War, where police dispersed a crowd and wounded thirty people in the process. The Islamic activists remained active in provincial elections and political influence.

The low number of violations against the preservation of religion and the mind explains the fact that Islamic activists were less active in Turkey than in the preceding year of analysis.

November 1991–October 1992

The pattern of preserving religion and the mind for the fourth year of analysis was as follows: The government opposed three Islamic issues that were raised and supported two issues. The government's support was mostly for spreading Islam in the new Turkish republics after the dismantling of the USSR. The government cracked down on Islamic activists domestically: For example, 1,000 officers and cadets were discharged for having Islamic views, and a pro-Islamic magazine's coordinator was attacked by police forces in his office. The Turkish government was simultaneously restricting religious freedom domestically and encouraging the rise of Islam in the new republics.

Islamic activism from November 1991 to October 1992 reflected the following patterns: approximately twenty Islamic activists were arrested, and the activists made approximately twelve attempted attacks, which included an attack on a synagogue and the killing of the security chief of the Israeli embassy. The approximate number of Islamic activists who joined demonstrations increased to 2,570 people, and all demonstrations were peaceful. Even though Islamic activists continued participating in the electoral process, their participation decreased in comparison with the four preceding years.

Although the Turkish government suppressed religious freedom domestically, the issues that were raised from November 1991 to October 1992 were not controversial enough to arouse public interest. The demonstrations mentioned focused on international issues rather than domestic ones. There were demonstrations to protest against the killing of a Shi'ite leader in Lebanon, an attack on the Yugoslav embassy, an anti-Israel demonstration during the visit of the Israeli president, and another anti-Serbian demonstration.

Thus the violent aspects of Islamic activism were low and stable, while nonviolent activism focused on international issues. The Islamic activists did not seem to hold the Turkish government accountable for their grievances. The decrease in violations of the preservation of religion and the mind was accompanied by a decrease in both violent and nonviolent Islamic activism.

November 1992–October 1993

The last year of analysis reflected the following patterns concerning the preservation of religion and the mind: the government rejected Islamic issues in four instances, supported an Islamic issue once, and referred an issue to a third party once. The government extradited a religious leader residing in Germany, an Islamic group was crushed by the police in Ankara, the prime minister warned muftis (religious scholars) against political involvement, and the education ministry sent investigative teams to inspect schools allegedly linked to the Hezbollah Party. A criminal court prohibited the circulation of excerpts from Salman Rushdie's *The Satanic Verses*, a book that was considered blasphemous and inflammatory by many Muslims.

The effect of those restrictions on the preservation of religion and the mind on Islamic activism was as follows: approximately 140 Islamic activists were arrested, and the approximate number of activist attacks increased to forty-six in all. The main attacks for November 1992 through October 1993 included student clashes between Islamists and secularists, the killing of a secular writer, and an attack on a hotel where a secular writer was holding a seminar on Salman Rushdie's work. The latter attack took place in Sivas and resulted in the death of thirty-six people. It accounts for most of the attacks for the year.

The approximate number of Islamic activists who demonstrated decreased to 770, about one-third of the demonstrators for the preceding year. All demonstrations were peaceful. Electoral activities continued but were limited, in comparison with the first and second years of analysis.

With the decrease in violations of the preservation of religion and the mind (reflected in the smaller number of Islamic issues rejected by the government), there was a corresponding decrease in violent and nonviolent Islamic activism—with the exception of the attack on the hotel in Sivas.

The patterns reflected in the five years indicate that Islamic activism in Turkey is responsive to the preservation of religion and the mind. The only exception to direct interaction between the preservation of religion and the mind and Islamic activism occurred during the second year but, as indicated above, violent actions of Islamic activism during the second year represent a delayed reaction to the turban bill, an issue that was highly controversial during the first year of analysis.

Preserving the Self

November 1988–October 1989

Data for the first year of analysis show that there were ten cases of *habeas corpus* violations and about forty people tortured/killed during imprisonment. There were no reported confrontations between the police and the demonstrating crowds.

Islamic activism reflected the following patterns: eighty Islamic activists were arrested, and activists made four attempted attacks on public officials, tourists, and secularists. Approximately 790 Islamic activists rallied; all demonstrations were peaceful. The election patterns reflect active involvement of Islamicists in the provincial and professional political process.

November 1989–October 1990

The second year of the analysis shows that *habeas corpus* violations remained constant in ten cases, while the approximate number of people tortured/killed during imprisonment decreased to thirty cases; there were no reported police clashes with demonstrators.

Islamic activism reflected the following patterns for the second year of analysis: The approximate number of Islamic activists arrested increased to 100 people, and the estimated number of attempted activist attacks jumped to the highest figure of the five years: fifty attacks. As noted above, most of those attacks targeted secular professionals who opposed the turban bill in the first year of analysis. Approximately 2,310 Islamic activists joined demonstrations, and all the demonstrations were peaceful. This year also reflects an increased involvement of Islamic activists in professional elections.

With the stability in the number of *habeas corpus* violations and the decrease in the number of people killed/tortured during imprisonment, there was an increase in nonviolent Islamic activism as reflected in the number of demonstrators, the kinds of demonstrations, and the election patterns.

November 1990–October 1991

The preservation of the self reflected the following patterns for the third year of analysis: *habeas corpus* violations increased to an estimated thirty cases, there were no reports of people tortured/killed, and there was a single skirmish with the police during a demonstration that resulted in wounding thirty people. With regard to the preservation of the self, the third year shows relatively few violent government actions than the first two years. The patterns of Islamic activism showed a slight increase in estimated arrests to 100 people, and a decrease in attempted attacks to twelve (less than half of the number of attacks in the preceding year). The latter attacks targeted foreign interests rather than public officials or secularists. The approximate number of Islamic activists who demonstrated decreased sharply to 420, and five out of six demonstrations were peaceful, with the exception of one clash with the police. The election patterns reflected a decrease in the Islamic activists' involvement in professional elections, though they were still active in provincial elections during this year. With the decrease in violations of the preservation of the self, there is a notable decrease in violent and nonviolent Islamic activism.

November 1991–October 1992

The fourth year of analysis reflected the following patterns for the preservation of the self: The approximate number of *habeas corpus* violations remained constant at thirty, and there were no reports of people killed/tortured during imprisonment. There were also no reports of clashes between the police and the demonstrators this year.

Islamic activism patterns from November 1991 to October 1992 reflected the following: The approximate number of Islamic activists arrested decreased to twenty people, and the estimated number of attempted activist attacks remained constant at twelve. The number of Islamic activists who joined demonstrations increased dramatically, to an estimated 2,570; all reported demonstrations were peaceful. The election patterns reflect a decrease in the involvement of Islamic activists in the election process.

There is a decrease in both the violation of preserving self and in Islamic activism. Moreover, as observed in the preceding section, the increase in the number of demonstrators relates to international issues, not domestic ones.

November 1992–October 1993

The last year of analysis had no reports of violating the preservation of the self. Islamic activism reflected the following patterns: There were approximately 140 Islamic activists arrested, and attempted attacks targeted forty-six people (thirty-six out of the forty-six people were killed in an attack on a secular writer who was lecturing in Sivas). The approximate number of Islamic activists who joined demonstrations decreased dramatically to 770; all the demonstrations were peaceful. The election patterns reflected a limited amount of interaction, especially in provincial elections.

The upsurge in violent Islamic activism was due entirely to the incident in Sivas. Otherwise nonviolent Islamic activism decreased in concurrence with the increase in the preservation of the self for November 1992–October 1993.

The patterns reflected in the five years of analysis indicate that there is an inverse relation between the preservation of the self and Islamic activism, as proposed in the hypothesis of this study. There are only two incidents for which the Islamic activism data do not follow this pattern. The first incident happened during the fourth year of analysis, when government violations of the self decreased but there was a large increase in the number of demonstrators. The demonstrations focused on international issues (the Gulf War and the Bosnian dilemma) rather than on domestic ones. The demonstrators were not reacting to the Turkish government's domestic policies.

The second exception happened during the fifth year of analysis, when the government was acting in favor of preservation of the self, yet the violent aspect of Islamic activism increased sharply. This rise was due to one specific incident where the people of Sivas attacked a secular writer in a hotel, killing thirty-six people. This incident was not directly linked to the government actions or to the expression of a long-standing grievance. Rather, it was a spontaneous act by the people of Sivas.

The increase in preservation-of-self violations in the data on Turkey is low in comparison with Egypt and Algeria. Therefore the escalation of violent confrontations between government and Islamic activists is limited in Turkey. Owing to the low levels of violating preservation of the self in Turkey, the conflict between Islamic activists and the government did not lead to violence and therefore did not create a conflict spiral of the sort observed in both Egypt and Algeria.

Preserving Posterity/Youth

November 1988–October 1989

In the first year of analysis, the patterns for the preservation of posterity reflected the following: The government rejected issues pertaining to Islamic education and practice on five of six occasions. Four of the five incidents of rejection related to the proposed turban bill that would have allowed female students to wear Islamic garb on campus. The government chose to oppose the bill and retaliate against its proponents. During this year, the government also expelled ninety-five military students from their schools for engagement in "fundamentalist" activity.

The patterns of Islamic activism showed about eighty Islamic activists arrested and four attempted attacks by activists. An estimated 790 Islamic activists demonstrated; all demonstrations were peaceful. Election patterns show that Islamic activists were active in both provincial and professional elections.

Even though the government was restricting Islamic education and practice, Islamic activism was relatively low during the first year of analysis. However, it is important to take the second year into account, since there was a lag in the Islamic activist reaction to the restrictions pertaining to the turban bill.

November 1989–October 1990

During the second year of analysis, only one issue pertaining to Islamic practice was raised: lifting the ban on Islamic dress worn by women students. Islamic activism reflected the following patterns: The approximate number of Islamic activists arrested remained constant, whereas the approximate number of attempted attacks increased dramatically. Demonstrators also increased to an estimated 2,310; all demonstrations were peaceful. The election patterns reflected consistent participation by Islamic activists, with more activity reflected in professional elections than in provincial elections. As noted above, the increase in Islamic activism was a response to government rejection of the turban bill in the previous year.

November 1990–October 1991

The third year of analysis reflects a positive response from the government to issues of Islamic education and practice. The council of ministers agreed to include three years of Qur'an courses as a compulsory requirement for primary education.

Islamic activism reflected the following patterns: The number of Islamic activists arrested increased slightly to an estimated 100 people, and the number of attempted attacks decreased dramatically to about twelve. There was also a sharp drop in Islamic activist demonstrators, to an estimated 420 individuals. The demonstrations were peaceful, with the exception of one incident in which police fired to disperse the crowds, wounding approximately thirty people. The election patterns for Islamic activism showed less activity during this year of analysis in comparison with the first two years.

Along with the government's positive response toward Islamic education, there was a drop in both violent and nonviolent Islamic activism. The January 1991 clash with the police was an aberration that needs to be clarified. It was one of a series of anti-Gulf War demonstrations in which the police fired shots to disperse the crowds, leading to confrontations; that is, the demonstration was at first peaceful and became violent in response to police action.

November 1991–October 1992

In the fourth year of analysis, there was only one reported incident of violating the preservation of posterity. This incident involved the arrest of Islamic activists in Istanbul for holding meetings and organizing seminars at a bookstore.

Islamic activism reflected the following patterns: Approximately twenty Islamic activists were arrested, and about twelve attempted activist attacks were reported. The number of Islamic activists who demonstrated increased dramatically to about 2,570 demonstrators; all demonstrations were peaceful. The Islamic activists' involvement in elections decreased in comparison with the other four years of analysis.

The rise in the number of demonstrators reflected an increased interest in international issues, mainly the Gulf War and the violence in Bosnia. Also, most attacks were aimed at foreigners rather than public officials. Therefore, patterns are consistent with my proposed hypothesis. The data indicate that the decline in violations of preserving posterity is accompanied by decreases in both violent and nonviolent Islamic activism.

November 1992–October 1993

The last year of analysis reflects a similar pattern to the previous year; the government opposed Islamic education in one episode: its concern about Hezbollah's alleged activity in schools in the southeast region of Anatolia.

Islamic activism shared an increase in numbers of activists arrested to about 140 people, and in attacks to forty-six incidents (mainly the Sivas incident). The number of Islamic demonstrators decreased dramatically to 770; all reported demonstrations were peaceful. The election patterns reflected a slight increase in Islamic activist involvement in provincial elections.

The patterns reflected over the five years of analysis support the proposed hypotheses: in years with few or no government actions adversely affecting the preservation of posterity there was a collateral decrease in Islamic activism, both violent and nonviolent.

Preserving Property/Wealth

The preservation of property is indexed by the stability in inflation rates, as given in the FBIS reports, for every year under study. Inflation remained constant during the five years, with the exception of the third and fourth years of analysis. In the third year inflation was reported to be stable; in the fourth year there were no reports of either stability or increase in inflation rates.

Whether one considers the number of attempted attacks, the number of demonstrators, or election patterns, it is clear that there was a marked decrease in Islamic activism during the third year of analysis. The implication is that, owing to the break in the upward trend of inflation, the Islamic activists' sense of a cumulative economic grievance lessened, along with their activity, during the last three years of analysis. This interpretation is reinforced when one compares the preservation of property variable across the three countries studied: in Egypt and Algeria, inflation rose almost continually—and so did Islamic activism.

Conclusion

A number of observations can be derived from analyzing the five years of data on Turkey (see Table 3 below). First, preserving religion, the mind, and posterity has a large impact on Islamic activism, as noted in the first two years of analysis. For example, as a result of increased government violation of religion, the mind, and posterity during the first year of analysis, there was a sharp increase in the number of attacks and number of Islamic activist demonstrators in the second year of analysis. Although the Islamic activist response seems delayed, the link between the first and second years of analysis becomes clear when one realizes that the turban bill issue was the cause of increase in Islamic activist demonstrators and the increase in attacks on secularists who opposed allowing female students to wear Islamic-style dress on college campuses.

The second and fourth independent variables, the preservation of the self and the preservation of property, seem to have a lesser impact on Islamic activism in comparison with preserving religion, the mind, and posterity/youth. The preservation of the self is slightly more consequential in its effect on Islamic activism. The evidence shows that with decreases in actions that violated the self, there was an accompanying decrease in violent and nonviolent Islamic activism. In Turkey's case, the decrease in government actions that violated the self led to the reduction of violence, unlike in Egypt and Algeria. The conflict spiral (exemplified in the increase in government violations of the self and Islamic activists' violence) did not develop in Turkey, as discussed in the conclusion of this study.

The last observation is general in nature but pertinent to Turkey's place in the Islamic world: the number of Islamic issues raised in Turkey are, generally, minimal in comparison with Egypt and Algeria, where the relationship between the four independent variables and Islamic activism is more pronounced. My results suggest that the Turkish government does not often interfere with the preservation of religion, the mind, the self, posterity, and property; moreover, the effects of interference when it does occur may be more muted because the Turkish people are less sensitive to Islamic activist grievances owing to their prolonged socialization to the separation of religion from public life and their political and economic affinity with Western Europe and the United States.

Even though the number of issues raised in Turkey were few, there were parallel changes in the independent and the dependent variables that indicated a link between the preservation of religion, the mind, the self, posterity, and property and the violent and nonviolent aspects of Islamic activism.

Table 3
Summary of Data on Islamic Activism in Turkey*

Year	Nov. 1988 - Oct. 1989				Nov. 1989 - Oct. 1990				Nov. 1990 - Oct. 1991				Nov. 1991 - Oct. 1992				Nov. 1992 - Oct. 1993			
Approximate number of Islamic activists arrested	80				80				100				20				140			
Approximate number of attempted attacks	4				50				12				12				46			
Approximate number of Islamic activists who rallied/ demonstrated	790				2,310				420				2,570				770			
Categories of kinds of demonstration	1	2	3	4	1	2	3	4	1	2	3	4	1	2	3	4	1	2	3	4
Frequency of kinds of demonstration	4	0	0	0	7	0	0	0	5	0	1	0	4	0	0	0	2	0	0	0
Categories of election patterns	1	2	3	00	1	2	3	00	1	2	3	00	1	2	3	00	1	2	3	00
Frequency reflecting election patterns	2	1	0	0	1	3	0	0	2	0	0	0	1	0	0	0	2	0	0	0

* See Appendix 3 for information on the categories and scales used to code the data.

CHAPTER 7

The Imperatives and Implications of a Cultural Revolution: A Conclusion

Observations on the Data

In drawing a conclusion to this research, a summary of the findings in the country studies is in order. The general hypothesis is that Islamic activism is a function of the extent to which the state in an Islamic society falls short of the principles of Islamic social justice as embodied in the end goals of the Shari'ah (*al maqāṣid*).

The following observations were consistent across the board: first, changes in the indicators measuring the preservation of religion and the mind, together with the indicator measuring the preservation of posterity, affect nonviolent Islamic activism. That is, violations of preserving religion, the mind, and posterity tended to increase nonviolent activism more than nonviolent activism.

It is important to note that the violation-of-self indicators in Egypt and Algeria, especially, exemplified endless spirals of conflict. In Algeria, after the cancellation of elections and the imprisonment of many FIS members, the Islamic movement went underground and changed its political tactics in its struggle against the regime. The movement became more violent, and the government also increasingly cracked down on the movement and its sympathizers. The escalation of violence on both sides needs to be recognized when interpreting the data in Algeria. In Egypt, the escalation of conflict in the last three years of the study is reflected in both the Islamic activists' and the government's actions.

The examination and interpretation of the data should not overlook the effect of conflict escalation on Islamic activism. The escalation is portrayed in the violation-of-self indicators, because they measure the government's violence against Islamic movements and the activists' violent demonstrations and assassination attempts.

The fact that the escalation of conflict affects Islamic activism needs to be reexamined at length, because the duration and the intensity of the conflict between Islamic activists and different regimes might help to explain Islamic activism (especially the violent aspects of Islamic activism). Egypt affords a good case study of the link between the duration of the conflict and Islamic activism, while Algeria provides a good case study of the link between the intensity of the conflict and Islamic activism.

A third observation is that Islamic activism increased in both violent and nonviolent aspects in Egypt (especially in the last three years, November 1990 to October 1993). In Algeria, nonviolent Islamic activism increased (especially in the two years preceding the December 1991 elections). Violent Islamic activism emerged in Algeria only after the cancellation of the elections and the dissolution of the FIS. Islamic activists in Turkey were only moderately active throughout the five years of analysis, with the exception of their activity in the first two years regarding the turban bill.

A fourth observation is that the data in the last year of analysis in Egypt and the fourth year of analysis in Algeria show dramatic increases in both violent and nonviolent Islamic activism in comparison with other years of analysis. The latter observation seems to suggest that there is a cumulative effect when the *maqāsid* are violated;[101] that is, the longer grievances are felt as a result of violations of the preservation of religion, the mind, the self, posterity, and property, the more vigorous Islamic activism becomes in expressing itself politically, through both violent and nonviolent means.

The general hypothesis of this study therefore, agrees with the observations based on the data collected for each country.

There are some differences in the degree of Islamic activism in each country examined. The tension between Islamic activists and the Turkish government, for example, is less obvious in comparison with Egypt and Algeria. One of the most important reasons for this is the Turkish people's

101. There is also a lag in the Islamic activist reaction to regime policies that was especially clear in Turkey in the first and second years of analysis.

perception of the role of religion in the public sphere. In Egypt and Algeria, the nationalist movements led by Nasser and Ben Bella were entwined with Islamic themes. That is, in those countries both nationalism and religion were used to engage the masses in fighting colonialism.

In Turkey, however, as the Ottoman Empire fell apart, its political and religious symbols became distinct from each other. The Turkish leader, Atatürk, preferred to detach Turkey and its people from their religious past in order to involve them in his movement. Thus in the Turkish political ethos, nationalism became the antithesis of the religious.

Although the data on Turkey reflect that Islamic activists responded to the violation of the *maqāṣid*, most people confined religion to its private sphere. It is not expected to play an active role in public, political life. Thus the difference between Turkey, Egypt, and Algeria stems not only from the extent of government violation of the *maqāṣid* but also from the people's perception.

Another factor affecting the degree of Islamic activism in Turkey is that Islamic themes have recently attracted a few anti-Kemalist elites. Along with the struggle against Kurdish separatists in the southeast, Turkey is also facing new international challenges. First, in its struggle to join the European Union (EU), Turkey has used its Islamic heritage to coerce the EC into accepting it as a member. That is, Turkey alleges that the EU is discriminating against it because of its ethno-religious background. Second, Turkey is also engaged in a race with Iran to establish close ties with the new, mostly Muslim, Central Asian republics. Therefore, some elites are interested in reviving Islam in the public arena, as indicated in Chapter 6.

Current Thought on Islamic Activism

In recounting the basic ideas presented in my research, I would like to relate the hypothesis and the results of this study to current writings on Islamic activism. The approaches offered in the literature to explain Islamic activism, as presented in Chapter 1, are the modernization/economic development approach, the cultural approach, and the popular discontent/mass mobilization approach. I have argued that the popular discontent/mass mobilization approach better explains Islamic activism because it is more comprehensive. The study also adapts the popular discontent approach to the particulars of Islamic movements and their grievances.

There is an increasing interest in Islamic activism in both academic and media circles. Baker (1991, p. 45), the author of *Sadat and After: Struggles for Egypt's Political Soul,* notes that "causal studies, despite their veils of distance and objectivity, carry indirect but potent political messages. Their claims to objectivity are always suspect." The basic theme that Baker (1991, p. 47) invokes in his article is best captured in this statement:

> We chose to avoid the complications of being drawn into different human political worlds. In the quest for causes, we avoided encounters and dialogues—with the radicals, and perhaps of more importance, even with the moderate mainstream of the Muslim current.

The ideas propounded by Baker are evident in Lewis's and Huntington's arguments. For example, Lewis (1990, p. 60) writes:

> We are facing a mood and a movement far transcending the level of issues and politics and the governments that pursue them. This is no less than a clash of civilizations—the perhaps irrational but surely historic reaction of an ancient rival against our Judeo-Christian heritage, our secular present, and the world-wide expansion of both.

A similar argument is also made by Huntington (1993, pp. 34–35):

> In Eurasia the great historic fault lines between civilizations are once more aflame. This is particularly true along the boundaries of the crescent-shaped Islamic bloc of nations from the bulge of Africa to central Asia. Violence also occurs between Muslims, on the one hand, and Orthodox Serbs in the Balkans, Jews in Israel, Hindus in India, Buddhists in Burma and Catholics in the Philippines. Islam has bloody borders.

As Baker states, a convergence of opinions on the "green menace" (green being a traditionally favored color in Islam) exists in both academic and media circles. A journalist's perception of Islamic activism, and by association Islam, is reported in a *Foreign Affairs* article (Miller 1993, p. 46): "Why should one suspect the sincerity of the Islamists' commitment to truth, justice and the democratic way? In short, because of Arab and Islamic history and the nature and evolution of these groups."

Among those to whom the "green menace" is a threat, distinctions among separate Islamic activist movements are not considered. Instead, Islamic movements are lumped together, along with the Islamic civilization as a whole. The authors quoted above do not differentiate between the domestic and the international levels of analysis. An approach that assumes all Islamic activism to be a security threat obscures the analysis and understanding of specific movements.

My research emphasizes the need to listen to the Islamic activists' discourse in order to understand the predicament of current Middle Eastern societies. Given the underlying assumptions of Lewis, Huntington, and others, the task of understanding the Islamic activist movements is handicapped by political and cultural baggage. I have examined prevailing explanations of Islamic activism and distinguished the popular discontent approach as the most comprehensive. By choosing popular discontent as an approach, we focus our attention on the cultural and political nuances of different Islamic movements.

The need to develop the popular discontent approach is stated clearly in a very recent book on Islamic activism by Fuller (1995, p. 110):

> Domestic discontent in the Muslim world is the single most important prerequisite for the international growth of radical Islamist forces. When popular discontent with local conditions is at manageable levels, then international issues in and of themselves are not likely to rally major radical Islamist movements across international borders. Unfortunately, domestic discontent is prevalent in numerous Muslim countries: Deepening economic problems, unemployment and lack of opportunity, high population growth rates with which governments cannot keep pace in providing social services and infrastructure, poorly administered and inefficient state sectors, corruption, poor government, absence of representative government, all feature among the key grievances. Most regimes in the region suffer from a crisis of legitimacy because they are not elected and often have little basis for genuine legitimacy in time of crisis.

The popular discontent approach led me to focus on two issues. First is the search in Islamic discourse for the basic principles of a just society. Second is the correlation of Islamic activists' grievances with their theoretical arguments to isolate the reasons for violent and nonviolent Islamic activism. The study is grounded in religious themes (*uṣūl al fiqh*) that theoretically represent Islamic activists' grievances, in order to explain the rationale behind Islamic movements.

The concern for reforms that underlies this study is paralleled in Fuller's analysis. He states (Fuller 1995, p. 99):

> Two devices within Islam are available for this process of further reform: reinterpretation or extension of earlier legal precedents (*ijtihād*) and revision by consensus of Islamic scholars or even the sense of the community (*ijmā'*).

My study relies on a subcomponent of ijtihād in its analysis of the current Islamic movements: the end goals of Islamic law (*al maqāṣid*).

Fuller (1995, p. 104) stresses another main concern of my research, the Algerian and Egyptian regimes' failure to distinguish the variations in Islamic movements:

> Lumping all Islamic groups together in a wave of condemnation regardless of their views or means of operation risks placing established regimes in the unenviable position of seeming to war against Islam itself—a potentially fatal perception.

The latter point is strongly reinforced by the data analysis of this research. In governments' indiscriminate attempts to control Islamic activist movements, they give mixed messages to moderate Muslims who are not politically involved. For example, in Egypt there are usually two trucks of security forces parked at each major mosque, forces which are perceived as the guardians of the regime in power. The overbearing appearance of the police at mosques signals to ordinary Muslims that they are perceived as a threat to the regime just by the performance of their prayers.

Islamic Law and Politics

By taking into account the nuances of Islamic culture, popular discontent, and Islamic activists' grievances, I have couched my theoretical argument in Islamic legal concepts and tested the effects of violations of them on Islamic activist movements. The data analysis indicates that the number and extent of violations of the end goals of the Shari'ah (*al maqāṣid*) are closely linked to the extent and form of Islamic activism, as hypothesized.

The relation between the *maqāṣid* and Islamic activism has varied and useful implications. Separating the domestic and international elements of Islamic activism, for purposes of analysis, shows that domestic issues directly affect Islamic activist movements. Contrary to the perception of

Huntington and Lewis, the Islamic movements are more focused on domestic than international issues. One of the main pitfalls in current literature on Islamic activism is the failure to distinguish between the different levels of analysis. Writing about Islamic activist movements as threats to the West is flawed by the failure to distinguish Islam as the faith of an individual and Islamic activism as a movement that relates to the peoples of each individual country.

Current literature also dismisses the differences between Islamic activism as a domestic movement and Islamic activism as an international phenomenon. It is important to understand Islamic activism as a cultural expression of grievances and of Muslim peoples' understanding of rulership and justice. Although there is a link between the domestic issue of Islamic activism and its international aspects, one has to distinguish analytically the domestic from the international aspects of the movements.

There are many instances where differentiating the domestic and the international levels proves difficult. For example, during the Gulf War many Islamic movements demonstrated against their government's participation in the war against Iraq (data on Egypt and Turkey especially indicate numerous demonstrations against the Gulf War). The genocide of Muslims in Bosnia also mustered the support of many Islamic movements in Turkey, Algeria, Egypt, Pakistan, and elsewhere. Sheikh 'Umar 'Abd al Raḥmān's alleged involvement in the World Trade Center bombing also draws attention to the transnational implications of the Islamic movements. Thus, the transnational effect of Islamic movements affects local conditions; however, the weight of everyday problems in many cases supersedes the movements' reactions to transnational conditions.

The bond between Islamic activism as a domestic and transnational movement is conspicuous in Algeria's case. The French government is becoming increasingly conservative in its policies toward its Algerian immigrant population. The December 1991 elections in Algeria heightened French fears of more Algerian immigration. Thus the French government, as well as other Western countries, expressed relief upon the cancellation of these elections. In response, the FIS and other Islamic movements view the United States and other European countries as allies to local elites. Thus the fear of Islamic movements in the West becomes a self-fulfilling prophecy.

Even though Islamic movements are affected by and affect the international scene, it is important to address the causes rather than the manifestations of Islamic activism. Though I have hypothesized in this study that domestic conditions are causal to Islamic activism, one cannot deny the link between the international and domestic levels of analysis. The violent and nonviolent aspects of Islamic activism examined in this research nevertheless proved more responsive to domestic pressures than international ones.

Reliance on the dynamics of domestic politics to explain Islamic activism has three general implications. First, that we should consider Islamic movements as popular vehicles of change. Throughout the post-colonial era in Egypt and Algeria, Islamic movements seem to have had a wide base of mass support. Even though it is difficult to anticipate whether Islamic activist movements will work for or against reform, should they come to power, it is equally difficult to infer that the movements are doomed to fail.

Because Islamic movements have a wide base of support in a number of Muslim countries, it is more likely that free political expression will allow them to participate through legitimate political channels. Two obvious examples are events prior to the elections in December 1991 in Algeria and in the last parliamentary elections in Jordan. My research has highlighted the fact that Muslim people expect their leaders to be accountable, and above all to rule by the legal precepts advocated in Islamic law (the Shari'ah). The pertinence of accountability to Islamic activism is stressed in Haddad's writing (Haddad 1991) and by Anderson, who states (1991, p. 104), "By and large, the movements reflected the local circumstances in which they had developed. The increasing remoteness of the governments elicited demands for greater accountability."

Therefore, the peoples of each country are the sole definers of their ruler's accountability. The issue of accountability leads us to the commonplace question: Is democracy compatible with Islam? This in turn brings us to the second general implication of this study, namely that Western-style democracy might be different from the Muslim "just society." The concern about the compatibility of Islam and democracy was heightened after the Algerian elections of December 1991. The perception that Islam is incompatible with democracy is best captured by Huntington (1991, pp. 72–73):

> A strong correlation exists between Western Christianity and democracy. Modern democracy developed first and most vigorously in Christian countries . . . . Democracy was especially scarce among countries that were predominantly Muslim, Buddhist, or Confucian. This correlation does not prove causation. Western Christianity emphasizes, however, the dignity of the individual and the separate spheres of church and state. In many countries, Protestant and Catholic church leaders have been central in the struggles against repressive countries. It seems plausible to hypoth-

esize that the expansion of Christianity encourages democratic development.

In concluding his book, Huntington (1991, p. 307) also emphasizes that "to the extent that governmental legitimacy and policy flow from religious doctrine and religious expertise, Islamic concepts of politics differ from and contradict the premises of democratic politics."

The certainty with which Huntington states his opinion runs contradictory to the findings of my research. However, Huntington defines democracy in terms of its institutional and electoral processes. If democracy is defined in terms of the systematic satisfaction of peoples' needs and wants, one might begin to see the common ground that Western-style democracy has with Islam. For example, the current political debate presented by the Republican Party about a "contract with America" is an appeal made to United States citizens who have been estranged from the process of governing. The "contract" is a political tool used as an expression of the party's accountability to its voters. Likewise, the Islamic activists' grievances, together with their attempts to reinstate the Shari'ah as the law of the land, are their interpretation of how rulers have failed to be accountable, and/or how they (Islamic activists) would be accountable should they come to power.

The issues of self-rule and accountability become dependent on the respective peoples' perceptions of a good and just society. This argument implies that there are alternative paths to democratization and that the politico-cultural background of a mass movement reveals different interpretations of the idea of self-rule and democratization.

The third general implication of this research relates to the analysis of Islamic activism as an international religio-political movement. Islam's role in the international arena captured much attention, especially after the dismantling of the Union of Soviet Socialist Republics and the Gulf War crisis. From Fukuyama's "end of history" (Fukuyama 1992) and Gellner's "enlightenment-rational fundamentalism," the debate extended to the international relations arena. Huntington's article in *Foreign Affairs* titled "A Clash of Civilizations?" was one among many similar arguments. Huntington's hypothesis in the article (Huntington 1993, p. 22) is that: "The great divisions among humankind and the dominating source of conflict will be cultural . . . . The clash of civilizations will dominate global politics." One of the main threats to Western civilization, according to Huntington, is the Islamic civilization. He emphatically states (Huntington 1993, p. 35) that "Islam has bloody borders." Thus, Islamic movements are seen as a growing menace that will not only overcome the current regimes but will also affect "Western civilization."

The perception that there will be a clash of civilizations or an "end of the dialogue" is a self-fulfilling prophecy. As Fuller (1995, p. 50) suggests, "the emphasis on human rights may be an increasingly important area of common ground between the Islamic opposition groups and the West."

The implications of my study need further detailed analysis. However, it is important to note that this study has a number of limitations. The research presumes that the writings of Islamic activists are connected to the real causes of their grievances, thus assuming that there are no other unarticulated motives for their political actions. The study also presumes that there is a connection between Islamic activists' experiences and grievances and the public events coded.

An operational limitation of this study is its inability to measure adequately "prevailing wealth," since the indicator used to measure it proved imprecise. Further study of the concept of "wealth" and the means to preserve it in a modern economic system is necessary in order to examine its link to current Islamic activist movements.

My intention was to search for the religious bases of the expression of popular discontent in Muslim countries. By doing so, I found common ground between the West and the Islamic activists. Respect for the humanity of individuals and their need for freedom are among the many shared attributes between Islamic activists and the West.

The most important implication of this study is that we, as social scientists, need to be more vigilant in our analysis of Islamic activist movements, as Baker (1991, p. 47) indicated. Understanding the causation of Islamic activism depends on the close surveillance even of Islamic extremists ('Umar 'Abd al Raḥmān 1989, p. 154):

> The role of the learned people (*'ulamā'*) is a very important one in the Islamic world. It is their role to guide the Islamic movement: to adapt to modernity and the realities of life, and at the same time to concur with the Islamic law (the Shari'ah) and its end goals (*al maqāṣid*).

The "end of dialogue" academically will not further human research in anyway. Approaching Islamic activism with the mindset that these are radical, irrational, temporary and undemocratic movements distorts the analysis of and the conclusions drawn about the movements.

Appendices

Appendix 1: Data for Egypt

Variable I: Preserving Religion and the Mind[1]

November 1988–October 1989

Events	Code	FBIS Date & Page
1. Government official bans Islamic meetings.	3	7 Oct. 1988 p. 17
2. Interior Ministry asks opinion of al Azhar on issues of dispute with Islamic activists.	2	19 Jan. 1988 pp. 7-8
3. President gives speech on Preacher's day.	1	7 Mar. 1989 pp. 8-9
4. Islamic activists are taken to meet with Awqaf Minister.	2	7 Mar 1989 pp. 11-12
5. Islamic activists leaders are arrested on account of disturbing the peace and shouting anti-government slogans.	3	10 Apr. 1989 p. 12
6. Several Islamic activists are put in custody for 15 days on account of distributing anti-government publications on a train to Sinnuris.	3	17 Apr. 1989 p. 12
7. Interior minister issues directives to implement the law prohibiting attaching religious stickers to cars.	3	25 Apr. 1989 p. 16
8. Interior minister orders arrest of 50-year-old mother of a sought Islamic activist and the is kept as hostage until her son appears.	3	4 May 1989 p. 16

[1] Preserving religion and the mind is measured as follows: (1) The regime supports the Islamic activists' argument or acts in favor of defending/representing Islam; (2) The regime refers the issue to a third party; (3) The regime clearly states its conflicting stand on the issue; (00) No information.
The second category refers to incidents where religious authorities act or make statements that are congruent with governmental policies. Thus, religious authorities use the state's political ideas and language in addressing Islamic activists.
The information used to code all the data depends on articles published in the Foreign Broadcast Information Service, *Near East Daily Reports*, for the five years studied: November 1988 to October 1993.

9. A number of Islamic activists are arrrested while distributing leaflets in front of al Rahman mosque.	3	30 May 1989 p. 23
10. The Ministries of Interior and Religious Endowment	2&3	30 May 1989
11. Security officers storm al Rahman mosque and demolish one of its walls, seize its contents and prevent people from praying there.	3	15 May 1989 p. 8
12. After being released, one of the Islamic activist leaders, Sheikh 'AbdelRahman, is prevented from praying at the mosque.	3	16 Aug. 1989 p. 13
13. A number of Islamic activists are arrested for luring children under the guise of religion to instill in them extremist ideas.	3	5 Sept. 1989 p.11
14. A number of Muslim Brotherhood members are arrested after attending a news conference held by the Doctors' Union.	3	27 Sept. 1989 pp. 13-14

November 1989–October 1990

Events	Code	FBIS Date & Page
1. Security forces storm the Hamid Jawdat mosque and fire on worshippers (two people are injured).	3	20 Nov. 1980 pp. 9-10
2. Security police interfere in student elections by striking off two hundred names of Islamic activist candidates.	3	27 Nov. 1989 pp. 15-16
3. Two Islamic activist students are arrested for praying in the faculty garden and 43 are dismissed on account of being affiliated with Islamic groups.	3	19 Dec. 1989 p. 18
4. Religious endowment minister warns youth against sectarian sedition.	2	4 Apr. 1990 p. 15

November 1990–October 1991

Events	Code	FBIS Date & Page
1. In the security crackdown on Islamic students, scores of students are dismissed and veiled women students denied access to the university in Tanta, while Islamic clubs' activities are banned in Manufiyah University.	3	13 Nov. 1990 p. 10
2. Hundreds of houses in al Fayyum governorate are raided by police forces in search of al Muhajib's (Speaker of the People's Assembly) murderers.	3	20 Nov. 1990 p. 15
3. Security forces interfere in student election processees in al Azhar, Alexandria, and al Zaqaziq universities.	3	21 Nov. 1990 p. 12
4. Chief editor of *al Sha'b* newspaper (affiliated with the Muslim Brotherhood) is arrested because of his rejection of the Gulf War.	3	6 Feb. 1991 p. 6
5. Security forces prevent opposition members from the Socialist Labor Party (affiliated with the Muslim Brotherhood) from conducting a peaceful demonstration against the Gulf War.	3	8 Feb. 1991 p. 6
6. Police clash with students because they demonstrated against the Gulf War.	3	25 Feb. 1991 p. 13
7. Police clash again with students demonstrating against the Gulf War.	3	26 Feb. 1991 p. 4
8. Police clash again with students demonstrating against the Gulf War.	3	1 Mar. 1991 p. 2
9. Police disperse students demonstrating against the Gulf War.	3	6 Mar. 1991 p. 10
10. An Islamic activist is arrested for possessing leaflets with the intention of distributing them after prayers.	3	27 June 1991 p. 8f
11. State Security Investigation (SSI) arrests hundreds of Islamic activists on the occasion of 'Id al Adha (Muslim holiday).	3	10 July 1991 p. 9

12. A higher Council for the Islamic Call is established under the authority of al Azhar's imam. The council will draw up a unified plan for all institutions active in the field of Islamic call under al Azhar leadership (The council was set up on the instructions of President Mubarak)	2	25 July 1991 p. 14
13. Thirty-seven people are arrested for distributing leaflets against the Peace Conference in Madrid.	3	28 Oct. 1991 p. 13

November 1991–October 1992

Events	Coding	FBIS Date & Page
1. Interior minister says that 67 people were arrested because they were preparing pamphlets opposing the Peace Conference in Madrid.	3	7 Nov. 1991 p. 19
2. Counter-terrorism experts are sent to Algeria to control FIS unrest.	3	4 Feb. 1992 p. 14
3. Court upholds ban on the Muslim Brotherhood party.	3	7 Feb. 1992 p. 7
4. Security officials arrest worshipers at al Shahid mosque.	3	11 Feb. 1992 p. 23
5. Security forces beat up Islamic activists who were trying to close a movie rental store.	3	21 Feb. 1992 p. 18
6. Islamic activists are arrested for distributing anti-regime leaflets.	3	25 Mar. 1992 p. 23
7. Security forces storm Umar ibn al Khattab mosque to arrest Islamic activists.	3	19 May 1992 p. 9
8. The grand sheikh of al Azhar reprimands extremism.	3	20 May 1992 p. 9

9. The Egyptian Organization for Human Rights (EOHR) charges the government with human rights violations, including freedom of expression and freedom of thought violations.	3	22 May 1992 p. 12
10. Muslim Brotherhood members are arrested in al Sharqiyah governorate for holding a meeting and distributing anti-government leaflets.	3	8 June 1992 p. 19
11. Muslim Brotherhood leader condemns violence but accuses the government of giving writers freedom to attack Islam.	3	10 June 1992 p. 11
12. Religious endowment minister announces the need for a "united front" to counter terrorism.	2	17 June 1992 p. 5
13. Religious endowment minister urges students in Alexandria University to fight terrorism.	2	17 June 1992 pp. 21-22
14. Secretary General of the National Democratic Party (NDP) states firm opposition to extremism.	3	20 July 1992 pp. 18-19
15. Security forces storm mosque in Dayrut and seize anti-government pamphlets.	3	27 July 1992 p. 18
16. Security forces conduct house-to-house searches in Dayrut, seizing anti-government pamphlets among other things.	3	30 July 1992 pp. 12-13
17. Paper reports humiliation of people and arrest of peaceful citizens in a number of governorates as a result of the police crackdown on Islamic activists.	3	26 Aug. 1992 p. 16
18. Leader of Muslim Brotherhood blames government for recent terrorist attacks, stating that "people get killed in broad daylight for no other reason than opposing the government."	3	28 Aug. 1992 p. 11

November 1992–October 1993

Events	Coding	FBIS Date & Page
1. Eight hundred professors (who are affiliated with the Muslim Brotherhood) from Asyut University protest against the security personnel's "systematic searches."	3	12 Nov. 1992 p. 21
2. Security forces arrest a Muslim Brotherhood leader in Bani Suwayf and seize a photocopying machine, radios, and anti-government pamphlets.	3	20 Nov. 1992 p. 11
3. State publishes first edition of a religious paper run by the state.	1&2	1 Dec. 1992 p. 16
4. Security forces arrest extremists trying to organize a seminar in al Shadir mosque.	3	7 Dec. 1992 p. 23
5. Muslim Brotherhood writer accuses the government of relying on tourism which encourages gambling, drinking, prostitution, and nudist beaches.	3	9 Dec. 1992 p. 18
6. An Islamic activist is arrested for possessing anti-government leaflets and 300 religious cassettes.	3	16 Dec. 1992 p. 16
7. Qina governor suspends liquor sale licenses.	1	18 Dec. 1992 p. 11
8. Fourteen Muslim Brotherhood members are arrested for giving statements to foreign news agencies that distort Egypt's image and incite citizens to undermine the state's security.	3	21 Dec. 1992 p. 19

9. Security forces arrest more Muslim Brotherhood members for involvement with foreign news agencies and their promotion of an ideology that threatens to destabilize Egypt.	3	5 Jan. 1993 p. 14
10. The High Court upheld a ban on an Islamic party, "al Sahwah."	3	1 Feb. 1993 p. 16
11. The minister of religious endowment announces that private mosques will be placed under state control.	3	11 Feb. 1993 p. 10
12. Police arrest Islamic activists and seize anti-government leaflets.	3	18 Feb. 1993 p. 16
13. President Mubarak signs a new law imposing restrictions on union and professional syndicate elections.	3	19 Feb. 1993 pp. 14-15
14. A senior official of the Religious Endowment Ministry comments on government control of mosques.	2&3	24 Feb. 1993 p. 10
15. Government confronts professional syndicate leaders for their rejection of new law restricting elections.	3	2 Mar. 1993 p. 14
16. Government reinforces security around the TV station, night clubs and cinemas in fear of Islamic activist attacks.	3	4 Mar. 1993 p. 13
17. Minister of education dismisses four students and transfers a teacher because they listened to a tape inciting sedition in class.	3	5 Mar. 1993 pp. 8-9
18. Islamic activists are arrested for possessing anti-government leaflets.	3	9 Mar. 1993 p. 20
19. A number of worshippers are attacked by security forces in a mosque in Aswan.	3	10 Mar. 1993 pp. 14-15
20. Students protesting the transfer of a school teacher are arrested.	3	15 Mar. 1993 p. 13
21. Heavily armed soldiers search and watch over Friday prayer-goers.	3	16 Mar. 1993 p. 20
22. Security officials arrest and deport four Westerners inciting religious sedition.	1	17 Mar. 1993 p. 17

23. Al Azhar imam denies that the Egyptian regime is secular.	2	25 Mar. 1993 p. 7
24. Egyptian mufti states that the Islamic group is ignorant of Islamic law.	2	30 Mar. 1993 p. 21
25. Eleven Islamic activists are jailed for distributing Sheikh 'Abdel-Rahman leaflets.	3	30 Mar. 1993 p. 25
26. University bans a faculty member's work because it was blasphemous.	1	1 Apr. 1993 p. 19
27. Religious endowment minister states the need to protect Islam from Islamic activist terrorism.	2	16 Apr. 1993 p. 14
28. Religious endowment minister condemns Islamic activists involved in killing and destruction.	2	22 Apr. 1993 p. 15
29. Police plan crackdown on distributors of cassettes in front of mosques.	3	23 Apr. 1993 p. 21
30. Eight hundred and twenty-two Islamic activists detained for involvement in an "outlawed" Islamic Conquest Vanguard movement (among the arrested were many professors and army officers).	3	20 May 1993 pp. 10-11
31. Arrest of several Islamic activists and seizure of videocassettes and books banned by al Azhar.	3	20 May 1993 p. 11
32. Amnesty International reports wide-scale human rights violations by Egyptian security forces.	3	26 May 1993 p. 12
33. Government shuts down the Muslim Brotherhood paper.	3	2 June 1993 p. 9
34. Religious endowment minister asks ulema (religious scholars) to confront terrorism.	2	4 June 1993 p. 11
35. Ten Muslim Brotherhood members are arrested for possessing anti-government leaflets.	3	16 June 1993 p. 19
36. Security agencies confiscate a London-based newspaper for publishing an interview with Sheikh 'Umar 'Abdel-Rahman.	3	4 Aug. 1993 p. 8

37. Court charges Islamic activists with obtaining 1,000 copies of a banned book.	3	8 Sept. 1993 p. 14
38. State security confiscates a book about al Sheikh Umar 'Abdel-Rahman.	3	10 Sept. 1993 p. 12
39. State allows the Muslim Brotherhood paper to resume publication.	1	10 Sept. 1993 p. 14
40. Police storm al Rahmah mosque in Asyut.	3	15 Sept. 1993 p. 15
41. The councils of universities ban political and religious activities on campus.	3	6 Oct. 1993 p. 19
42. The United States State Department suggests change in the religious concepts in school curricula.	3	6 Oct. 1993 p. 27
43. Interrogation of Islamic activists (party officials and journalists) because their paper insulted the president and jeopardized stability.	3	13 Oct. 1993 p. 27

Variable II. Preserving the Self

A. The Practice of *Habeas Corpus*[2]

Year	Nov. Oct. '88 – '89	Nov. Oct. '89 – '90	Nov. Oct. '90 – '91	Nov. Oct. '91 – '92	Nov. Oct. '92 – '93
Approximate number of violations	260	120	390	280	1,310

[2] The category scale developed to code this variable is as follows: (1) 1–20 incidents of habeas corpus violations; (2) 21–40 incidents; (3) 41–40 incidents; (4) 61–80 incidents; (5) More than 80 incidents; (00) No information.

Each FBIS report of *habeas corpus* violation was categorized using the intervals indicated above. When available, exact numbers were reported. Categories were used because many of the FIBS reports give only estimates or have several reports of the same incident. This issue is common in all the variables that have numerical estimates (i.e., in variables II.B., II.C., V.A., V.B., and V.C.). The approximate annual totals were calculated using the following scale values: (1) 1–20 incidents = 10; (2) 21–40 incidents = 30; (3) 41–60 incidents = 50; (4) 61–80 incidents = 70; (5) More than 80 = 90.

Variable II.B. Torture and Death during Imprisonment[3]

Year	Nov. Oct. '88 – '89	Nov. Oct. '89 – '90	Nov. Oct. '90 – '91	Nov. Oct. '91 – '92	Nov. Oct. '92 – '93
Approximate number tortured and killed during imprisonment	50	1,410	945	1,323	1,610

Variable II.C. Utilizing Police Forces and Military to Disperse/Deter[4] Islamic Activists[5]

Year	Nov. Oct. '88 – '89	Nov. Oct. '89 – '90	Nov. Oct. '90 – '91	Nov. Oct. '91 – '92	Nov. Oct. '92 – '93
Approximate no. killed/wounded by police	180	330	300	300	998

[3] The category scale developed to code this variable is as follows:

(1) 1–20 cases of torture/death
(2) 21–40 cases
(3) 41–60 cases
(4) 61–80 cases
(5) 81–100 cases
(6) 101–300 cases
(7) 301–500 cases
(8) 501–700 cases
(9) 701–900 cases
(10) More than 900 cases
(00) No information

Please refer to footnote 2 in variable II.A.

The approximate annual totals were calculated using the following scale values:

(1) 1–20 incidents = 10
(2) 21–40 incidents = 30
(3) 41–60 incidents = 50
(4) 61–80 incidents = 70
(5) 81–100 = 90
(6) 101–300 = 200
(7) 301–500 = 400
(8) 501–700 = 600
(9) 701–900 = 800
(10) More than 900

[4] The word "deter" is mentioned to stress the use of force to crush Islamic activism without incidents, i.e., the police forces storm mosques and houses to kill/deter Islamic activists. The consequences usually result in a war of attrition between security forces and Islamic activists.

[5] The category scale developed to code this variable is as follows:

(1) Crowd was harmless, but police used brutal force (i.e. killed/wounded people) to disperse them. The number of people killed/wounded is: (a) Less than or equal to 50; (b) 51–100; (c) 101–500; (d) More than 500.
(2) Crowd was harming property/people, the police used force. The number of people killed/wounded is: (a) Less than or equal to 50; (b) 51–100; (c) 101–500; (d) More than 500. Please refer to variable II.A., footnote 2.

The approximate annual totals were calculated using the following scale values: (1) Less than or equal to 50 = 30; (2) 51–100 = 75; (3) 100–500 = 300; (4) More than 500 = 700.

Kind of crowd action that caused police brutality	1	2	1	2	1	2	1	2	1	2
Frequency of such actions	3	4	5	6	9	1	3	7	11	20

Variable III. Preserving Posterity/Youth[6]

November 1988–October 1989

Events	Coding	FBIS Date & Page
1. Interior minister bans activities of Islamic groups in universities and mosques and orders investigators to follow up the activities of Islamic activist students inside and outside campuses.	2	7 Oct. 1988 p. 17
2. Interior minister issues a warrant to arrest 19 children who were on an "educational trip" with Islamic activists (their ages range from 10 to 16 years).	2	15 Aug. 1989 p. 8
3. A number of people are arrested for instilling extremist ideas in children age 6 to 7.	2	5 Sept. 1989 p. 11

November 1989–October 1990

Events	Coding	FBIS Date & Page
1. Security forces interfere in university elections.	2	27 Nov. 1989 pp. 15-16
2. A number of Islamic activist students are arrested after they won in student elections.	2	19 Dec. 1989 p. 18

[6] This variable is similar to preserving religion and the mind in its method of measurement. The scale developed for it is as follows: (1) The regime encourages religious education/practice; (2) The regime openly discourages religious education/practice; (00) No information.

November 1990–October 1991

Events	Coding	FBIS Date & Page
1. Police crack down on Islamic activist students who won recent elections.	2	13 Nov. 1990 p. 19
2. Campus violence increases as police use force to abort student protest.	2	21 Nov. 1990 p. 12
3. Security forces do not intervene in student rally against the Gulf War.	2	19 Feb. 1991 p. 25
4. Security forces clash with student protesters.	2	25 Feb. 1991 p. 13
5. Increase in campus violence because of police/student clashes	2	26 Feb. 1991 p. 14
6. More university disturbances between security forces and students	2	1 Mar. 1991 p. 2
7. Hundreds of youths affiliated with Islamic Activism on campus are rounded up on a Muslim holiday ('Id al Adha).	2	10 July 1991 p. 9
8. 185 Islamic activist students are arrested for protesting against the Peace Conference in Madrid.	2	28 Oct. 1991 p. 13

November 1991–October 1992

Events	Coding	FBIS Date & Page
1. University professors object to measures taken by campus police and request more freedom.	2	14 Jan. 1992 p. 15
2. Militants clash with police over closing a video rental store.	2	21 Feb. 1992 p. 18
3. Sheikh of al Azhar notes insufficient religious curricula in schools and universities.	2	20 May 1992 p. 9

November 1992–October 1993

Events	Coding	FBIS Date & Page
1. Islamic activist professors protest against campus security measures.	2	12 Nov. 1992 pp. 21-22
2. Arrest of Islamic activists because they train children in means of communication.	2	20 Nov. 1992 p. 11
3. Islamic activists criticize tourism and its effect on cultural mores and values.	2	9 Dec. 1992 p. 18
4. Muslim Brotherhood members arrested for defaming Egypt and contacting foreign news agencies by using the computer company Salsabil.	2	5 Jan. 1993 p. 14
5. Minister of education discourages teachers from requesting girls to wear headscarves.	2	18 Feb. 1993 p. 16
6. Minister of education dismisses four female students and transfers a teacher for playing a cassette inciting religious sedition in class.	2	5 Mar. 1993 pp. 8-9
7. Police forces raid the Imbabah district, killing a woman and a child and two Islamic activists.	2	10 Mar. 1993 pp. 14-15
8. Students protesting against the transfer of their teacher are arrested.	2	15 Mar. 1993
9. Education minister warns against the influence of Islamic activists in schools.	2	22 Apr. 1993 pp. 15-16
10. Education minister alerts the National Democratic Party of Islamic activist attempts to infiltrate the educational system.	2	28 Apr. 1993 p. 26
11. Minister of education removes hundreds of Islamic activist educators from their posts.	2	5 May 1993 p. 14

12. Minister of education removes a number of Islamic activist teachers from private schools.	2	10 May 1993 p. 19
13. Minister of education reveals that the removal of Islamic activist teachers was due to their control of schools in a number of governorates where they were teaching a different curriculum than the one designed by the ministry.	2	12 May 1993 pp. 18-19
14. A report details the Islamic activist infiltration of high schools and universities.	2	19 May 1993 pp. 12-13
15. A few university students are arrested for distributing cassettes and religious books banned by al Azhar.	2	20 May 1993 p. 12
16. Education minister warns against "terrorist plan" to control education and states that the National Democratic Party's Educational Committee, the Education Ministry, and the State's executive body are cooperating to abort the "plan."	2	25 May 1993 p. 12
17. Amnesty International decries human rights violations in the regime's crackdown on Islamic Activism, stating that some of the detainees were as young as 15 years.	2	26 May 1993 p. 12
18. University councils ban any religious/political activities on campus.	2	6 Oct. 1993 p. 19
19. Report states that the maintenance of US aid to Egypt is dependent on removing "outdated" religious concepts from the educational curricula.	2	6 Oct. 1993 p. 19
20. One hundred students are arrested in Alexandria University because they were protesting against the expulsion of 500 students linked to Islamic activism.	2	26 Oct. 1993 p. 20

Variable IV. Preserving Property/Wealth[7]

Year	Nov. Oct. '88 – '89	Nov. Oct. '89 – '90	Nov. Oct. '90 – '91	Nov. Oct. '91 – '92	Nov. Oct. '92 – '93
Degree of inflation rate stability	2	2	00	2	2

Variable V. The Degree of Islamic Activism
A. The Approximate Number of Islamic Activists Arrested Each Year[8]

Year	Nov. Oct. '88 – '89	Nov. Oct. '89 – '90	Nov. Oct. '90 – '91	Nov. Oct. '91 – '92	Nov. Oct. '92 – '93
Approx. number of IAs arrested	2,340	3,660	3,710	2,800	10,450

7 This variable is measured through the analysis of articles published in the Foreign Broadcast Information Service throughout the five years of analysis. The categories under which this variable is coded are as follows: (1) Inflation varies according to international market fluctuations; (2) Inflation is continuously increasing; (00) No information.

8 The category scale used to code this variable is as follows: (1) Less than or equal to 50; (2) 51–100; (3) 101–900; (4) More than 900; (00) No information. Please refer to variable II.A., footnote 2. The approximate annual totals are calculated using the following scale values: (1) Less than or equal to 50 = 20; (2) 51–100 = 70; (3) 101–900 = 500; (4) More than 900.

Variable V.B. Approximate Number of Attempted Attacks against Public Figures, Police Forces, Secularists, and Tourists[9]

Year	Nov. Oct. '88 – '89	Nov. Oct. '89 – '90	Nov. Oct. '90 – '91	Nov. Oct. '91 – '92	Nov. Oct. '92 – '93
Approx. no. of attempted attacks	35	44	47	124	668
Additional notes on the targets of attacks	1 attempt on the interior minister's life.	Assembly speaker assassinated.	1 attempt on the interior minister's life.	a) A number of tourists. b) Faraj Fudah (a secular writer) was assassinated.	a) Attacks on Copts. b) Attacks on policemen. c) Attempt to assassinate information minister. d) Threat to assassinate the president. e) Attempt to assassinate Arafat.

Variable V.C. Approximate Number of Islamic Activists Who Join and Instigate Rallies/ Demonstrations Each Year[10]

Year	Nov. Oct. '88 – '89	Nov. Oct. '89 – '90	Nov. Oct. '90 – '91	Nov. Oct. '91 – '92	Nov. Oct. '92 – '93
Approx. number of IAs who rally/ demonstrate	1,255	2,220	3,890	190	7,110

[9] The category scale used for coding is as follows: (1) 1–10 attacks; (2) 11–20 attacks; (3) 21–40 attacks; (00) No information. Please refer to variable II.A., footnote 2.
The approximate annual totals are calculated using the following scale values: (1) 1–10 = 4; (2) 11–20 = 15; (3) 21–40 = 30.

[10] The category scale developed to code this variable is as follows: (1) Less than or equal to 50; (2) 51–100; (3) 101–500; (4) 501–1000; (5) More than 1000. Please refer to variable II.A., footnote 2.
The approximate annual totals are calculated using the following scale values: (1) Less than or equal to 50 = 20; (2) 51–100 = 60; (3) 101–500 = 300; (4) 501–1000 = 750; (5) More than 1000 = 1000.

Variable V.D. Kinds and Frequencies of Demonstrations in Which Islamic Activists Are Involved[11]

Year	Nov. Oct. '88 – '89	Nov. Oct. '89 – '90	Nov. Oct. '90 – '91	Nov. Oct. '91 – '92	Nov. Oct. '92 – '93
Categories	1 2 3 4	1 2 3 4	1 2 3 4	1 2 3 4	1 2 3 4
Frequency	7 - 4 1	6 6 3 4	10 - 4 2	1 5 2 7	9 11 1 7

Variable V.E. Islamic Activists Winning or Gaining Influence on Provincial or Professional Level[12]

Year	Nov. Oct. '88 – '89	Nov. Oct. '89 – '90	Nov. Oct. '90 – '91	Nov. Oct. '91 – '92	Nov. Oct. '92 – '93
Categories of election patterns	1 2 3 00	1 2 3 00	1 2 3 00	1 2 3 00	1 2 3 00
Frequency reflecting election patterns	1 - - -	- 2 2 -	- - 1 -	- 1 - -	3 2 2 -

11 The scale used to define the kinds of demonstrations is as follows: (1) Peaceful; (2) Harmed property; (3) Entangled in a clash with police forces, military, or any other state agency; (4) Harmed other individuals not related to the state.

12 This variable is qualitative in nature and estimates the degree of involvement of Islamic Activists in the public elections processes. The categories used to define this variable are as follows: (1) Winning an election or gaining acceptance in 1–2 provinces; (2) Winning an election or gaining acceptance in a certain syndicate; (3) Losing elections in a certain province/syndicate due to the regime's interference; (00) No information.

Appendix 2: Data for Algeria

Variable 1: Preserving Religion and the Mind[1]

November 1988–October 1989

Events	Coding	FBIS Date & Page
1. Military tanks surround a mosque in Chevally, and armed soldiers steer worshipers as they leave the mosque.	3	11 Oct. 1988 p. 9
2. The Higher Islamic Council issues an appeal to the Algerian people to unite.	2	11 Oct. 1988 p. 23
3. The Ministry of Religious Affairs bars politics from the mosques.	2&3	3 Apr. 1989 p. 10

November 1989–October 1990

Events	Coding	FBIS Date & Page
1. The National Liberation Front (FLN) requests the public to march in order to call for separating party elections from mosques.	3	17 Apr. 1990 p. 3

1 Preserving Religion and the Mind is measured as follows: (1) The regime supports the Islamic activists' argument or acts in favor of defending/representing Islam; (2) The regime refers the issue to a third party; (3) The regime clearly states its conflicting stand on the issue; (00) No information.

The second category refers to incidents where religious authorities act or make statements that are congruent to governmental policies. Thus, religious authorities use the state's political ideas and language in addressing Islamic activists.

The information used to code all the data depends on articles publised in the Foreign Broadcast Information Service, *Near East Daily Reports* for the five years studied: November 1988 to October 1993.

2. A mosque association does not authorize the celebration of a religious festival.	2&3	24 Apr. 1990 p. 4
3. On winning elections in Constantine, the Islamic Salvation Front (FIS) makes general changes in education and prohibits bars, brothels, wearing shorts/swimming suits, etc.	1	17 July 1990 p. 5

November 1990–October 1991

Events	Coding	FBIS Date & Page
1. The government does not react to Islamic activists' recruitment of hundreds of youths to fight a "holy war" against Israel.	3	17 Dec. 1990 p. 5
2. President Hamrouche condemns the Gulf War.	1	30 Jan. 1991 p. 10
3. Police use tear gas to disperse demonstrators against the Gulf War.	3	19 Feb. 1991 p. 20
4. New election law is designed to prevent the use of mosques for electoral campaigning.	3	27 Mar. 1991 p. 4
5. The Algerian Cultural and Informational Center refuses to curtail its activities during Ramadan, as requested by FIS.	3	27 Mar. 1991 p. 4
6. Interior minister describes a strike by the FIS and other political parties as illegal and tantamount to civil disobedience.	3	22 Apr. 1991 p. 6
7. Police evacuate Islamic activists from Khalid ibn al Walid Mosque.	3	11 June 1991 p. 12
8. Annaba University is closed because of a strike by Islamic activist professors and students.	3	13 June 1991 p. 2
9. The police committee for protecting public order has to approve space for and time of the 'Id prayers.	2	24 June 1991 p. 5

10. Amidst violent clashes, the army removes Islamic emblems from the fronts of town halls.	3	26 June 1991 p. 4
11. Ulema call on Algerian people to unite and stop the shedding of Muslim blood.	2	28 June 1991 p. 5
12. Madani, leader of the FIS, states that the military is "committing a mortal sin by threatening to shoot those wanting to go to the mosque."	3	1 July 1991 p. 5
13. One of the ulema calls on the Algerian people to abandon violence.	1	1 July 1991 p. 6
14. Islamic activists (FIS) are expelled by security forces from the Great Mosque and the mosque is closed.	3	2 July 1991 p. 5
15. Security officials search Islamic Activists' headquarters and Khadra mosque.	3	8 July 1991 p. 6
16. A "Qur'an Radio" begins its broadcast.	1	12 July 1991 pp. 2-3
17. Paratroopers open fire on thousands of FIS demonstrators who gathered around the mosque for Friday prayers.	3	15 July 1991 p. 4
18. The military bans all marches and public gatherings	3	18 July 1991 p. 5
19. Authorities stress that the ban on public gatherings and meetings in public squares is still in place.	3	22 July 1991 p. 1
20. One of the FIS religious leaders (sheikhs) is arrested in his office.	3	30 Sept. 1991 p. 14

November 1991–October 1992

Events	Coding	FBIS DATE & Page
1. FIS members are arrested near a mosque, and police carry out systematic identity checks of drivers with beards.	3	21 Jan. 1992 p. 11
2. An imam of one of the mosques is arrested on account of urging citizens to rebel against state institutions.	3	22 Jan. 1992 p. 13

3. A FIS leader is arrested in a security crackdown on Islamic activists.	3	23 Jan. 1992 p. 11
4. Algiers governor bans gatherings near mosques.	3	23 Jan. 1992 p. 12
5. Two journalists linked to the FIS are arrested.	3	24 Jan. 1992 p. 20
6. Police open fire on 500 people outside a mosque on Friday and arrest several journalists (including French, Spanish, and Turkish journalists).	3	27 Jan. 1992 pp. 11-12
7. Interior Ministry calls on citizens to conduct their prayers inside the mosques in their districts.	3	28 Jan. 1992 pp. 11-12
8. Police arrest two imams of mosques in Badjarah.	3	29 Jan. 1992 p. 18
9. State takes over the Sunna mosque, a FIS stronghold.	3	30 Jan. 1992 p. 19
10. Algiers governor bans public gatherings.	3	31 Jan. 1992 p. 19
11. Approximately 27 Islamic activists are injured while demonstrating and chanting anti-government slogans.	3	3 Feb. 1992 pp. 13-16
12. A number of imams are arrested in civil unrest.	3	3 Feb. 1992 p. 15
13. A number of imams and FIS leaders are arrested.	3	5 Feb. 1992 p. 5
14. The government bans a peaceful march called for by FIS.	3	6 Feb. 1992 p. 8
15. Minister of interior states the government intends to fight hard against disorder caused by Islamicists.	3	7 Feb. 1992 p. 4
16. Army surrounds Ben Badis mosque in Kouba quarter of Algiers.	3	7 Feb. 1992 p. 5
17. State of Emergency is declared and the FIS is dissolved by the government.	3	10 Feb. 1992 pp. 7-11
18. Several imams are arrested, and clashes continue between the police and the people, especially after Friday prayers.	3	10 Feb. 1992 pp. 12-16

19. People report that intense gunfire was heard at dawn near el-Annassers mosque.	3	11 Feb. 1992 p. 16
20. The latest issue of FIS's newspaper is seized by the National Gendarmerie.	3	12 Feb. 1992 p. 8
21. People gathering near Katchaoua mosque are fired on by police; a child is wounded	3	14 Feb. 1992 p. 6
22. A pro-FIS newspaper is confiscated for containing subjects that affect the country's security.	3	20 Feb. 1992 p. 15
23. 14,000 FIS members are arrested and a pro-Islamic newspaper al Nahdah is confiscated.	3	21 Feb. 1992 pp. 14-14
24. Algerian Human Rights League urges an end to arbitrary arrests of IAs.	3	25 Feb. 1992 p. 14
25. 800 people, including women and children, stage a procession; police fire into the air to disperse them.	3	2 Mar. 1992 p. 14
26. Chairman of the Higher State Council defends the decision to dissolve FIS.	3	5 Mar. 1992 p. 9
27. Religious affairs minister meets mosque imams and states that mosques should be used exclusively for worship.	3	11 Mar. 1992 p. 7
28. Police surround al Ansar mosque to apprehend its imam after Friday prayers.	3	23 Mar. 1992 p. 13
29. Army chief is dismissed for his hostility to Islamic activists.	1	31 Mar. 1992 p. 8
30. Hachani, an FIS leader, is charged with inciting the crowds.	3	22 Apr. 1992 pp. 8-9
31. Ministry of Religious Affairs bans "unauthorized" imams from mosques.	2&3	24 Apr. 1992 p. 6
32. State confiscates a paper because it interviewed an Tunisian IA leader (Rashed al Ghannoushi).	3	27 Apr. 1992 p. 10
33. Supreme Court upholds the ban on the FIS.	3	30 Apr. 1992 p. 18
34. Religious affairs minister condemns acts of sabotage and disturbances carried out by Islamic activists.	2	7 May 1992 pp. 2-3

35. Imam arrested following Friday prayers in Tlemcen.	3	19 May 1992 p. 8
36. The local inspector of the Ministry of Religious Affairs appoints a new imam before Friday prayers, thus arousing the people's opposition.	2&3	26 May 1992 p. 6
37. Crowds performing the 'Id prayers outside a mosque are tear gassed by police forces.	3	12 June 1992 p. 6
38. Crowds attempt to organize protest against military court sentences on FIS leaders but are dispersed by police.	3	20 July 1992 pp. 6-7
39. Police arrest pro-FIS demonstrators.	3	27 July 1992 p. 14
40. A foreign news agency correspondent is warned not to publish FIS letter.	3	24 Aug. 1992 p. 13
41. Several youths are killed during police dispersal of groups after Friday prayers.	3	8 Sept. 1992 pp. 11-12

November 1992–October 1993

Events	Coding	FBIS Date & Page
1. Police arrest a gang of terrorists and seize their fax machines, radio sets and political pamphlets.	3	23 Nov. 1992 p. 18
2. Religious Affairs Ministry condemns the demolition of a mosque in India.	1	9 Dec. 1992 p. 14
3. Interior minister suspends 6 Islamic organizations.	3	14 Dec. 1992 p. 8
4. Ministry of Culture and Information bans a paper and punishes two journalists because they spread rumors and falsify the truth.	3	21 Dec. 1992 p. 14
5. Minister of religious affairs orders demolition of unofficial mosques.	3	30 Dec. 1992 p. 10
6. Arab interior ministers meet in Tunisia to discuss struggle against terrorism. (Algeria's minister of interior attends.)	3	7 Jan. 1993 p. 1

7. The Algerian government establishes diplomatic ties with Bosnia.	1	25 Jan. 1993 p. 6
8. Bosnian war casualties arrive in Algeria for treatment.	1	23 Feb. 1993 p. 7
9. Article notes that the mere possession of Islamicist literature in Algeria is punishable by law.	3	5 Mar. 1993 pp. 7-8
10. Governor of Setif province suspends 195 religious associations on account of religious incitement.	3	11 Mar. 1993 p. 12
11. One of the main FIS leaders and his defense lawyer stand trial for signing and distributing seditious leaflets.	3	4 May 1993 p. 7
12. The Ministry of Religious Affairs requires muezzins (callers to prayer) to get permission from local authorities to call for dawn prayers. Citizens must pray at home, owing to curfew regulations.	3	15 June 1993 pp. 12-13

Variable II. Preserving the Self
A. The Practice of *Habeas Corpus*[2]

Year	Nov. Oct. '88 – '89	Nov. Oct. '89 – '90	Nov. Oct. '90 – '91	Nov. Oct. '91 – '92	Nov. Oct. '92 – '93
Approx. number number of violations	160	00	280	1,030	450

2 The category scale developed to code this variable is as follows: (1) 1–20 incidents of *habeas corpus* violations; (2) 21–40 incidents; (3) 41–60 incidents; (4) 61–80 incidents; (5) More than 80 incidents; (00) No information.

Each FBIS report of *habeas corpus* violations was categorized using the intervals indicated above. When available, exact numbers were reported. Categories were used because many of the FIBS reports give only estimates or have several reports of the same incident. This issue is common in all the variables that have numerical estimates (i.e., in variables II.B., II.C., V.A., V.B., and V.C.). The approximate annual totals were calculated using the following scale values: (1) 1–20 incidents = 10; (2) 21–40 incidents = 30; (3) 41–60 incidents = 50; (4) 61–80 incidents = 70; (5) More than 80 = 90.

Variable II.B. Torture and Death During Imprisonment[3]

Year	Nov. Oct. '88 – '89	Nov. Oct. '89 – '90	Nov. Oct. '90 – '91	Nov. Oct. '91 – '92	Nov. Oct. '92 – '93
Approximate number tortured and killed during imprisonment	220	00	30	1,930	1,845

Variable II.C. Utilizing Police Forces and Military to Disperse/Deter[4] Islamic Activists[5]

Year	Nov. Oct. '88 – '89	Nov. Oct. '89 – '90	Nov. Oct. '90 – '91	Nov. Oct. '91 – '92	Nov. Oct. '92 – '93
Approximate number killed/ wounded by police	60	0	645	1,350	1,620

[3] The category scale developed to code this variable is as follows:

(1) 1–20 cases of torture/death
(2) 21–40 cases
(3) 41–60 cases
(4) 61–80 cases
(5) 81–100 cases
(6) 101–300 cases
(7) 301–500 cases
(8) 501–700 cases
(9) 701–900 cases
(10) More than 900 cases
(00) No information

Please refer to footnote 2 in variable II.A.

The approximate annual totals were calculated using the following scale values:

(1) 1–20 incidents = 10
(2) 21–40 incidents = 30
(3) 41–60 incidents = 50
(4) 61–80 incidents = 70
(5) 81–100 = 90
(6) 101–300 = 200
(7) 301–500 = 400
(8) 501–700 = 600
(9) 701–900 = 800
(10) More than 900

[4] The word "deter" is mentioned to stress the use of force to crush Islamic activism without incidents, i.e., the police forces storm mosques and houses to kill/deter Islamic activists. The consequences usually result in a war of attrition between security forces and Islamic activists.

[5] The category scale developed to code this variable is as follows:

(1) Crowd was harmless, but police used brutal force (i.e. killed/wounded people) to disperse them. The number of people killed/wounded is: (a) Less than or equal to 50; (b) 51–100; (c) 101–500; (d) More than 500.
(2) Crowd was harming property/people, the police used force. The number of people killed/ wounded is: (a) Less than or equal to 50; (b) 51–100; (c) 101–500; (d) More than 500. Please refer to variable II.A., footnote 2.

Kind of crowd action that caused police brutality	1	2	1	2	1	2	1	2	1	2
Frequency of such actions	2	-	-	-	9	10	17	23	50	7

Variable III. Preserving Posterity/Youth[6]

November 1988–October 1989

Events	Coding	FBIS Date & Page
0		

November 1989–October 1990

Events	Coding	FBIS Date & Page
1. After winning the elections, FIS banned mixed schooling in Constantine city.	1	17 July 1990 p. 5

November 1990–October 1991

Events	Coding	FBIS Date & Date
1. The Algerian Cultural Center refuses a request by the city council of Bab el-Oued and the Algerian popular council to cancel art performances during Ramadan.	2	27 Mar. 1991 p. 5
2. Annaba University remains closed owing to a strike held by Islamic Activist students and professors.	2	13 June 1991 p. 2

[6] This variable is similar to preserving religion and the mind in its method of measurement. The scale developed for it is as follows: (1) The regime encourages religious education/practice; (2) The regime openly discourages religious education/practice; (00) No information.

November 1991–October 1992

Events	Coding	FBIS Date & Page
1. Police arrest people in a mosque, including youths.	2	21 Jan. 1992 p. 11
2. Youths warned against gathering near mosques.	2	23 Jan. 1992 p. 12
3. Shots are fired and tear gas is used by the police after Friday prayers.	2	27 Jan. 1992 p. 11
4. Skirmishes reported between rioting youths and police in a suburb of Algiers.	2	29 Jan. 1992 p. 18
5. State takes over a mosque in Algiers.	2	29 Jan. 1992 p. 19
6. Police forces fire shots to disperse youths going to Friday prayers in a university mosque.	2	31 Jan. 1992 p. 19
7. Groups of youths are injured by police gunfire for demonstrating in Bab el-Oued.	2	3 Feb. 1992 pp. 13-16
8. Adolescents, among others, clash with police, who use tear gas to disperse the demonstrators.	2	5 Feb. 1992 p. 5
9. Tensions continue in Batna, and the State Council issues a comminiqué warning security forces not to commit excesses against civilians.	2	6 Feb. 1992 pp. 7-8
10. FIS quotes witnesses as saying that the police forces spared nobody in the arrests, including the mentally ill, children and the elderly.	2	21 Feb. 1992 pp. 14-15
11. Paramilitary forces fire warning shots in order to disperse Islamic activist students at Bab Ezzouar University.	2	24 Feb. 1992 pp. 14-15

12. Ain Bey University in Constantine is affected by student unrest when students demand the release of arrested students and professors. Meanwhile, students try to organize marches in Batna University.	2	24 Feb. 1992 p. 15
13. Setif University council decides to cancel classes owing to student unrest.	2	25 Feb. 1992 p. 14
14. Protests continue on campuses, including Blida, Ain Bey, and Annaba universities.	2	2 Mar. 1992 pp. 14-15
15. Tensions continue, and another campus suffers unrest: Mostaganes University where 15 students from the "Movement for the Protection of the People's Choice" are arrested.	2	3 Mar. 1992 p. 16
16. Police forces are called to end the Setif University campus disturbances.	2	17 Mar. 1992 p. 6
17. Security forces intervene to disperse students at Setif secondary schools.	2	17 Mar. 1992 p. 12
18. Rumors circulate that the mosque at Bab Ezzouar University is going to be demolished.	2	23 Mar. 1992 pp. 13-14
19. The people of Laraba municipality try to set fire to the administrative section of one primary and two secondary schools.	2	7 May 1992 p. 2
20. In dispersing the crowds after Friday prayers at Sheikh Brahimi mosque, the security forces kill a 17-year-old.	2	8 Sept. 1992 pp. 11-12

November 1992–October 1993

Events	Coding	FBIS Date & Page
0		

Variable IV. Preserving Property/Wealth[7]

Year	Nov. Oct. '88 – '89	Nov. Oct. '89 – '90	Nov. Oct. '90 – '91	Nov. Oct. '91 – '92	Nov. Oct. '92 – '93
Degree of inflation rate stability	2	2	00	2	2

Variable V. The Degree of Islamic Activism[8]

Year	Nov. Oct. '88 – '89	Nov. Oct. '89 – '90	Nov. Oct. '90 – '91	Nov. Oct. '91 – '92	Nov. Oct. '92 – '93
Approx. number of IAs arrested	725	120	4,720	1,820	1,800

Variable V.B. Approximate Number of Attempted Attacks Against Public Figures, Police Forces, Secularists and Tourists[9]

Year	Nov. Oct. '88 – '89	Nov. Oct. '89 – '90	Nov. Oct. '90 – '91	Nov. Oct. '91 – '92	Nov. Oct. '92 – '93
Approx. no. of attempted attacks.	0	0	68	272	300
Additional notes on the targets of attack.	0	0	0	1) Bomb is planted in mosque when Boudiaf (presi-	1) Attack on ex-Defense Minister Nezzar. 2) Ex-educa-

[7] This variable is measured through the analysis of articles published in the Foreign Broadcast Information Service throughout the five years of analysis. The categories under which this variable is coded are as follows: (1) Inflation varies according to international market fluctuations; (2) Inflation is continuously increasing; (00) No information.

[8] The category scale used to code this variable is as follows: (1) Less than or equal to 50; (2) 51–100; (3) 101–900; (4) More than 900; (00) No information. Please refer to variable II.A., footnote 2. The approximate annual totals are calculated using the following scale values: (1) Less than or equal to 50 = 20; (2) 51–100 = 70; (3) 101–900 = 500; (4) More than 900.

[9] The category scale used for coding is as follows: (1) 1–10 attacks; (2) 11–20 attacks; (3) 21–40 attacks; (00) No information. Please refer to variable II.A., footnote 2. The approximate annual totals are calculated using the following scale values: (1) 1–10 = 4; (2) 11–20 = 15; (3) 21–40 = 30.

				dent), Ghozali (prime minister), and other officials are praying. 2) Boudiaf assassinated in Annaba while giving a public speech, and 141 people are wounded.	tion Minister is assassinated. 3) Labor and sports ministers are wounded. 4) Public prosecutor is assassinated. 5) Minister of equipment escapes assassination. 6) Ex-prime minister is assassinated and members of his family and his driver are killed.

Variable V.C. Approximate Number of Islamic Activists Who Join and Instigate Rallies/ Demonstrations Each Year[10]

Year	Nov. Oct. '88 – '89	Nov. Oct. '89 – '90	Nov. Oct. '90 – '91	Nov. Oct. '91 – '92	Nov. Oct. '92 – '93
Approx. number of IAs who rally/ demonstrate	3,300	4,340	12,850	6,550	0

10 The category scale developed to code this variable is as follows: (1) Less than or equal to 50; (2) 51–100; (3) 101–500; (4) 501–1000; (5) More than 1000. Please refer to variable II.A., footnote 2.
The approximate annual totals are calculated using the following scale values: (1) Less than or equal to 50 = 20; (2) 51–100 = 60; (3) 101–500 = 300; (4) 501–1000 = 750; (5) More than 1000 = 1000.

Variable V.D. Kinds and Frequencies of Demonstrations in Which Islamic Activists Are Involved[11]

Year	Nov. Oct. '88 – '89	Nov. Oct. '89 – '90	Nov. Oct. '90 – '91	Nov. Oct. '91 – '92	Nov. Oct. '92 – '93
Categories	1 2 3 4	1 2 3 4	1 2 3 4	1 2 3 4	1 2 3 4
Frequency	3 - - -	2 1 1 -	16 7 11 4	14 12 16 2	- 6 - 1

Variable V.E. Islamic Activists Winning or Gaining Influence on Provincial or Professional Level[12]

Year	Nov. Oct. '88 – '89	Nov. Oct. '89 – '90	Nov. Oct. '90 – '91	Nov. Oct. '91 – '92	Nov. Oct. '92 – '93
Categories of election patterns	1 2 3 00	1 2 3 00	1 2 3 00	1 2 3 00	1 2 3 00
Frequency reflecting election patterns.	- - - -	4 - - -	1 - - -	1 - - -	- 1 - -

N.B.: The Islamic Salvation Front (FIS) won the first round of elections on December 30–31, 1991 However, the Security Council canceled the second round of elections and dissolved the FIS, and the president resigned on January 11, 1992.

[11] The scale used to define the kinds of demonstrations is as follows: (1) Peaceful; (2) Harmed property; (3) Entangled in a clash with police forces, military, or any other state agency; (4) Harmed other individuals not related to the state.

[12] This variable is qualitative in nature and estimates the degree of involvement of Islamic Activists in the public elections processes. The categories used to define this variable are as follows: (1) Winning an election or gaining acceptance in 1–2 provinces; (2) Winning an election or gaining acceptance in a certain syndicate; (3) Losing elections in a certain province/syndicate owing to the regime's interference; (00) No information.

Appendix 3: Data for Turkey

Variable I. Preserving Religion and the Mind[1]

November 1988–October 1989

Events	Coding	FBIS Date & Page
1. Prime Minister Özal explains President Evren's veto of the turban bill that would have allowed female students to wear veils on campus.	3	2 Dec. 1988 p. 39
2. Prime Minister Özal encourages the building of a mosque on the Turkish-Russian border at Sarp.	1	7 Dec. 1988 p. 74
3. Inonu, the Social Democratic Party (SDP) leader, criticizes the government for upholding Articles 141, 142, and 163 of the constitution (the last is the law that restricts religious freedom of expression).	1	7 Dec. 1988 p. 27
4. An imam of a mosque in Kundali district is sentenced to five and a half years in prison for delivering a sermon against the state.	3	28 Dec. 1988 p. 27
5. Evren states that he is against the turban bill because it violates the constitution and the spirit of Atatürk's reforms.	3	10 Jan. 1989 p. 27

[1] Preserving Religion and the Mind is measured as follows: (1) The regime supports the Islamic activists' argument or acts in favor of defending/representing Islam; (2) The regime refers the issue to a third party; (3) The regime clearly states its conflicting stand on the issue; (00) No information.

The second category refers to incidents where religious authorities act or make statements that are congruent to governmental policies. Thus, religious authorities use the state's political ideas and language in addressing Islamic activists.

The information used to code all the data depends on articles published in the Foreign Broadcast Information Service, *Near East Daily Reports* for the five years studied: November 1988 to October 1993.

6. The minister of culture attends an international Islamic meeting	1	31 Jan. 1989 p. 44
7. The Religious Affairs Department does not comment on Khomeini's fatwa against Salman Rushdie, while other religious authorities voice agreement with Khomeini's fatwa.	2	23 Feb. 1989 p. 61
8. The constitutional court abolishes the law allowing women to wear the veil on campus.	3	9 Mar. 1989 p. 37
9. Religious Affairs director opposes the publication of *The Satanic Verses.*	1	14 Mar. 1989 *p. 42*
10. Demonstrators against the abolition of the turban bill are detained in Istanbul.	3	17 Mar. 1989 p. 42
11. Officials voice alarm about boarding houses that teach students religion and train them for combat.	3	24 Mar. 1989 p. 39
12. An Islamic activist mayor has his house searched by police forces in Sanliurfa, and they seize 287 of his books. The mayor is also detained because he stated that he is "neither Kemalist, nor secularist - just Muslim."	3	18 Apr. 1989 p. 41 and 19 Apr. 1989 p. 24
13. Another four mayors who belong to the Islamist Prosperity Party are questioned by the assistant prosecutor of the State Security Court.	3	19 Apr. 1989 p. 24

November 1989–October 1990

Events	Coding	FBIS Date & Page
1. The turban ban in universities is lifted.	1	2 Jan. 1990 p. 26
2. The chairman of the Department of Religious Affairs states that the lottery is forbidden in Islam.	1&2	31 Jan. 1990 p. 29

3. The State Security Court suspends publication of a pro-Islamic magazine.	3	20 Mar. 1990 p. 14
4. Justice minister encourages a dialog on the pros and cons of revoking Article 163, among other articles.	3	11 Apr. 1990 pp. 53-55
5. Foreign minister attends the ICO (Islamic Conference Organization) foreign ministers meeting in Cairo.	3	31 Oct. 1990 pp. 10-11
6. Authorities investigate a prayer held for an Islamic activist leader, attended by 15,000 Muslims in Anatolia.	3	31 Oct. 1990 p. 44

November 1990–October 1991

Events	Coding	FBIS Date & Page
1. Security forces disperse and arrest anti–Gulf War demonstrators (Islamic activists) in Sanliurfa.	3	22 Jan. 1991 p. 58
2. Police use tear gas bombs to disperse Islamic activist demonstrators against the Gulf War in several cities and towns throughout Turkey.	3	28 Jan. 1991 pp. 50-51
3. The Religious Affairs director states that a call for "jihad" by Islamic activists against the allies in the Gulf War is inappropriate.	2&3	31 Jan. 1991 p. 50
4. Police clash with anti-war demonstrators; several demonstrators are arrested.	3	4 Feb. 1991 p. 54
5. Seventeen members of an "illegal" rightist group are arrested for trying to overthrow the secular regime in Turkey.	3	19 Feb. 1991 p. 60

6. The Turkish Grand National Assembly approves a bill that allows the release of prisoners on probation and abolishes Article 163, among other articles.	1	12 Apr. 1991 pp. 38-39
7. A large number of Islamic activist bureaucrats are dismissed and others are investigated for gathering and praying on Friday, keeping copies of the Qur'an in their desks, wearing silver wedding bands, and carrying prayer beads.	3	9 Sept. 1991 pp. 39-43

November 1991–October 1992

Events	Coding	FBIS Date & Page
1. 1,000 officers, non-commissioned officers, and military cadets are discharged for holding Islamist and leftist views.	3	Nov. 1991 p. 61
2. President Özal leaves for the Islamic Conference Organization summit meeting in Senegal.	1	9 Dec. 1991 p. 50
3. Twelve Islamic activists are arrested in Istanbul for trying to overthrow the secular regime.	3	27 Apr. 1992 p. 44
4. The Religious Affairs Department will build mosques in the new Turkish republics.	1	14 July 1992 pp. 43-44
5. The pro-Islamic magazine Bizim Dergah's general coordinator is attacked by police in his office.	3	8 Sept. 1992 p. 59

November 1992–October 1993

Events	Coding	FBIS Date & Page
1. Police issue an arrest warrant for a religious leader residing in Germany.	3	3 Mar. 1993 p. 61

2. The National Education Ministry will send investigative teams to schools to inspect educational institutions for alleged links to Hezbollah Party.	3	5 Mar. 1993 p. 58
3. The Islamic Movement Group is crushed by police in Ankara.	3	8 Mar. 1993 p. 60
4. The Prime Minister warns muftis (religious scholars) against involvement in politics.	3	8 Mar. 1993 pp. 60-61
5. A criminal court in Istanbul seizes a publication with excerpts from the book *The Satanic Verses*.	1	28 may 1993 p. 43
6. The head of the Religious Affairs Department criticizes *The Satanic Verses* and challenges the idea that the book poses any threat to the Qur'an and Islam in general.	2	28 May 1993 p. 44

Variable II. Preserving the Self

A. The Practice of *Habeas Corpus*[2]

Year	Nov. Oct. '88 – '89	Nov. Oct. '89 – '90	Nov. Oct. '90 – '91	Nov. Oct. '91 – '92	Nov. Oct. '92 – '93
Approx. number of violations	10	10	30	30	0

[2] The category scale developed to code this variable is as follows: (1) 1–20 incidents of *habeas corpus* violations; (2) 21–40 incidents; (3) 41–60 incidents; (4) 61–80 incidents; (5) More than 80 incidents; (00) No information.

Each FBIS report of habeas corpus violations was categorized using the intervals indicated above. When available, exact numbers were reported. Categories were used because many of the FIBS reports give only estimates or have several reports of the same incident. This issue is common in all the variables that have numerical estimates (i.e., in variables II.B., II.C., V.A., V.B., and V.C.). The approximate annual totals were calculated using the following scale values: (1) 1–20 incidents = 10; (2) 21–40 incidents = 30; (3) 41–60 incidents = 50; (4) 61–80 incidents = 70; (5) More than 80 = 90.

Variable II.B. Torture and Death During Imprisonment[3]

Year	Nov. Oct. '88 – '89	Nov. Oct. '89 – '90	Nov. Oct. '90 – '91	Nov. Oct. '91 – '92	Nov. Oct. '92 – '93
Approximate number tortured and killed during imprisonment	40	30	0	0	0

Variable II.C. Utilizing Police Forces and Military to Disperse/Deter[4] Islamic Activists[5]

Year	Nov. Oct. '88 – '89	Nov. Oct. '89 – '90	Nov. Oct. '90 – '91	Nov. Oct. '91 – '92	Nov. Oct. '92 – '93
Approximate number killed/ wounded by police	0	0	30	0	0

[3] The category scale developed to code this variable is as follows:

(1) 1–20 cases of torture/death
(2) 21–40 cases
(3) 41–60 cases
(4) 61–80 cases
(5) 81–100 cases
(6) 101–300 cases
(7) 301–500 cases
(8) 501–700 cases
(9) 701–900 cases
(10) More than 900 cases
(00) No information

Please refer to footnote 2 in variable II.A.

The approximate annual totals were calculated using the following scale values:

(1) 1–20 incidents = 10
(2) 21–40 incidents = 30
(3) 41–60 incidents = 50
(4) 61–80 incidents = 70
(5) 81–100 = 90
(6) 101–300 = 200
(7) 301–500 = 400
(8) 501–700 = 600
(9) 701–900 = 800
(10) More than 900

[4] The word "deter" is mentioned to stress the use of force to crush Islamic activism without incidents, i.e., the police forces storm mosques and houses to kill/deter Islamic activists. The consequences usually result in a war of attrition between security forces and Islamic activists.

[5] The category scale developed to code this variable is as follows:

(1) Crowd was harmless, but police used brutal force (i.e. killed/wounded people) to disperse them. The number of people killed/wounded is: (a) Less than or equal to 50; (b) 51–100; (c) 101–500; (d) More than 500.
(2) Crowd was harming property/people, the police used force. The number of people killed/wounded is: (a) Less than or equal to 50; (b) 51–100; (c) 101–500; (d) More than 500. Please refer to variable II.A., footnote 2.

Kind of crowd action that caused police brutality	1	2	1	2	1	2	1	2	1	2
Frequency of such actions	0	0	0	0	0	0	0	0	0	0

N.B.: There were no confrontations between the crowds and the police forces. Everything was peaceful until January 28, 1991, when the police in dispersing the crowds wounded 30 people (FBIS January 28, 1991, pp. 50–51).

Variable III. Preserving Posterity/Youth[6]

November 1988–October 1989

Events	Coding	FBIS Date & Page
1. Prime Minister Özal comments on President Everen's veto of the turban bill (in universities).	2	2 Dec. 1988 p. 39
2. President states that he vetoed the law lifting the ban on women wearing the Islamic veil in university classes.	2	10 Jan. 1989 p. 27
3. Women wearing headscarves march in Istanbul to protest against the Constitutional Court's decision to abolish the law allowing women to wear the veil.	2	9 Mar. 1989 p. 37
4. A group of demonstrators are detained after Friday prayers for voicing their opposition to the turban law.	2	17 Mar. 1989 p. 42
5. An article investigates the growing impact of imam and preacher schools in Turkey.	1	23 Mar. 1989 pp. 26-28

[6] This variable is similar to preserving religion and the mind in its method of measurement. The scale developed for it is as follows: (1) The regime encourages religious education/practice; (2) The regime openly discourages religious education/practice; (00) No information.

6. Chief of Staff announces that 95 military students were expelled for engaging in "fundamentalist" activities in military schools.	2	12 Apr. 1989 p. 24

November 1989–November 1990

Events	Coding	FBIS Date & Page
1. The ban on women students wearing the veil is lifted.	1	12 Jan. 1990 p. 26

November 1990–October 1991

Events	Coding	FBIS Date & Page
1. The Council of Ministers decides to include three years of Qur'an courses as part of compulsory education after primary schooling.	1	2 Oct. 1991 p. 29

November 1991–October 1992

Events	Coding	FBIS Date & Page
1. Security forces arrest 12 Islamic activists in Istanbul for holding meetings and organizing seminars at a bookstore.	2	27 Apr. 1992 p. 44

November 1992–October 1993

Events	Coding	FBIS Date & Page
1. The National Education Ministry investigates alleged Hezbollah activity in schools in the southeast region of Anatolia.	2	5 Mar. 1993 p. 58

Variable IV. Preserving Property/Wealth[7]

Year	Nov. Oct. '88 – '89	Nov. Oct. '89 – '90	Nov. Oct. '90 – '91	Nov. Oct. '91 – '92	Nov. Oct. '92 – '93
Degree of inflation rate stability	2	2	1	00	2

Variable V. Degree of Islamic Activism

A. Approximate Number of Islamic Activists Arrested Each Year[8]

Year	Nov. Oct. '88 – '89	Nov. Oct. '89 – '90	Nov. Oct. '90 – '91	Nov. Oct. '91 – '92	Nov. Oct. '92 – '93
Approx. number of IAs arrested.	80	80	100	12	140

Variable V.B. Approximate Number of Attempted Attacks Against Public Figures, Police Forces, Secularists, and Tourists.[9]

Year	Nov. Oct. '88 – '89	Nov. Oct. '89 – '90	Nov. Oct. '90 – '91	Nov. Oct. '91 – '92	Nov. Oct. '92 – '93
Approx. number of attempted attacks	4	50	12	12	46

7 This variable is measured through the analysis of articles published by the Foreign Broadcast Information Service throughout the five years of analysis. The categories under which this variable is coded are as follows: (1) Inflation varies according to international market fluctuations; (2) Inflation is continually increasing; (00) No information.

8 The category scale used to code this variable is as follows: (1) Less than or equal to 50; (2) 51–100; (3) 101–900; (4) More than 900; (00) No information. Please refer to variable II.A., footnote 2. The approximate annual totals are calculated using the following scale values: (1) Less than or equal to 50 = 20; (2) 51–100 = 70; (3) 101–900 = 500; (4) More than 900.

9 The category scale used for coding is as follows: (1) 1–10 attacks; (2) 11–20 attacks; (3) 21–40 attacks; (00) No information. Please refer to variable II.A., footnote 2. The approximate annual totals are calculated using the following scale values: (1) 1–10 = 4; (2) 11–20 = 15; (3) 21–40 = 30.

Additional notes on the targets of attacks.		1) An assassination attempt on the president's and the prime minister's lives. 2) An assassination attempt on the head of the Religious Affairs Department and the supreme education chairman. 3) Many attempts on professors and secular journalists.	1) Most attacks are on foreigners: e.g. an American officer, an Egyptian press attaché, an Iraqi attaché, the vice president of a British–Turkish company.	1) An attack on a synagogue in Istanbul. 2) A bomb kills the security chief of the Israeli Embassy.	1) Student clashes between secularists and Islamicists. 2) A bomb kills a secular writer. 3) An attack on a hotel in Sivas because of the invitation of a secular writer ends in killing 36 people.

Variable V.C. Approximate Number of Islamic Activists Who Join and Instigate Rallies/ Demonstrations Each Year[10]

Year	Nov. Oct. '88 – '89	Nov. Oct. '89 – '90	Nov. Oct. '90 – '91	Nov. Oct. '91 – '92	Nov. Oct. '92 – '93
Approx. number of IAs who rally/ demonstrate	790	2,310	420	2,570	770

10 The category scale developed to code this variable is as follows: (1) Less than or equal to 50; (2) 51–100; (3) 101–500; (4) 501–1000; (5) More than 1000. Please refer to variable II.A., footnote 2.

The approximate annual totals are calculated using the following scale values: (1) Less than or equal to 50 = 20; (2) 51–100 = 60; (3) 101–500 = 300; (4) 501–1000 = 750; (5) More than 1000 = 1000.

Variable V.D. Kinds and Frequencies of Demonstrations in Which Islamic Activists Are Involved[11]

Year	Nov. Oct. '88 – '89	Nov. Oct. '89 – '90	Nov. Oct. '90 – '91	Nov. Oct. '91 – '92	Nov. Oct. '92 – '93
Categories	1 2 3 4	1 2 3 4	1 2 3 4	1 2 3 4	1 2 3 4
Frequency	4 0 0 0	7 0 0 0	5 0 1 0	4 0 0 0	2 0 0 0

Variable V.E. Islamic Activists Winning or Gaining Influence on Provincial or Professional Level[12]

Year	Nov. Oct. '88 – '89	Nov. Oct. '89 – '90	Nov. Oct. '90 – '91	Nov. Oct. '91 – '92	Nov. Oct. '92 – '93
Categories of election patterns	1 2 3 00	1 2 3 00	1 2 3 00	1 2 3 00	1 2 3 00
Frequency reflecting election patterns	2 1 0 0	1 3 0 0	2 0 0 0	1 0 0 0	2 0 0 0

[11] The scale used to define the kinds of demonstrations is as follows: (1) Peaceful; (2) Harmed property; (3) Entangled in a clash with police forces, military, or any other state agency; (4) Harmed other individuals not related to the state.

[12] This variable is qualitative in nature and estimates the degree of involvement of Islamic Activists in the public elections processes. The categories used to define this variable are as follows: (1) Winning an election or gaining acceptance in 1–2 provinces; (2) Winning an election or gaining acceptance in a certain syndicate; (3) Losing elections in a certain province/syndicate due to the regime's interference; (00) No information.

Glossary of Arabic Terms[1]

āyah (pl. *āyāt*): Verse from the Qur'an.

fiqh/*fuqahā'*: Fiqh is the origin of the noun *Fuqahā'*. Fiqh is the process of inferring Islamic law from the Qur'an and the Hadith (Prophet Muhammad's sayings). The *fuqahā'*, therefore, are the legal scholars who perform such a task.

ḥadīth (pl. *aḥādīth*): The words spoken by the Prophet that were reported by his companions. The *ḥadīth* is an integral part of Islamic law that is second in importance after the Qur'an.

ḥasan: The origin of words like *istiḥṣān, aḥṣan, muḥṣin*. It means good or beneficial.

ijmā': The consent of legal scholars concerning a certain issue. It is considered to be one of the sources of Islamic law.

istiḥṣān: Its origin is *ḥaṣin*. A legal principle invoked as a general guideline in Muslim legal thought.[2]

istiṣhāb: A legal principle invoked to maintain a certain practice, until the practice is repealed by a more accurate explanation of the law.

istiṣlāḥ: A legal principle that applies public good or public welfare as a guideline for legislating Islamic law.

khalīfah: Historically, the leader of the Muslim Ummah.

---

1. Transliteration makes it difficult to convey the meaning of the Arabic words because it is a phonetic representation of them. However, generally speaking, Semitic languages usually have a root for each word. This root is composed of three letters (for example, *fi'l* in Arabic and *pal* in Hebrew). When the word is conjugated in other forms (for example, *istaf'al, fā'il, maf'ūl*, etc.), the meaning changes accordingly but it retains its similarity to the origin (*fi'l*). The form *istaf'al* means indirect involvement in the act of doing. *Fā'il* means the person directly involved in the act of doing. *Maf'ūl* means the object to which the act is done.

2. A more theoretical and detailed discussion of the principle is provided in Chapter 2.

khilāfah: In theological terms, humanity is the follower and caretaker of the Earth, after God. Therefore, each individual is *khalīfat Allāh fī al Arḍ* (God's vicegerent on Earth).

madhhab (pl. *madhāhib*): A legal school of law. The main four Sunni *madhāhib* are: *Mālikī, Ḥanafī, Shāfi'ī, and Ḥanbalī.*

al maqāṣid: The end goals of Islamic law. That is, the spirit of the law and its guiding principles.

maṣlaḥah (pl. *maṣāliḥ*): Public welfare or the public good, sought by practicing *istiṣlāḥ* according to Islamic law. In Islamic legal thought, the public good is qualified according to the Qur'an and the Sunnah.

maṣlaḥah mursalah: The *maṣlaḥah* that has nothing for or against it according to the Qur'an, Sunnah, and ijmā'.

mujtahid: The origin of the word is *juhd.*[3] *Mujtahid* is a Muslim theologian who knows enough about the religion to be able to extrapolate reasonable judgments on different issues.

al naṣṣ (pl. *al nuṣūṣ*): The Text, i.e., the Qur'an and the *ḥadīth.*

qaṭ'īyāt: The word is the plural of *qaṭ'ī,* and the opposite of *ẓanī,* which in fiqh means that the issue is clearly addressed in the Text (*al naṣṣ*).

al qiyās: A method used in Muslim law to extrapolate legal reasoning by analogy. For example, if drinking alcohol is prohibited because it obscures rational behavior, therefore narcotics are prohibited as well.

ṣaluḥa: The origin of *istiṣlaḥ* and *al aṣlaḥ*, meaning the good, the beneficial, the useful.

Al Shari'ah (pl. *Sharā'i'*): The canonical revealed Islamic law that is found in the Qur'an, the Sunnah, the consensus of legal scholars, and from their use of analogical reasoning.

Sīrah: The biography of the Prophet, i.e., the entirety of the Prophet Muhammad's acts and sayings.

Sunnah: The Prophet Muhammad's acts and sayings that were recognized by his followers as part of his customary practice.

'ulamā': Plural of *'ālim*. Religious scholars (see *fuqahā'*).

'urf: Local customs. In legal Islamic thought some scholars agreed that local customs should be incorporated in the body of the law.

uṣūl al fiqh: The foundations of Muslim law. According to the Sunnis these are the Qur'an, the Sunnah, the consensus of religious scholars, and their analogical reasoning.

ẓannīyāt: The plural of *ẓanī,* which in fiqh means a doubtful issue. That is, an issue that (a) is open to debate and (b) is not clearly ruled as a forbidden or favored act in Islamic law.

---

3. It is also related to the words ijtihād and jihād, which mean, respectively, making more effort and exploiting all resources.

Bibliography

Abd al Raḥmān, 'Umar. *Mīthāq al 'Amal al Islāmī* (An Islamic Social Contract). Cairo: Maktabat Ibn Kathīr, 1989.

Al 'Ābidī, Ḥamādī. *Al Shāṭibī and Maqāṣid al Sharī'ah*. Beirut: Dār Qutaybah, 1992.

Abū Zahrā', Muḥammad. *Abū Ḥanīfah*. Cairo: Dār al Fikr al 'Arabī, 1947.

-----. *Mālik*. Cairo: Maktabat al Anglū al Maṣrīyah, 1952.

-----. *Uṣūl al Fiqh* (The Origins of Fiqh). Cairo: Dār al Fikr al 'Arabī, n.d.

Ageron, Charles-Robert. *Modern Algeria: A History from 1830 to the Present*. Trenton, NJ: Africa World Press, Inc., 1991.

Ahmad, Feroz. *The Turkish Experiment in Democracy 1950–1975*. London: The Royal Institute of International Affairs, 1977.

Ahmad, Shaikh Mahmud. *Social Justice in Islam*. Pakistan: Institute of Islamic Culture, 1975.

Akarli, Engin D., and Gabriel Ben-Dor. *Political Participation in Turkey*. Istanbul: Bogazici University, 1975.

Akhavi, Shahrough. "Egypt: Diffused Elite in a Bureaucratic Society." In *Political Elites in Arab North Africa*. New York: Longman Inc., 1982.

'Ālim, Yūsif H. al. *Al Maqāṣid al 'Āmmah li al Sharī'ah al Islāmīyah* (The End Goals of the Islamic Shari'ah). Herndon, VA: International Institute of Islamic Thought, 1991.

'Alwānī, Ṭāhā Jābir al. *Uṣūl al Fiqh al Islāmī* (The Origins of Fiqh in Islam). Herndon, VA: International Institute of Islamic Thought, 1981.

'Āmidī, Sayf al Dīn al. *Al Iḥkām fī Uṣūl al Aḥkām* (Mastering the Origins of the Law. N.p., n.d.

Amnesty International. *Amnesty International Report 1988*. London: Amnesty International Publications, 1988.

-----. *Amnesty International Report 1989*. London: Amnesty International Publications, 1989.

-----. *Amnesty International Report 1990*. London: Amnesty International Publications, 1990.

-----. *Amnesty International Report 1992*. London: Amnesty International Publications, 1992.

-----. *Amnesty International Report 1993*. London: Amnesty International Publications, 1993.

-----. *Egypt: Violations of Human Rights*. London: Amnesty International Publications, 1989.

-----. *Egypt: Arbitrary Detention and Torture under Emergency Powers*. London: Amnesty International Publications, 1989.

-----. *Turkey: Brutal and Systematic Abuse of Human Rights*. London: Amnesty International Publications, 1989.

Anderson, Lisa, "Obligation and Accountability: Islamic Politics in North Africa." *Daedalus* 120, no. 3 (Summer 1991).

An-Na'im, 'Abdullahi Ahmed, and Francis M. Deng. *Human Rights in Africa: Cross Cultural Perspectives*. Washington, DC: The Brookings Institution, 1990.

-----. *Toward an Islamic Reformation*. Syracuse: Syracuse University Press, 1990.

-----. *Human Rights in Cross-Cultural Perspectives: A Quest for Consensus*. Philadelphia: University of Pennsylvania Press, 1991.

Arjomand, Said Amir. *From Nationalism to Revolutionary Islam*. Albany: State University of New York Press, 1984.

'Aṭīyah, Jamāl al Dīn. *Al Naẓarīyah al 'Āmmah li al Sharī'ah al Islāmīyah* (The General Theory of Islamic Shari'ah). N.p.: al Madinah Printers, 1988.

Baghdādī, Sayf al Dīn al. "Qawā'id al Uṣūl." In *Majmū' Mutūn Uṣūlīyah* (The Canons of the Origins of the Law). Damascus: Al Maktabah al Hāshimīyah, n.d.

Baker, Raymond William. *Sadat and After: Struggles for Egypt's Political Soul*. Cambridge, MA: Harvard University Press, 1990.

-----. "Afraid of Islam: Egypt's Muslim Centrists between Pharaohs and Fundamentalists." In *Daedalus* 120, no. 3 (Summer 1991).

Barraclough, Colin. "Roll Over Ataturk: Turkey's Refah Seems Poised to Remake the Nation's Secular Image." In *Middle East Insight* 11, no. 2 (Jan.–Feb. 1995).

Batran, Aziz A. *Islam and Revolution in Africa*. Brattleboro, VT: Center for Arab–Islamic Studies, 1983.

Bayūmī, Ibrāhīm al. *Al Fikr al Siyāsī li al Imām Ḥasan al Bannā'* (The Political Thought of Hasan al Bannā). Cairo: Dār al Tawzī' wa al Nashr al Islāmīyah, 1992.

Beberoglu, Berch. *Power and Stability in the Middle East*. London: Zed Books Ltd., 1989.

Becker, Howard S. *Writing for Social Scientists: How to Start and Finish Your Thesis, Book, or Article*. Chicago: The Unversity of Chicago Press, 1986.

Bennoune, Mahfoud. *The Making of Contemporary Africa, 1830–1987*. Cambridge, UK: Cambridge University Press, 1988.

Bianchi, Robert. *Interest Groups and Political Development in Turkey*. Princeton: Princeton University Press, 1984.

-----. "Interest Groups and Politics in Mubarak's Egypt." In *The Political Economy of Egypt*, edited by Ibrahim Oweiss. Washington, DC: Center for Contemporary Arab Studies, Georgetown University, 1990.

Binder, Leonard. *Islamic Liberalism: A Critique of Development Ideologies*. Chicago: University of Chicago Press, 1988.

Birand, Mehmet Ali. *The General's Coup in Turkey*. London: Brassey's Defence Publishers, 1987.

The Boston Globe, December 1995–March 1995.

Burgat, François. *The Islamic Movement in North Africa*. Austin: Center of Middle Eastern Studies, University of Texas, 1993.

Burke, Edmund, and Ira M. Lapidus. *Islam, Politics, and Social Movements*. Berkeley: University of California Press, 1988.

Burrell, R. M. *Islamic Fundamentalism*. London: The Royal Asiatic Society, 1989.

Burrell, R. Michael, and Abbas R. Kelidar. *Egypt: The Dilemmas of a Nation, 1970–1977*. Beverly Hills: Sage Publications, 1977.

Butterworth, Charles. "Prudence Versus Legitimacy: The Persistent Theme in Islamic Political Thought." In *Islamic Resurgence in the Arab World*, edited by Ali Hillal Dessouki. New York: Praeger Publishers, 1982.

Butterworth, Charles, and William Zartman. *The Annals of the American Academy of Political and Social Science* 524 (1992).

Būṭī, Muḥammad Sa'īd al. *Ẓawābit al Maṣlaḥah fī al Sharī'ah al Islāmīyah*. Damascus: al Maktabah al Amawīyah, 1966.

Charnay, Jean-Paul. *Islamic Culture and Socio-Economic Change*. Leiden: E. J. Brill, 1971.

The Chicago Manual of Style. Chicago: The University of Chicago Press, 1982.

Choueiri, Youssef M. *Islamic Fundamentalism*. Boston: Twayne Publishers, 1990.

Cole, Juan R. I. *Comparing Muslim Societies: Knowledge and the State in a World Civilization*. Ann Arbor: University of Michigan Press, 1992.

Collier, David. "New Perspectives on the Comparative Method." In *Comparative Political Dynamics: Global Research Perspectives*, edited by Dankwart Rustow and Kenneth Paul Erickson. New York: Harper Collins Publishers, 1991.

Colona, Fanny. "Cultural Resistance and Religious Legitimacy in Colonial Algeria." *Economy and Society* 3 (1974).

Commission on Security and Cooperation in Europe. *Human Rights in Turkey*. Washington, DC: Commission of Security and Cooperation in Europe, 1993.

Coulson, Noel J. *Conflicts and Tensions in Islamic Jurisprudence*. Chicago: The University of Chicago Press, 1969.

Dabashi, Hamid. *Theology of Discontent: The Ideological Foundation of the Islamic Revolution in Iran*. New York: New York University Press, 1993.

Darīnī, Fatḥī al. *Khaṣā'iṣ al Tashrī' al Islāmī* (The Specifics of Islamic Shari'ah). Beirut: Mu'asasat al Risālah, 1982.

Darwīsh, Ṣāliḥ al. *Hiwārāt Rāshid al Ghanūshī* (A Collection of Dialogs with Rāshid al Ghanūshī). London: Khalil Media Service, 1992.

Davis, Eric. "Ideology, Social Class and Islamic Radicalism in Modern Egypt." In *From Nationalism to Revolutionary Islam*, edited by Said Arjomand. Albany: State University of New York Press, 1984.

Deeb, Mary-Jane. "Militant Islam and the Politics of Redemption." *The Annals of the American Academy of Political and Social Science* 524 (1992).

Dekmejian, Richard Hrair. *Egypt under Nasser: A Study in Political Dynamics*. Albany: State University of New York Press, 1971.

-----. *Islam in Revolution: Fundamentalism in the Arab World*. Syracuse: Syracuse University Press, 1985.

Dessouki, Ali E. Hillal. *Islamic Resurgence in the Arab World*. New York: Praeger Publishers, 1982.

Dessouki, Ali E. Hillal, and Alexander S. Cudsi. *Islam and Power*. Baltimore: Johns Hopkins University Press, 1981.

Dodd, C. H. *Democracy and Development in Turkey*. Hull: University of Hull, 1979.

Dogan, Mattei, and Dominique Pelassy. *How to Compare Nations: Strategies in Comparative Politics*. Chatham: Chatham House Publishers, 1984.

Donahue, John J., and John L. Esposito. *Islam in Transition: Muslim Perspectives*. New York: Oxford University Press, 1982.

Donnelly, Jack, and Rhoda E. Howard. *International Handbook of Human Rights*. New York: Greenwood Press, 1987.

Egyptian Organization for Human Rights. *Torture in Egypt in 1989*. New York: Lawyers Committee for Human Rights–Middle East, 1990.

Encyclopedia of Islam (Second Edition). Leiden: E. J. Brill, 1960.

Entelis, John P. *Comparative Politics of North Africa: Algeria, Morocco, and Tunisia*. Syracuse: Syracuse University Press, 1980.

-----. "Elite Political Culture and Socialization in Algeria: Tensions and Discontinuities." *The Middle East Journal* 35 (1981).

-----. "Algeria: Technocratic Rule, Military Power." In *Political Elites in Arab North Africa*. New York: Longman Inc., 1982.

Esposito, John L. *Islam and Development: Religion and Sociopolitical Change*. New York: Syracuse University Press, 1980.

-----. *Voices of Resurgent Islam*. New York: Oxford University Press, 1983.

-----. *Islam: The Straight Path*. Oxford: Oxford University Press, 1988.

-----. *The Islamic Threat: Myth or Reality?* Oxford: Oxford University Press, 1992.

-----. "Political Islam: Beyond the Green Menace." *Current History,* 1994.

Evin, Ahmet. *Modern Turkey: Continuity and Change*. Leske: Schriften des Deutschen Orient-Instituts, n.d.

Fallers, Lloyd A. *The Social Anthropology of the Nation-State*. Chicago: Aldine Publishing Company, 1974.

Farsoun, Karen. "State Capitalism in Algeria." *Middle East Research and Information Project Reports* (MERIP) 35 (1975).

Fāsī, 'Allāl al. *Difā'an 'an al Sharī'ah* (In Defense of the Shari'ah). Rabat: Manshūrāt al 'Aṣr al Ḥadīth, 1972.

-----. *Maqāṣid al Sharī'ah al Islāmīyah wa Makārimihā* (The Maqāṣid of the Islamic Sharī'ah and Its Benefits). Casablanca: Maktabat al Wiḥdah al 'Arabīyah, 1963.

Finkel, Andrew, and Nukhet Sirman. *Turkish State, Turkish Society*. London: Routledge, 1990.

Foreign Broadcast Information Service (FBIS). *Near East Daily Reports.* November 1988–October 1993.

-----. *West Europe Daily Reports.* November 1988–October 1993.

Fukuyama, Francis. *The End of History and the Last Man.* New York: Press Press, 1992.

Fuller, Graham E. *Islamic Fundamentalism in the Northern Tier Countries.* Santa Monica: National Defense Research Institute, 1991.

-----. "Has Political Islam Failed?" *Middle East Insight* 11, no. 2 (Jan.–Feb. 1995).

Fuller, Graham E., and Ian O. Lesser. *A Sense of Siege: The Geopolitics of Islam and the West.* Boulder: Westview Press,1995.

Funk, Wilfred, and Norman Lewis. *30 Days to a More Powerful Vocabulary.* New York: Pocket Books, 1970.

Gellner, Ernest. *Postmodernism, Reason and Religion.* London: Routledge, 1992.

Gerber, Haim. *Islam, Guerilla War, and Revolution.* Boulder: Lynne Rienner Publishers, 1988.

Geyikdagi, Mehmet Yasar. *Political Parties in Turkey: The Role of Islam.* New York: Praeger Publishers, 1984.

Ghānim, al Bayūmī. *Al Fikr al Siyāsī li al Imām Ḥasan al Bannā'* (The Political Thought of Imām Ḥasan al Bannā'). Cairo: Dār al Tawzī' wa al Nashr al Islāmīyah, 1992.

Ghazālī, Abū Ḥamīd al. *Al Mustaṣfā'* (The Eclectic Source of the Law). Cairo: al Maṭba'ah al Amīrīyah, n.d.

Ghazālī, Muḥammad al. *Al Ṭarīq min Hunā* (The Way Starts Here). Cairo: al Bashīr, 1987.

Glasse, Cyrill. *The Concise Encyclopedia of Islam.* San Francisco: Harper Collins Publishers, 1989.

Goldberg, Ellis. "Smashing Idols and the State: The Protestant Ethic and Egyptian Sunni Radicalism." In *Comparing Muslim Societies: Knowledge and the State in a World Civilization,* edited by Juan R. I. Cole. Ann Arbor: University of Michigan Press, 1992.

Goldstone, Jack A., Ted Robert Gurr, and Garrokh Moshiri. *Revolutions of the Late Twentieth Century.* Boulder: Westview Press, 1991.

Guenena, Nemat. *The Jihad: An Islamic Alternative in Egypt.* Cairo: The American University in Cairo Press, 1988.

Gurr, Ted Robert. *Why Men Rebel.* Princeton: Princeton University Press, 1970.

-----. *Handbook of Political Conflict: Theory and Research.* New York: The Free Press, 1980.

Gurr, Ted Robert, and Barbara Harrf. *Ethnic Conflict in World Politics.* Boulder: Westview Press, 1994.

Hadar, Leon T. "What Green Peril?" *Foreign Affairs* (Spring 1993).

Haddad, Yvonne Yazbeck, John Obert Voll, and John L. Esposito. *The Contemporary Islamic Revival: A Critical Survey and Bibliography.* New York: Greenwood Press, 1991.

Hale, William M. *Aspects of Modern Turkey.* London: Bowker Publishing Company, 1976.

Hamond, Andrew. "Interview with Egytian Islamist Banned" in *Egypt-Net* (an Internet forum).

Harris, Lillian Craig. *Egypt: Internal Challenges and Regional Stability.* London: Routledge and Kegan Paul, 1988.

Ḥasan, Bahīy al Dīn. *Difāʻan ʻan Ḥuqūq al Insān* (In Defense of Human Rights). Cairo: al Munaẓamah al Miṣrīyah li Ḥuqūq al Insān, 1993.

Ḥasan, Ḥusīn Ḥamīd. *Naẓarīyat al Maṣlaḥah fī al Fiqh al Islāmī* (The Theory of *Maṣlaḥah* in Muslim Fiqh). Cairo: Dār al Nahḍah al ʻArabīyah, 1971.

Hawwā, Saʻīd al. *Al Islām.* 4 vols. Cairo: Maktabat Wahba, 1977.

Heikal, Mohammed. *Autumn of Fury.* London: Andre Deutsch Ltd., 1983.

Helms, Christine M. *Arabism and Islam: Stateless Nations and Nationless States.* Washington, DC: The Institute of National Strategic Studies, 1990.

Helsinki Watch. *Human Rights in Turkey's Transition to Democracy.* New York: Helsinki Watch Committee, 1983.

-----. *Straws in the Wind: Prospects for Human Rights and Democracy in Turkey.* New York: Helsinki Watch Committee, 1984.

-----. *Critique: Review of the Department of State's Country Reports on Human Rights Practices for 1984.* New York: Hensinki Watch, 1985.

-----. *Freedom and Fear: Human Rights in Turkey.* New York: Human Rights Watch, 1986.

-----. *Violations of the Helsinki Accords: Turkey.* New York: Helsinki Watch Committee, 1986.

-----. *State of Flux: Human Rights in Turkey.* New York: Helsinki Watch Committee, 1987.

-----. *Paying the Price: Freedom of Expression in Turkey.* New York: Helsinki Watch Committee, 1989.

-----. *Prison Conditions in Turkey*. New York: Helsinki Watch Committee, 1989.

-----. *Broken Promises: Torture and Killings Continue in Tur-key*. New York: Human Rights Watch, 1992.

Heper, Martin, and Raphael Israeli. *Islam and Politics in the Modern Middle East*. New York: St. Martin's Press, 1984.

Heper, Metin. *Readings in Turkish Politics*. N.p.: 1980.

-----. "Recent Instability in Turkey." *International Journal of Turkish Studies* 1 (1980).

Hill, Enid. "Law and Courts in Egypt: Recent Issues and Events Concerning Islamic Law." In *The Political Economy of Egypt*, edited by Ibrahim Oweiss. Washington, DC: Center for Contemporary Arab Studies, Georgetown University, 1990.

Hinnebusch, Raymond A. *Egyptian Politics under Sadat: The Post-Populist Development of an Authoritarian-Modernizing State*. Cambridge: Cambridge University Press, 1985.

-----. "The Formation of the Contemporary Egyptian State from Nasser and Sadat to Mubarak." In *The Political Economy of Egypt*, edited by Ibrahim Oweiss. Washington, DC: Center for Contemporary Arab Studies, Georgetown University, 1990.

Hiro, Dilip. *Holy Wars: The Rise of Islamic Fundamentalism*. New York: Routledge, 1989.

Hirst, David, and Irene Beeson. *Sadat*. London: Faber and Faber Ltd., 1981.

Hopwood, Derek. *Egypt: Politics and Society 1945–1990*. London: Harper Collins Academic, 1991.

Hourani, Albert. *A History of the Arab Peoples*. New York: Warner Books, 1991.

Hourani, George F. *Reason and Tradition in Islamic Ethics*. Cambridge: Cambridge Unversity Press, 1985.

Huḍībī, Ḥasan al. *Dustūrunā?* (Our Constitution?). Cairo: Dār al Anṣār, 1978.

Hudson, Michael C. "Islam and Political Development." In *Islam and Development: Religion and Sociopolitical Change*, edited by John L. Esposito. Syracuse: Syracuse University Press, 1980.

Humana, Charles. *World Human Rights Guide*. London: The Economist Publications, 1986.

Human Rights Watch. *The Persecution of Human Rights Monitors: December 1986 to December 1987*. New York: Human Rights Watch, 1987.

-----. *The Persecution of Human Rights Monitors: December 1987 to December 1988*. New York: Human Rights Watch, 1988.
-----. *The Persecution of Human Rights Monitors: December 1988 to December 1989*. New York: Human Rights Watch, 1989.
-----. *Human Rights Watch World Report 1990*. New York: Human Rights Watch, 1991.
-----. *Human Rights Watch World Report 1992*. New York: Human Rights Watch, 1992.
-----. *Indivisible Human Rights: The Relationship of Poli-tical and Civil Rights to Survival, Subsistence and Poverty*. New York: Human Rights Watch, 1992.
-----. *Human Rights Watch World Report 1993*. New York: Human Rights Watch, 1993.
-----. *Human Rights Watch World Report 1994*. New York: Human Rights Watch, 1994.
Hunter, Shireen T. *The Politics of Islamic Revivalism: Diversity and Unity*. Bloomington: Indiana University Press, 1988.
Huntington, Samuel P. *The Third Wave: Democratization in the Late Twentieth Century*. Norman: University of Oklahoma Press, 1991.
-----. "A Clash of Civilizations?" *Foreign Affairs* (Summer 1993).
Ibn 'Ashūr, Muḥammad al Ṭāhir. *Maqāṣid al Sharī'ah al Islāmīyah* (The End Goals of the Islamic Shari'ah). Tunis: al Sharikah al Tūnisīyah li al Tawzī', 1978.
Ibn al Subkī, 'Abd al Wahab. *Mutūn Jām'i al Jawāmi'* (A Collection of Uṣūl). Cairo: Maṭba'at al Bāb al Ḥalabī and Sons, n.d.
Ibn Taymīyah, Aḥmad. *Majmū' Fatāwī* (A Collection of Legal Opinions). Vols. 20, 28, and 32. N.p., n.d.
Ibrahim, Ibrahim. "Religion and Politics under Nasser and Sadat: 1952–1981." In *The Islamic Impulse*, edited by Barbara Freyer Stowasser. Washington, DC: Center for Contemporary Arab Studies, Georgetown University, 1987.
Ibrāhīm, Nājih. *Mīthāq al 'Amal al Islāmī* (An Islamic Social Contract). Cairo: Maktabat Ibn Kathīr, 1989.
Ibrahim, Saad Eddin. "Islamic Military as a Social Movement: The Case of Two Groups in Egypt." In *Islamic Resurgence in the Arab World*, edited by Ali E. Hillal Dessouki. New York: Praeger Publishers, 1982.
Imām, Sāmīyah Sa'īd. *Man Yamluk Miṣr?* (Who Owns Egypt?). Damascus: Dār Kan'ān li al Dirāsāt wa al Nashr, 1991.

Islahi, Amin Ahsan. *Islamic Law: Concept and Codification*. Pakistan: Islamic Publications Ltd., 1979.

Jabine, Thomas B., and Richard P. Claude. *Human Rights and Statistics: Getting the Record Straight*. Philadelphia: University of Pennsylvania Press, 1992.

Jackson, Henry F. *The FLN in Algeria: Party Development in a Revolutionary Society*. Westport: Greenwood Press, 1977.

Jamā'ah al Islāmīyah al. *Al Muwājahah Hatmīyah* (Confrontation Is Inevitable). Cairo: n.d.

Jawzīyah, Abū Bakr Ibn al Qayyim al. *I'lām al Muwāqi'īn* (Advice to the 'Ulamā'). 4 vols. Cairo: Maktbat Ibn Taymīyah, n.d.

Jūwaynī, Abū al Ma'ālī al (Imām al Ḥaramayn). *Al Burhān* (Evidence in the Origins of the Law). Qatar: n.d.

Keddie, Nikki R., *The Revolt of Islam and Its Roots*. Berlin: Berlin Institute for Comparative Social Research, 1989.

Kenz, Ali el. *Algerian Reflections on Arab Crises*. Austin: Center for Middle Eastern Studies, 1991.

Kepel, Gilles. *The Prophet and Pharaoh: Muslim Extremism in Egypt*. London: AlSaqi Books, 1985.

Khallāf, 'Abd al Wahhāb. *Al Siyāsah al Sharī'yah* (Ruling According to Islamic Law). Cairo: Dār al Anṣār, 1977.

Knauss, Peter R. "Algeria under Boumedienne." In *The Performance of Soldiers as Governors: African Politics and the African Military*, edited by Isaac James Mowoe. Washington, DC: University Press of America, 1980.

Larzeg, Marnia. *The Emergence of Classes in Algeria: A Study of Colonialism and Socio-Political Change*. Boulder: Westview Press, 1976.

Lawless, Richard. *North Africa: Contemporary Politics and Economic Development*. London: Croom Helm, 1984.

Lawrence, Bruce B. *Defenders of God: The Fundamentalist Revolt against the Modern Age*. San Francisco: Harper and Row Publishers, 1989.

Leder, Arnold. *Catalysts of Change: Marxist versus Muslim in a Turkish Community*. Austin: University of Texas, 1976.

Lewis, Bernard. "The Roots of Muslim Rage." *Atlantic Monthly* 266 (September 1990).

Lijphart, Arend. "Comparative Politics and the Comparative Method." *American Political Science Review* KXV (1971).

Lippman, Thomas W. *Egypt after Nasser: Sadat, Peace and the Mirage of Prosperity*. New York: Paragon House, 1989.

Long, David E., and Bernard Reich. *The Government and Politics of the Middle East and North Aftica*. Boulder: Westview Press, 1986.

MacDonald, Duncan B. *Development of Muslim Theology, Jurisprudence and Constitutional Theory*. New York: Charles Scribner's Sons, 1903.

Mardin, Serif. "Ideology and Religion in the Turkish Revolution." *International Journal of Middle East Studies* 2 (1971).

-----. "Religion in Modern Turkey." *International Social Science Journal* 29 (1977).

-----. *Religion and Social Change in Modern Turkey*. Albany: State University of New York Press, 1989.

-----. "The Just and the Unjust." *Daedalus* 120, no. 3 (Summer 1991).

Martin, B. G. *Muslim Brotherhoods in Nineteenth-Century Africa*. Cambridge: Cambridge University Press, 1976.

Masud, Muhammad Khalid. *Islamic Legal Philosophy*. Islamabad: Islamic Research Institute, 1977.

Mayer, Ann Elizabeth. *Islam and Human Rights: Tradition and Politics*. Boulder: Westview Press, 1991.

Mitwalī, 'Abd al Ḥamīd. *Al Sharī'ah al Islāmīyah Ka Maṣdar Asāsī li al Dustūr* (Islamic Sharī'ah: A Basic Source of Law for the Constitution). Alexandria, Egypt: Mansha'at al Ma'ārif, 1975.

Middle East Watch. *Behind Closed Doors: Torture and Detention in Egypt*. New York: Human Rights Watch, 1992.

Miller, Judith. "The Challenge of Radical Islam." *Foreign Affairs* (Spring 1993).

Morris, Mary E. *New Political Realities and the Gulf: Egypt, Syria, and Jordan*. Santa Monica: National Defense Research Institute, 1993.

-----. *The Persistence of External Interest in the Middle East*. Santa Monica: National Defense Research Insititute, 1993.

Mortimer, Robert. "Islam and Multiparty Politics in Algeria." *The Middle East Journal* 45 (1991).

Mowoe, Isaac James. *The Performance of Soldiers as Governors: African Politics and the African Military*. Washington, DC: University Press of America, 1980.

Muller, Edward N. "Income Inequality, Regime Repressiveness and Political Violence." *American Sociological Review* 50 (1980).

Munson, Henry. *Islam and Revolution in the Middle East*. New Haven: Yale University Press, 1988.

Murphy, Caryle. "Egypt: An Uneasy Portent of Change." *Current History* (1994).

Nādī, Fu'ād Muḥammad al. *Mabda' al Mashrū'īyah* (The Fundamentals of Legitimacy). Cairo: Dār Nashr al Thaqāfah, 1970.

Naseef, 'Abdullah Omar. *Today's Problems, Tomorrow's Solutions*. London: Mansell Publishing Limited, 1988.

Nasr, Seyyed Hossein. *Ideals and Realities of Islam*. London: George Allen and Unwin Publishers, 1985.

Netton, Ian Richard. *A Popular Dictionary of Islam*. Atlantic Highlands, NJ: Humanities Press International, Inc., 1992.

Noori, Ayatollah Yahya, and Sayed Hassan Amin. *Legal and Political Structure of an Islamic State*. Glasgow: Royston Limited, 1987.

Onulduran, Ersin. *Political Development and Political Parties in Turkey: The Implications for Iran and Pakistan*. Ankara: University of Ankara Press, 1974.

Ovendale, Ritchie. *The Middle East Since 1914*. London: Longman Group UK, Ltd., 1992.

Oweiss, Ibrahim M. The *Political Economy of Contemporary Egypt*. Washington, DC: Center for Contemporary Arab Studies, Georgetown University, 1990.

Ozbudun, Ergun. *Turkey in the Year 2000*. Ankara: Turkish Political Science Association, 1989.

Parker, Richard B. *North Africa: Regional Tensions and Strategic Concerns*. New York: Praeger Publishers, 1987.

-----. *The Politics of Miscalculation in the Middle East*. Bloomington: Indiana University Press, 1993.

Pearl, David. *A Textbook on Muslim Law*. London: Croom Helm Ltd., 1979.

Peretz, Don. *The Middle East Today*. New York: Praeger Publishers, 1988.

Pevsner, Lucille W. *Turkey's Political Crisis*. Washington, DC: The Center for Strategic and International Studies, 1984.

Piscatori, James P. *Islam in a World of Nation-States*. Cambridge: Cambridge University Press, 1986.

-----. *Islamic Fundamentalisms and the Gulf Crisis*. Chicago: The American Academy of Arts and Sciences, 1991.

Pitman, Paul M. *Turkey: A Country Study*. Washington, DC: Federal Research Division, Library of Congress, 1988.

Pullapilly, Cyriac K. *Islam in the Contemporary World*. Notre Dame, IN: Cross Roads Books, 1980.

Qa'ūd, Ḥilmī Muḥammad al. *Al Niẓām al 'Askarī fī al Jazā'ir Māzāl Yukhaṭiṭ li Ightiyāl al Irādah al Islāmīyah* (The Algerian Military Regime Continues Its Plan of Eradicating the Islamic Will). Cairo: Dār al I'tiṣām, 1993.

Qaraḍāwī, Yūsif al. *Al Saḥwah al Islāmīyah bayn al Juḥūd wa Taṭarruf* (The Islamic Awakening: Between Rejection and Extremism). Qatar: Dār al Ummah, 1981.

-----. *Sharī'at al Islām: Khulūdahā wa Salāḥuhā li al Taṭbīq fī kul Zamān wa Makān* (Islamic Shari'ah: Its Applicability Regardless of Time and Place). Beirut: Al Maktab al Islāmī, 1973.

Qarāfī, Shihāb al Dīn al. *Mukhtaṣar Tanqīh al Fuṣūl in Majmū' Mutūn Uṣūlīyah* (Revising the Details of the Origins of the Law). Damascus: al Maktabah al Hāshimīyah, n.d.

Quṭb, Muḥammad. *Ḥawl Taṭbīq al Sharī'ah* (Implementing the Shari'ah). Cairo: Maktabat al Sunnah, 1991.

Quṭb, Sayyid. *Al Mustaqbal li Haẓa al Dīn* (The Future for This Religion). N.p., n.d.

-----. *Fī al Tārīkh Fikratān wa Minhājān* (History: Thought and Discourse). Cairo: Dār al Shurūq, 1983.

-----. *Naḥwa Mujtama' Islāmī* (Toward an Islamic Society). Cairo: Dār al Shurūq, 1988.

Raysūnī, Aḥmad al. *Naẓarīyat al Maqāṣid 'ind al Imām al Shāṭibī* (The Theory of Maqāṣid According to al Shāṭibī). Herndon, VA: International Institute of Islamic Thought, 1991.

Rāzī, Fakhr al Dīn al. *Al Maḥṣūl fī 'Ilm Uṣūl al Fiqh* (The Harvest of the Origins of the Law), 6 vols. Beirut: Mu'assassat al Risālah, 1992.

Rosen, Lawrence. *The Anthropology of Justice: Law as Culture in Islamic Society*. Cambridge: Cambridge University Press, 1989.

Ruedy, John. *Modern Algeria: The Origins and Development of a Nation*. Bloomington: Indiana Univeristy Press, 1992.

Rustow, Dankwart and Kenneth Paul Erickson. *Comparative Political Dynamics: Global Research Perspectives*. New York: Harper Collins Publishers, 1991.

Ṣadr, Muḥammad Bāqir al. *Durūs fī 'Ilm al Uṣūl* (Lessons in the Origin of the Law). Cairo: Dar al Kitab al Masri, 1978.

Said, Edward W. *Culture and Imperialism*. New York: Alfred A. Knopf Inc., 1993.

-----. *Orientalism*. New York: Vintage Books, 1979.

Salmī, 'Izz al Dīn al. *Qawā'id al Aḥkām fī Maṣāliḥ al Anām* (The Rules for Perfecting the Interest of the People). Cairo: Maṭba'at al Istiqāmah, n.d.

Sardar, Ziauddin. *Islamic Futures: The Shape of Ideas to Come*. New York: Mansell Publishing Limited, 1985.

Sarayi, Sabri. "Politicization of Islamic Re-traditionalism: Some Preliminary Notes." In *Islam and Politics in the Modern Middle East*, edited by Martin Heper and Raphael Israeli. New York: St. Martin's Press, 1984.

Sayed, Moustapha El-. "The Islamic Movement in Egypt." In *The Political Economy of Egypt*, edited by Ibrahim Oweiss. Washington, DC: Center for Contemporary Arab Studies, Georgetown University, 1990.

Schacht, Joseph. *An Introduction to Islamic Law*. Oxford: The Clarendon Press, 1964.

Schem, Paul. "Algeria's Return to Its Past: Can the FIS Break the Vicious Cycle of History?" *Middle East Insight* 11, no. 2 (Jan.–Feb. 1995).

Shabon, Anwar M., and Isik U. Zeytinoglu. *The Political, Economic, and Labor Climate in Turkey*. Philadelphia: University of Pennsylvania, 1985.

Shāfi'ī al. *Al Umm* (The Origin). N.p., n.d.

Shalabī, Muḥammad Muṣṭafā. *Ta'līl al Aḥkām* (Deducing the Law). Cairo: Maṭba'at al Azhar, 1943.

Sharabi, Hisham B. *Government and Politics of the Middle East in the Twentieth Century*. Westport: Greenwood Press Publishers, 1987.

Shāṭibī, Abī al Iṣḥāq al. *Al I'tiṣām* (Seeking Sancturary), 2 vols. Cairo: Dār al Barāq, n.d.

-----. *Al Muwāfaqā*t (The Treatise). 4 vols. Cairo: Dār al Fikr, n.d.

Shīshānī, 'Abd al Wahhāb al. *Ḥuqūq al Insān wa Ḥurīyatuh al Asāsīyah fī al Niẓām al Islāmī wa al Nuẓūm al Mu'āṣirah* (Human Rights: A Comparison between Islam and Contemporary Legal Statutes). N.p., 1980.

Shāwkānī, Muḥammad Ibn 'Alī al. *Irshād al Fuḥūl* (A Guide for Eminent Scholars). N.p., n.d.

Singer, Hanaa Fikry. *The Socialist Labor Party: A Case Study of a Contemporary Egyptian Opposition Party*. Cairo: The American University in Cairo Press, 1993.

Skocpol, Theda, and Margaret Somers. "The Uses of Comparative History in Macrosocial Inquiry." *Comparative Studies in Society and History* 22 (1980).

Slugett, Peter, and Marion Farouk-Slugett. *Tuttle Guide to the Middle East.* Boston: Charles E. Tuttle Company Inc., 1991.

Springborg, Robert. *Mubarak's Egypt: Fragmentation of the Political Order*. Boulder: Westview Press, 1989.

Stowasser, Barbara F. *The Islamic Impulse*. Washington, DC: Center for Contemporary Arab Studies, 1987.

-----. "The Society and Its Environment." In *Turkey: A Country Study*, edited by Paul M. Pitman. Washington, DC: Federal Research Division, Library of Congress, 1988.

Strunk, William and E. B. White. *The Elements of Style*. New York: The MacMillan Company, 1972.

Tachau, Frank. *Turkey: The Politics of Authority, Democracy, and Development*. New York: Praeger Publishers, 1984.

Tapper, Richard. *Islam in Modern Turkey: Religion, Politics and Literature in a Secular State*. London: I. B. Tauris and Company Ltd., 1991.

Taylor, Stan. *Social Science and Revolutions*. New York: St. Martin's Press, 1984.

Telemcānī, 'Umar al. *Ba'd Mā 'Alamanī al Ikhwān al Muslimīn* (Some of What I Have Learned from the Muslim Brotherhood). N.p., 1982.

-----. *Al Islām wa al Ḥukūmah al Dīnīyah* (Islam and Religious Government). Cairo: Dār al Tawzī' wa al Nashr al Islāmīyah, 1985.

Tibi, Bassam. *Islam and the Cultural Accommodation of Social Change*. Boulder: Westview Press, 1990.

Tlemcani, Rachid. *State and Revolution in Algeria*. Boulder: Westview Press, 1986.

Toprak, Binnaz. "Politicisation of Islam in a Secular State: The National Salvation Party in Turkey." In *From Nationalism to Revolutionary Islam*, edited by Said Arjomand. Albany: State University of New York Press, 1984.

Ṭūfī, Najm al Dīn al. *Risālah fī al Maṣāliḥ al Mursalā* (A Treatise on *Maṣāliḥ*). Beirut: al Matba'ah al Ahliyah, n.d.).

Turābī, Ḥasan al. *Tajdīd Uṣūl al Fiqh al Islāmī* (Renewing Islamic Fiqh). Beirut: Dār al Jīl, 1980.

Turner, Bryan S. *Weber and Islam: A Critical Study*. London: Routledge and Kegan Paul Ltd., 1974.

'Uthmān, Muḥammad Fathī. *Ḥuqūq al Insān bayn al Sharī'ah al Islāmīyah wa al Fikr al Qānūnī al Gharbī* (Human Rights: A Comparison between the Islamic Shari'ah and Western Legal Thought). Cairo: Dār al Shurūq, 1982.

Utvik, Bjorn Olav. "Filling the Vacant Throne of Nasser: The Economic Discourse of Egypt's Islamist Opposition." In *Middle East Insight* 11, no. 2 (Jan.–Feb. 1995).

Vatikiotis, P. J. "Islamic Resurgence: A Critical View." In *Islam and Power*, edited by Alexander S. Cudsi and Ali E. Hillal Dessouki. Baltimore: Johns Hopkins University Press, 1981.

Von Sivers, Peter. "National Integration and Traditional Rural Organization in Algeria." In *From Nationalism to Revolutionary Islam*, edited by Said Arjomand. Albany: State University of New York Press, 1984.

Wagstaff, Malcom. *Aspects of Religion in Secular Turkey*. Durham: University of Durham, 1990.

Weiker, Walter. *The Modernization of Turkey: From Atatürk to the Present Day*. New York: Holmes and Meier Publishers, 1981.

Williams, John Alden. "Veiling in Egypt as a Political and Social Phenomenon." In *Islam and Development: Religion and Sociopolitical Change*, edited by John L. Esposito. Syracuse: Syracuse University Press, 1980.

Yapp, M. E. *The Near East Since the First World War*. London: Longman, Inc., 1991.

Zarkā', Muṣṭafā Aḥmad al. *Al Madkhal al Fiqhī al 'Ām* (A General Introduction to Fiqh). Damascus: Maṭba'at al Hayāa, 1964.

Zayd, Muṣṭafā. *Al Maṣlaḥah fi al Tashrī' al Islāmī wa Najm al Dīn al Ṭūfi* (*Maṣlaḥah* in the Islamic Shari'ah According to Najm al Dīn al Ṭūfi). Cairo: Dār al Fikr al Arabī, 1964.

Zubaida, Sami. *Islam, the People and the State: Essays on Political Ideas and Movements in the Middle East*. London: Routledge, 1989.

-----. "Islam, the State and Democracy." *The Middle East Report* 22 (1992).

Zuḥaylī, Wahba al. *Naẓarīyat al Ḍarūrah al Shar'īyah Muqāranah ma'a al Qānūn al Waḍ'ī* (A Comparison between the Theory of Basic Needs in the Shari'ah and Civil Law). Damascus: 1969.

IIT Publications

(English Language)

Islamization of Knowledge

- **Towards Islamic Anthropology: Definitions, Dogma, and Directions**, *Akbar S. Ahmed*, 1st ed., 1986
- **Toward Islamic English**, *Ismail Raji al Faruqi*, 2nd ed., 1986.
- **Modeling Interest-Free Economy**, *Muhammad Anwar*, 1st ed., 1987.
- **Islam: Source and Purpose of Knowledge**, 1st ed., 1988.
- **The Organization of the Islamic Conference: An Introduction to an Islamic Political Institution**, *Abdullah al Ahsan*, 1st ed., 1988.
- **Islamization of Attitudes and Practices in Science and Technology**, *M. A. K. Lodhi (ed.)*, 1st ed., published jointly with the Association of Muslim Scientists and Engineers (AMSE), 1989.
- **Toward Islamization of Disciplines**, 1989.
- **Resource Mobilization and Investment in an Islamic Economic Framework**, *Zaidi Sattar*, 1st ed., 1990.
- **The Education Conference Book: Planning, Implementation, Recommendations and Abstract of Papers**, *Fathi Malkawi / Hussein Abdul-Fattah (ed.)*, 1st ed., 1991.
- **Where East Meets West**, *Mona Abul-Fadl*, 1st ed., 1992.
- **Qur'anic Concepts of Human Psyche**, *Zafar Afaq Ansari*, 1st ed., 1992.
- **Islam and the Economic Challenge**, *M. Umer Chapra*, 1st ed., published jointly with The Islamic Foundation (UK), 1992.
- **Toward an Islamic Theory of International Relations: New Directions for Methodology and Thought**, *AbdulHamid A. AbuSulayman*, 2nd ed., 1993.
- **Islam and Economic Development**, *M. Umer Chapra*, published jointly with the Islamic Research Institute (Pakistan), 1st ed., 1993.
- **An Introduction to Islamic Economics**, *M. Akram Khan*, 1st ed., 1993.

- **Islamization of Knowledge: General Principles and Work Plan**, *International Institute of Islamic Thought,* 3rd ed., 1995.
- **Guidelines to Islamic Economics: Nature, Concepts and Principles**, *M. Raihan Sharif*, 1996.
- **Islamization of Academic Disciplines**, 1997.
- **Contribution of Islamic Thought to Modern Economics (Vol. 2)**, *Misbah Oreibi (ed.),* 1998.
- **Islam and Other Faiths,** *Ismail Raji al-Faruqi,* published jointly with The Islamic Foundation, 1998.
- **Islamization of Knowledge: Conceptual Background, Vision and Tasks,** *Salisu Shehu,* 1998.
- **Islamization of Knowledge: Historical Background and Recent Developments,** *Danjuma Abubakar Maiwada,* 1999.
- **Economic Guidelines in the Qur'an,** *S.M. Hasanuz Zaman*, 1999.

Issues in Contemporary Islamic Thought

- **The Ethics of Disagreement in Islam**, *Taha Jabir al Alwani*, 3rd ed., 2000.
- **Islamic Thought and Culture**, *Ismail Raji al Faruqi (ed.),* 1st ed., 1982.
- **Essays in Islamic and Comparative Studies**, *Ismail Raji al Faruqi (ed.),* 1st ed., 1982.
- **Islamic Awakening Between Rejection and Extremism**, *Yusuf al Qaradawi*, published jointly with American Trust Publications (USA), 2nd ed., 1991.
- **A Young Muslims Guide to Religions in the World**, *Syed Sajjad Husain*, 1992.
- **Economic Growth and Human Resource Development in an Islamic Perspective**, *Ehsan Ahmad (ed.)*, published jointly with the Association of Muslim Social Scientists (AMSS), 1st ed., 1993.
- **Proceedings of the Twenty First Annual Conference Association of Muslim Social Scientists**, *Mona Abul-Fadl (ed.)*, published jointly with the Association of Muslim Social Scientists (AMSS), 1st ed., 1993.
- **Civilization and Society**, *Syed Sajjad Husain*, 1994.

- **Trialogue of the Abrahamic Faiths**, *Ismail Raji al Faruqi (ed.)*, published jointly with Amana Publications (USA), 4th ed., 1995.
- **Madinan Society at the Time of the Prophet**, *Akram Diya' al Umari*, (2 Parts in one volume), 2nd ed.,1995.
- **Tawhid : Its Implications for Thought and life**, *Ismail Raji al Faruqi*, published jointly with International Islamic Publishing House, 5th ed. 2000.
- **Role of Private and Public Sectors in Economic Development in an Islamic Perspective**, *Ehsan Ahmad*, 1st ed., 1996.
- **Thematic Commentary of the Qur'an (Vol. 1)**, *Shaikh Muhammad al Ghazali*, 1997.
- **Thematic Commentary of the Qur'an (Vol. 2)**, *Shaikh Muhammad al Ghazali*, 1998.
- **Proceedings of the IIIT Lunar Calendar Conference**, 2nd ed., *Imad-ad-Dean Ahmad*, 1998.

Research Monographs

- **Islam and the Middle East**, *Mona Abul-Fadl*, 1st ed., 1990.
- **Sources of Scientific Knowledge : The Geological Concepts of Mountains in the Qur'an**, *Z. R. El-Naggar*, 1st ed., 1991.
- **Indexation of Financial Assets: An Islamic Evaluation**, *S.M. Hasanuz Zaman*, 1st ed., 1993.
- **Source Methodology in Islamic Jurisprudence**, *Taha Jabir al Alwani*, 2nd ed., 1994.
- **The Making of a Religious Discourse: An Essay in the History and Historiography of the 'Abbasid Revolution**, *Muhammad Qasim Zaman*, 1st ed., 1995.
- **Origin and Development of Experimental Science**, *Muin-ud-Din Ahmad Khan*, 1997.
- **Social Laws of Islam**, *Shah Abdul Hannan*, 2nd ed., 1997.

Occasional Papers

- **Outlines of a Cultural Strategy**, *Taha Jabir al Alwani*, 1st ed., 1989.

- **Islamization of Knowledge: A Methodology**, *Imad al Din Khalil*, 1st ed., 1989.
- **The Qur'an and the Sunnah: The Time-Space Factor**, *Taha Jabir al Alwani/Imad al Din Khalil*, 1st ed., 1991.
- **Knowledge: An Islamic Perspective**, *Bakhtiar Husain Siddiqui*, 1st ed., 1991.
- **Islamization of Knowledge : A Critical Overview**, *Seyyed Vali Reza Nasr*, 1st ed., 1992.
- **Ijtihad**, *Taha Jabir al Alwani*, 1st ed., 1993.
- **Laxity, Moderation and Extremism in Islam**, *Aisha B. Lemu*, 1st ed., 1993.
- **Islamization: Reforming Contemporary Knowledge**, *AbdulHamid AbuSulayman*, 1st ed., 1994.
- **Toward Global Cultural Renewal**, *Mona Abul-Fadl*, 1st ed.,1995.
- **The Islamization of Knowledge: Yesterday and Today**, *Taha Jabir al Alwani*, 1st ed., 1995.
- **Missing Dimensions in Contemporary Islamic Movements**, *Taha Jabir al Alwani*, 1st ed., 1996.

Human Development

- **Training Guide for Islamic Workers**, *Hisham Altalib*, 3rd ed.,1993.
- **Leadership: Western and Islamic**, *Muhammad Anisuzzaman / Md. Zainul Abedin Majumder*, 1996.
- **Islamic Business Ethics**, *Rafik Issa Beekun*, 1997.

Perspectives on Islamic Thought

- **National Security and Development Strategy**, *Arshad Zaman*, 1st ed., 1990.
- **Nationalism and Internationalism in Liberalism: Marxism and Islam**, *Tahir Amin*, 1st ed., 1991.
- **Theories of Islamic Law: The Methodology of Ijtihad**, *Imran Ahsan Khan Nyazee*, 1994.

Islamic Methodology

- **Crisis in the Muslim Mind**, *AbdulHamid AbuSulayman*, 2nd ed., 1997.

Academic Dissertations

- **Through Muslim Eyes: M. Rashid Rida and the West**, *Emad Eldin Shahin*, 1st ed., 1993.
- **Business Ethics in Islam**, *Mushtaq Ahmad*, published jointly with International Institute of Islamic Economics (Pakistan), 1995.
- **Qur'anic Text: Towards a Retrieval System**, *Hani Attiyah*, 1st ed.,1996.
- **Teachers' Training: The Islamic Perspective**, *M. Zafar Iqbal*, published jointly with Institute of Policy Studies (Pakistan), 1st ed.,1996.
- **Economic Doctrines of Islam: A Study in The Doctrines of Islam and their Implications for Poverty, Employment and Economic Growth**, *Irfan Ul Haq*, 1st ed., 1996.
- **Working Principles for an Islamic Model in Mass Media Communication**, *Suhaib Jamal al Barzinji*, 1998.
- **The Variant Readings of the Qur'an : A Critical Study of Their Historical and Linguistic Origins**, *Ahmad A. M. 'Abdallah*, 1998.

Supplementary Social Studies Teaching Units

- **I am a Muslim: A Modern Storybook** (kindergarten), *Susan Douglas*, published jointly with Kendall/Hunt Publishing Company, 1st ed., 1995.
- **Eid Mubarak! Islamic Celebration Around the World** (1st grade), *Susan Douglas*, published jointly with Kendall/Hunt Publishing Company, 1st ed., 1995.
- **Muslims in Our Community & Around the World** (2nd grade), *Susan Douglas*, published jointly with Kendall/Hunt Publishing Company, 1st ed., 1995.

- **Traders & Explorers in Wooden Ships** (5th grade), *Susan Douglas*, published jointly with Kendall/Hunt Publishing Company, 1st ed., 1995.
- **Islam & Muslim Civilization** (6th grade), *Susan Douglas*, published jointly with Kendall/Hunt Publishing Company, 1st ed., 1995.
- **Muslims Cities Then & Now** (3rd grade), *Susan Douglas*, published jointly with Kendall/Hunt Publishing Company, 1st ed., 1996.
- **Introduction to Geography: Where in the World Do Muslims Live?** (4th grade*), Susan Douglas*, published jointly with Kendall/Hunt Publishing Company, 1st ed., 1996.

Islamic Law and Jurisprudence

- **Islamic Law of Business Organization Partnerships**, *Imran Ahsan Khan Nyazee*, 1997.